I0813058

How to Find and Photograph *Kentucky Wildflowers*

How to Find and Photograph *Kentucky Wildflowers*

Thomas Barnes

Acclaim Press
MORLEY, MISSOURI

Acclaim Press
— Your Next Great Book —
P.O. Box 238
Morley, MO 63767
(573) 472-9800
www.acclaimpress.com

Book design: M. Frene Melton
Cover design: M. Frene Melton

Library of Congress Cataloging-in-Publication Data

Barnes, Thomas G., 1957-
How to find and photograph Kentucky wildflowers / by Thomas Barnes.
p. cm.
Includes index.
ISBN-13: 978-1-935001-68-3 (alk. paper)
ISBN-10: 1-935001-68-X (alk. paper)
1. Photography of plants. 2. Wild flowers--Kentucky--Pictorial works.
3. Natural areas--Kentucky--Guidebooks. I. Title.
TR724.B36 2011
778.9'434309769--dc22
2011008627

First Printing: 2011
Printed in the United States of America
10 9 8 7 6 5 4 3 2 1

Contents

Locating Wildflowers

Acknowledgments

How do you begin to thank all the people who have influenced you and helped create a vision in the mind that has come to fruition in the form of a book after many decades? It is a difficult task for sure.

I certainly need to say a big thanks to my parents who have supported me in countless ways and whose love and devotion to their son never ceased even when I faced the most difficult of times in my life.

To my children who have had to endure more trials and tribulations in their lives than any kids should have to endure, I love you and appreciate the interesting people you are growing into. I love you very much and always keep you in my thoughts and prayers.

For this particular project I am grateful for the multiple reviews of the manuscript by photographers, John Snell and James Archambeault; a naturalist, photographer and retired biology teacher Wally Roberts; a botanist extraordinaire, Dr. Ed Chester; a graphics designer, Dennis Duross who pointed out the errors in my thinking about color, and a technical editor, Linda Kiesel who always improves my grammar. Your thoughtful comments greatly improved the quality of this book.

To the folks at Acclaim Press for all their hard work in putting together an outstanding book I am truly thankful.

Thanks Lowell for your fellowship and assistance walking trails with me, you are a true friend indeed.

Finally, thanks to all the worthy souls around the state who love wildflowers and the natural world (Chris, Mary Alice, Susan, Ben, Deb, Marc, Tara and many, many others too numerous to mention) and who inspire me to continue to come to work on a daily basis.

God bless all of you and keep up the good work educating people about our wonderful biodiversity in this state.

Preface

Lydia M. Child wrote in 1843 Letters from New York, "Flowers have spoken to me more than I can tell in written words. They are the hieroglyphics of angels, loved by all men for the beauty of their character, though few can decipher even fragments of their meaning." And so it is with me as I wander in the woods every spring in search of wildflowers that speak to me of God's wonderful creation, renewal and rebirth after months of dark and dreariness and the coming of warmth and sunshine. Nothing amazes me more than to see a new flower I have yet to encounter and to study its intricate design, structure, and beauty.

One of my favorite flowers of all time that I photographed while working on *The Rare Wildflowers of Kentucky* is the diminutive kidney-leaf twayblade orchid. It is a tiny thing, growing only several inches tall, and can be found under rhododendron thickets in the southeastern Kentucky Mountains. It isn't all that showy, but when I look at that flower up close I see how it resembles an angel, and that brings me great pleasure every time I look at photos of it. As the old saying goes, "Beauty is in the eye of the beholder." But I have always liked things of beauty and by nature I am a visual person. What could be any more beautiful than a wildflower?

Wildflowers are among the most beautiful things any human could possibly encounter on this entire planet and that is why authors and poets such as Ralph Waldo Emerson who wrote in Hamatreya, "The earth laughs in flowers" – or Oliver Wendell Holmes who wrote, "The Amen of nature is always a flower." Flowers inspire art not only in words, but also in painting. The painter Georgia O'Keeffe wrote, "When you take a flower in your hand and really look at it, it's your world for the moment. I want to give that world to someone else. Most people in the city rush around so, they have no time to look at a flower. I want them to see it whether they want to or not." Flowers obviously inspired Mary Vaux Walcott to illustrate the five volumes of *North American Wildflowers* in 1925 that is commonly referred to as the "Audubon of Botany." And of course, flowers inspire photographers both amateur and professional and everyone in between.

Where do people obtain this inspiration to discover new and interesting wildflowers? For some it is an inherited trait. I think this was my route as my mother Donna and Grandmother Genevieve loved the prairie flowers. My grandfather and mentor, Johnnie Hynes, loved photographing the flowers in his yard with an old reflex camera. I will never forget the large patches of iris growing around our house as a child. But what really caught my attention photographically was when I was working on my doctorate at Texas A&M University and I saw the fields of bluebonnets and Indian paintbrush that would literally cover dozens and dozens of acres with beautiful color in the spring. What inspires others? Perhaps it is a quest for knowledge, understanding, and intrigue in trying to figure out exactly what species a particular flower is. Still for others it is the challenge of capturing them on film or with a brush, paint and canvas. Finally some have an interest just because they are beautiful. But

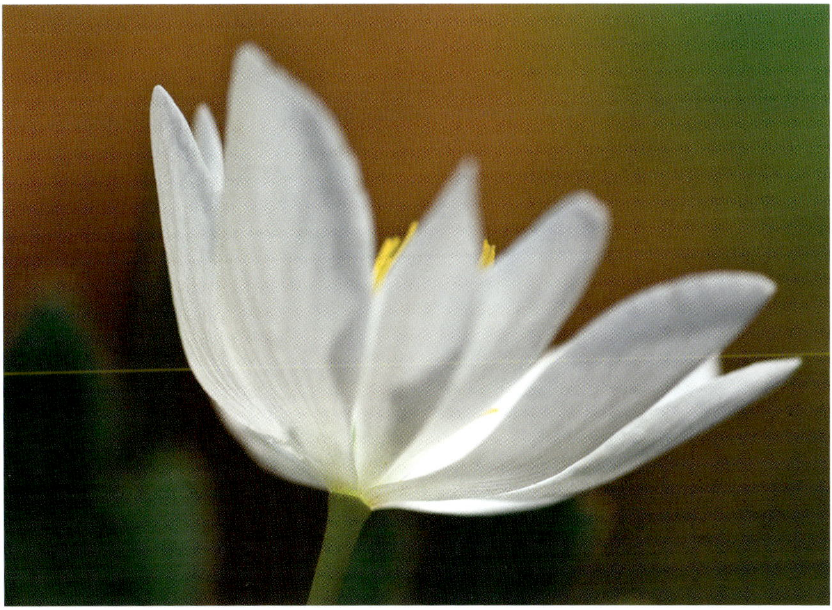

This backlit single flower of bloodroot set against the orange of the fallen leaves from the previous fall is one of the showiest of all the spring ephemeral wildflowers in the woods. This is a creative type of image that would not be useful in identifying the plant because it shows the lack of details in the leaf and flower. However, taken from beneath the flower with the light streaming through the petals with a nice background makes it a wonderful wildflower photograph.

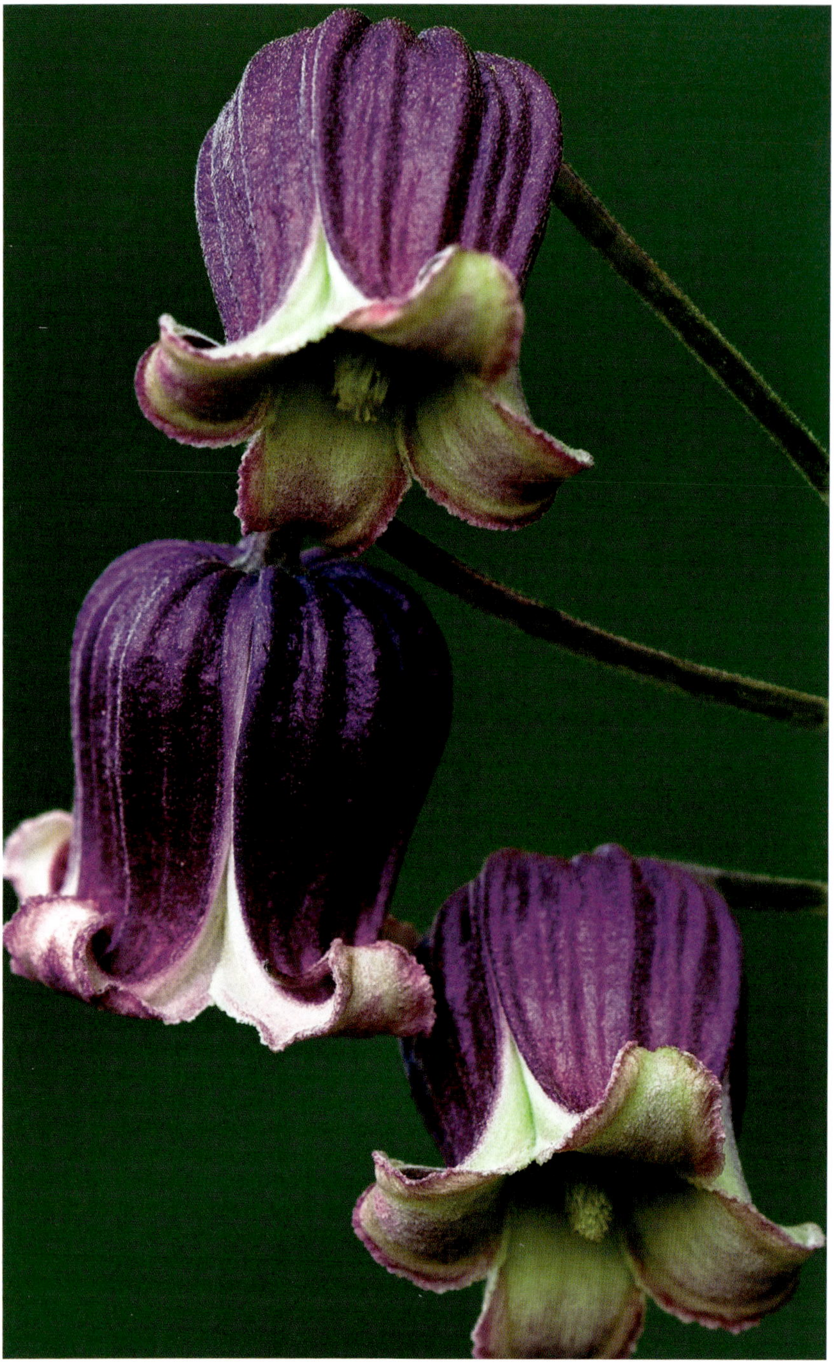

For some, it is all about the chase to find new species or color forms like this purple form of leather flower that occurs primarily in the mountains of Kentucky compared to the traditionally red form found in the rest of the state.

for whatever reasons, finding wildflowers is a major attraction for thousands of people all across Kentucky and this nation.

This book is quite simply about finding, appreciating and photographing wildflowers. It is also about taking your photographic skills to a higher skill level than just documenting what you saw in nature. When I am in the field, lying on the ground looking through the camera, and a casual observer approaches, he or she often inquires about what I am doing. When I reply that I am taking wildflower photos, it is amazing how many respond they too enjoy taking wildflower photos and seem to think it is quite an easy undertaking. Taking snapshots with a digital point-and-shoot camera is in fact quite easy, but capturing creative, artistic impressions of wildflowers is challenging. This book is for those who want to elevate their photography from taking documentary snapshots to making artistic flower portraits. However, those with point and shoot type cameras can definitely improve their images if they follow the guidelines presented throughout the book.

How is this book different from the dozens of books covering macro photography or digital photography? Quite honestly, this book is different because it is the only one to focus on wildflower photography from close-ups to flowers in the landscape; in addition, it is the only book that not only discusses my thoughts on equipment and how to use the equipment in the field, I also discuss some elementary principles of visual design or composition to aid you in thinking more creatively about how to photograph the wildflowers you find in the field, or even the horticultural flowers in the garden.

This section also includes information on color and the elements of visual design not to mention some basic photographic information about exposure, depth of field, etc. so that beginners do not feel lost when they pick up this book. In essence it covers the entire gamut of things to consider when photographing flowers. What doesn't it cover? It does not discuss what to do once the information is captured and stored on the media card, which is a subject for entire books. Why don't I discuss this information? Well to be quite frank, I don't do much post processing after it comes into the computer because I am not that good at it. After my session in the field, I download the files into Adobe Lightroom or Photoshop where I correct exposure, color, contrast and remove dust particles. That is pretty much it for post-processing. My strong belief is that most of the work should be done in the field, as explained in this book. That isn't to say that some images could not be improved in the digital darkroom because I am sure they could. But in the end, I do not have the time or skill necessary to do that much in the digital darkroom because I have an 8 to 5 type job at the University that requires much attention at this point in my life.

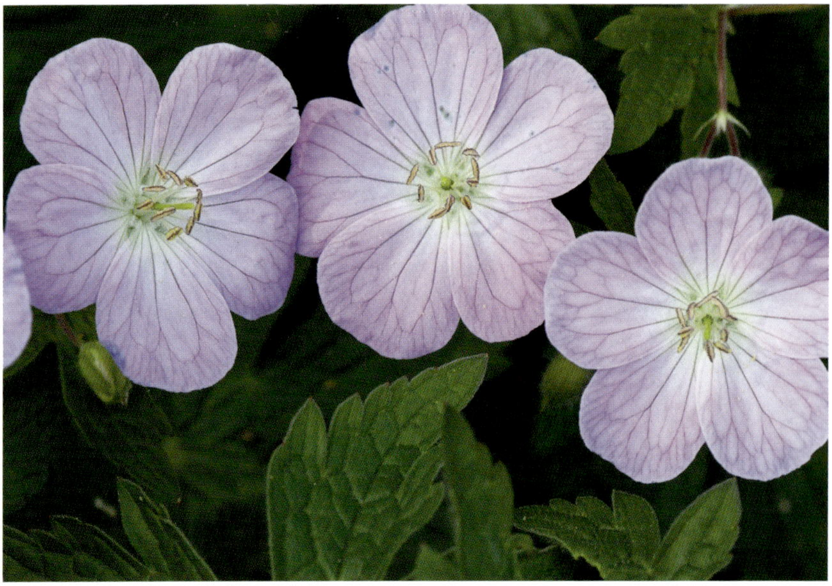

This trio of wild geraniums required no post-processing in the computer after the image was captured in the camera.

Dedication

In Loving Memory of my mother, Donna Genevieve Barnes, who loved prairie flowers and her favorite image was Harvey Dunn's painting, "The Prairie is My Garden."

How to Find and Photograph *Kentucky Wildflowers*

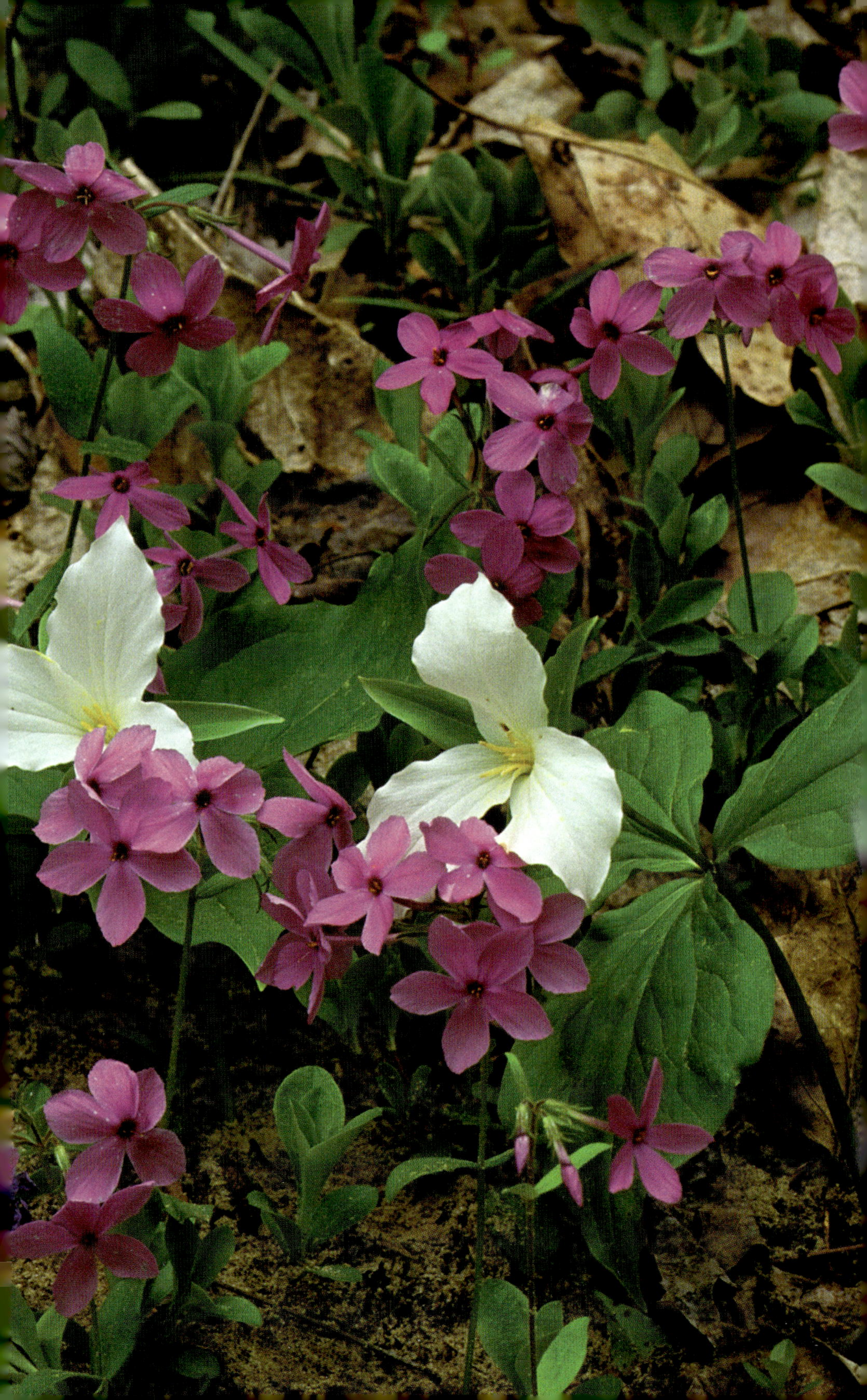

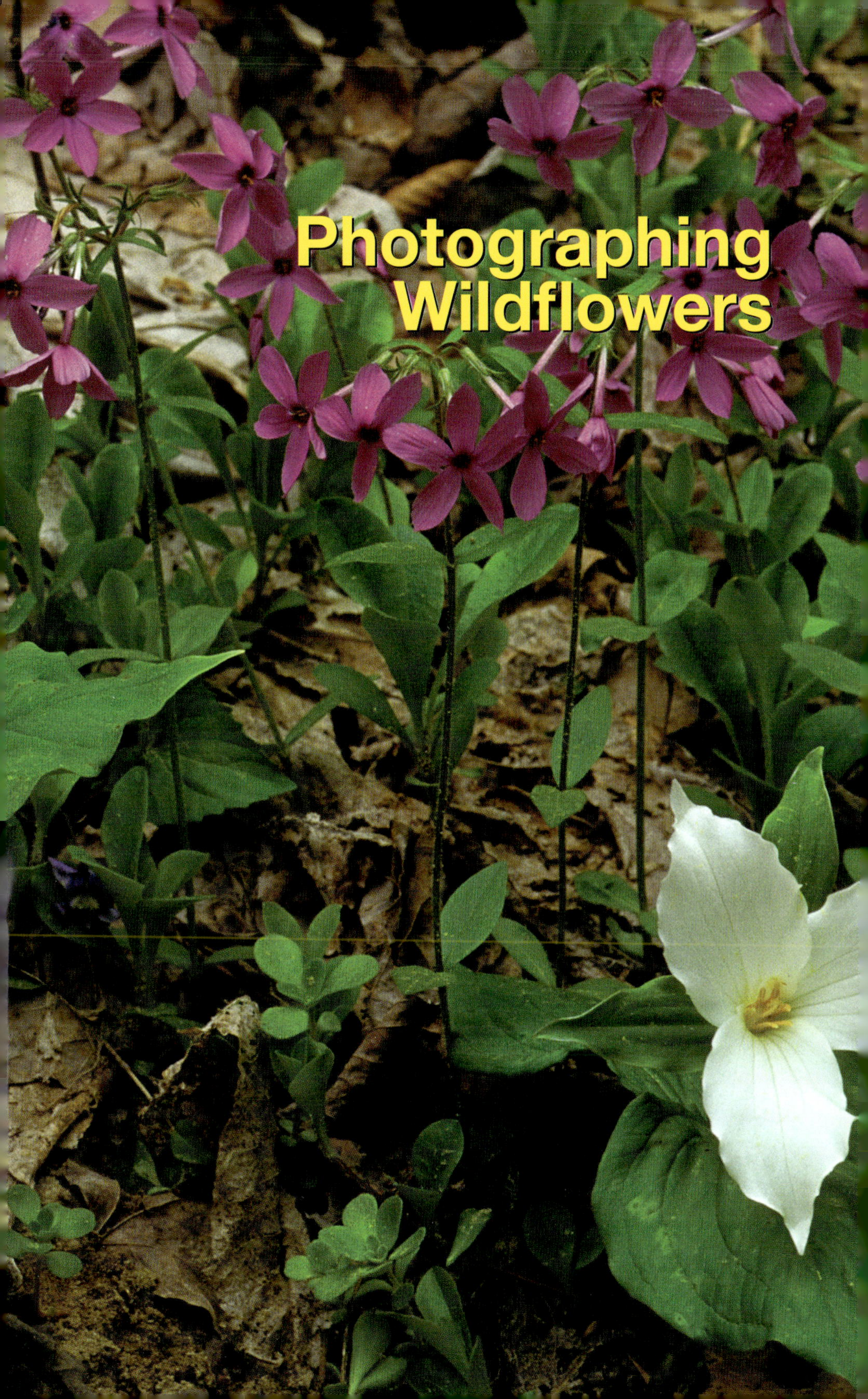
Photographing
Wildflowers

An Introduction to Photographing Wildflowers

While I enjoy doing all aspects of nature photography, I am perhaps best known for my wildflower photos that have been reproduced in countless books, pamphlets, websites, and other publications around the world. Because I have produced three books on wildflowers and taught about gardening with wildflowers and attracting wildlife with native plants, it seemed only natural to create a book on how I photograph wildflowers. I hope by providing this information, you will develop a greater appreciation for not only how difficult it is to photograph flowers, but also how wildflowers, like much in nature, are under assault. A recent U.S. Forest Service report documented that we are losing four acres of open space each minute to development, which equates to 6,000 acres a day. Once a site is developed, without a doubt, wildflowers lose out. It is pretty hard to grow trilliums and lady's slipper orchids without a forest canopy and the rich, humus-based soils they need to survive. Other factors are also stressing native ecosystems, and the primary reasons species become rare are habitat destruction, non-native organisms, and harmful human hobbies such as collecting for the garden, indiscriminate off-road vehicle use, and even something seemingly as benign as climbing rocks.

There is an even larger crisis looming on the horizon that will change everything: global warming. This will dramatically alter which species of plants survive, how abundant they are, and when they flower. Several research studies point to the real and potential threats to wildflowers in the future. A recent Cornell University study found that six of 15 wildflowers they studied produced flowers an average of 19.8 days earlier in the season. In another study, Stanford University scientists reported that up to 20 percent of our wildflowers will become extinct with an 8 percent decline in native plants in general. Not only is habitat loss a problem, but invasive, alien plants, are taking over the habitat of our native species. This is now

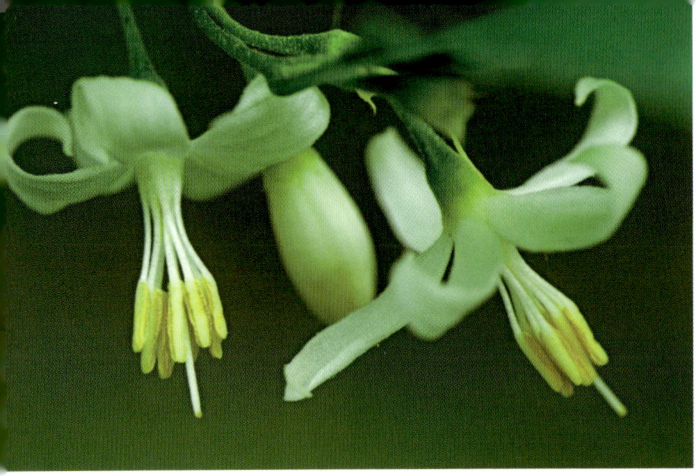

To photograph the American snowbell, a medium sized shrub, you must have some basic knowledge about where the plant grows and when it flowers. This species occurs in wet swampy woods and flowers in late spring. To become a better photographer, become a better naturalist.

the second most important reason that species become rare and it is poised to take over habitat loss as the number one reason.

What does it really take to make beautiful wildflower photos? It takes time, patience, and planning but it also takes technique, technique, technique, as well as good quality equipment, a beautiful subject and outstanding light. Every photographer eventually develops his or her own "style" and this certainly varies because we all are unique. How do you develop your technique and style? There are a couple of ways to accomplish this task and one is to take formal photography courses either in person or through correspondence or, as an alternative, attend one of the many workshops, seminars, or tours that are offered and listed in the back of magazines like *Outdoor Photographer* or from the North American Nature Photographers Association. You might also consider joining a local camera club and learning from other members. Another method – and this is how I taught myself – is to subscribe to magazines like *Outdoor Photographer* and *Popular Photography* and read them thoroughly. I also purchase photographic books of all different types including books by other photographers who have captured beautiful images. I then study these and try to figure out the composition, lighting, and other creative aspects of the image. It is not that I wish to make similar images, but they help stimulate my own creativity, and I may apply these ideas in similar situations. Perhaps that is one of the reasons you purchased this book: to enjoy the interesting and beautiful flowers and to learn, either from the visuals or the text. In either case the best way to learn is by doing. Never lose sight of the fact that one of the reasons you are doing this is because you enjoy it – participating in it either for the photographic challenge, the joy of being outdoors in nature, or the prospect of making money – and want to get better at it.

Have you read and studied your camera manual recently? I cannot stress enough how important it is for you to keep that owner's manual handy and read, re-read, and re-read it. This will help you master the use of your camera even though you may not use all the camera's features or functions. Familiarity with your equipment keeps you from having to figure out how to use some particular feature when the need arises in the field. It also allows you to focus your attention on the important part of wildflower photography, the creative aspect, because the technique of working the camera is second nature and completely comfortable. This approach also means fewer errors – for example finding that you shot the image with ISO 1600 instead of 100 or with the wrong white balance.

As you read through this book be reminded that, with digital photography, there are multiple methods of accomplishing any particular task. Keep in mind the information I present is just what I have had success using. It is certainly not indicative of what other author's or photographer's recommend. These are only my suggestions and it is certainly not inclusive by any stretch of the imagination. Perhaps the best advice I can give to any aspiring wildflower photographer is to spend as much time in the field as you can. Folks often inquire about how I got that shot, like the frog in the Kentucky lady's slipper orchid that graces the cover of *The Wildflowers and Ferns of Kentucky*. I explain to them that this is not all that uncommon and explain the ecology of lady's slipper orchid pollination which then explains why the frog was in the flower in the first place (attempting to get lunch). I then tell them that on one photographic trip some colleagues found a red spotted newt doing the same thing in a yellow lady's slipper orchid on Big Black Mountain. So how do you happen upon these situations? Spend as much time in the field as possible. Learn and understand the natural system: the biology and ecology of a species, whether you are on limestone or sandstone, whether the flower likes it wet or dry, and whether it likes sun or shade. This knowledge will help you become a better photographer, and your life will be richer for the experience. Then share this love of nature with everyone you encounter. Let them see your beautiful photos and teach them to love the earth and all her inhabitants so that my children and all the children of the world

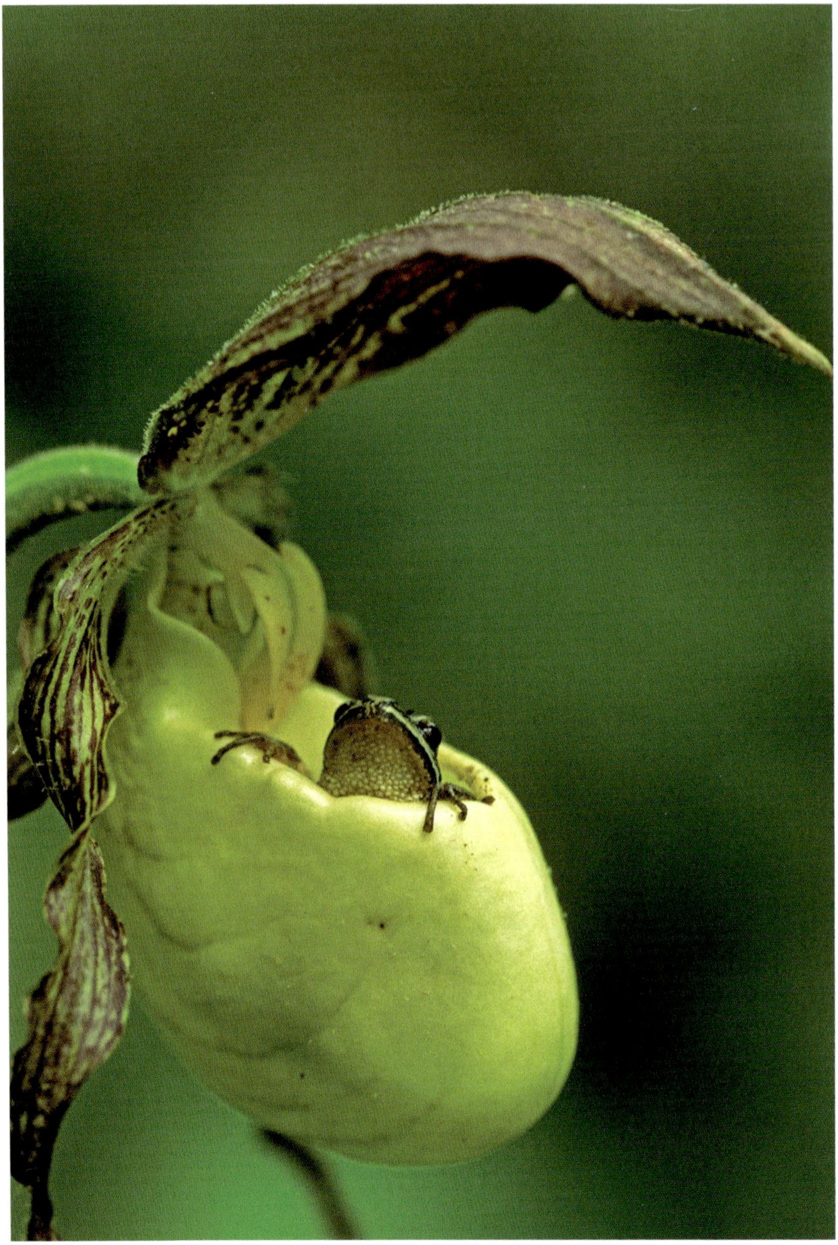

I was photographing a Kentucky Lady's Slipper Orchid using a 300mm lens with an extension tube on a tripod and had it focused on the lip of the flower. I had a cable release connected to the camera and I photographed the orchid noticing a black splotch near the back of the flower. I kept my hand on the cable release and approached the flower and I discovered a frog inside the flower. As I moved around the flower to look more closely, the frog began to move to the front and jumped out. All the time I was moving about the flower, I was also pressing the cable release, taking photos and ended up with three images of the frog just before it exited the flower.

will inherit a biologically rich world full of the beauty and grace that wildflowers bring to it.

What is Macro or Micro Photography?

What a simple question. Now the real question is why does it have such a complicated answer? One definition of macro photography is photography at life size and above. Anything that does not approach this level of magnification is called close-up photography. Another source says that macro photography is when the image depicted on the sensor is close to the same size as the subject. What this means is that a flower that is 15mm in size will be 15mm in size on the sensor. Others combine the two terms and say that term basically means close-up photography. That is why I did not write a book on macro photography. There are more than 800 books listed on Amazon.com that are completely dedicated to, or have a component of, the topic: Macro Photography.

Flower photography is a different sort of a breed (catch the pun all you plant types?). Flower photography can be macro or close-up or environmental habitat or landscape or in many cases, none of the above. This book will not delve into really high magnification

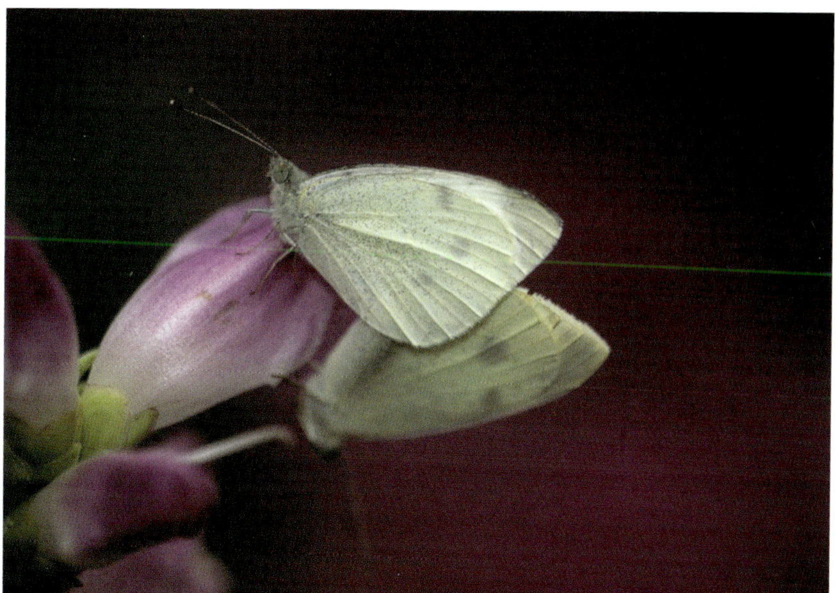

The cabbage butterfly is life-size as is the single flower of the pink turtlehead. However, this image is about one-fourth life-size as taken and most zoom lenses will typically give you this much magnification at the close-up setting.

macro photography. The flowers I deal with are big and conspicuous and showy and colorful and I want to capture all that grandeur with my camera. That is one of the big differences between this book and the other 800+ macro books in the market today. The other big difference is that I do not dwell on equipment, particularly specialized equipment for photographing tiny subjects. I am more interested in providing direction on photographing what most people see in nature and how to learn techniques about photographing flowers. Finally, most books do not focus on the creative or visual design side of photography, which for flowers becomes very important because flowers are bright and colorful and you should use this to your advantage.

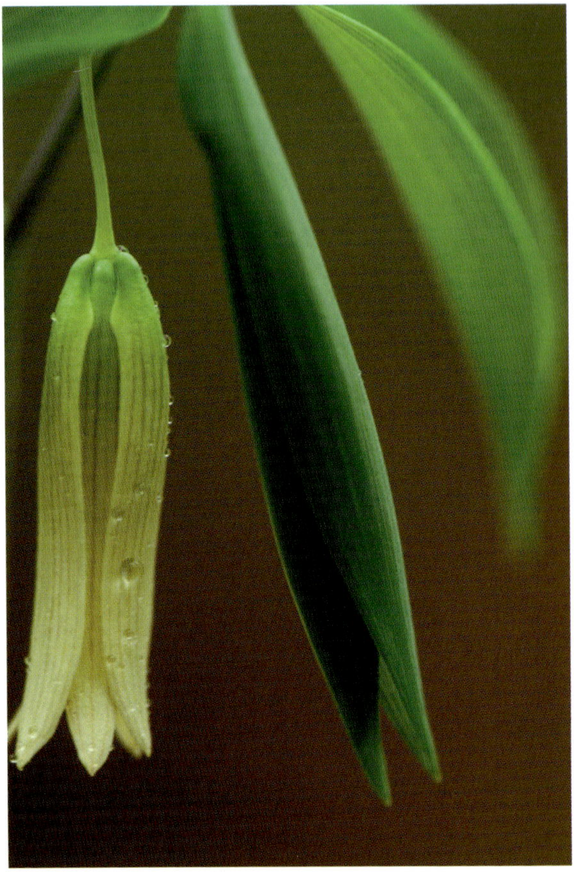

This sessile bellwort is life-size, meaning it is about the size of a quarter.

Making Little Things Big on the Sensor

Lets begin by dispelling the myth that you need a macro (or micro for us Nikon folks) lens to take high-quality wildflower photographs. Any, I repeat, any lens can take high-quality wildflower photos. Your creative vision and technique will be the key to getting nice images. Granted, you may not be able to make very tiny things really big on the sensor, but you can take numerous habitat or landscape photos with a normal or wide-angle lens. Furthermore, there are methods of making any lens focus closer which is all a macro lens does. I think some of my nicest wildflower photos were not taken with a macro lens but rather with short zoom in the range of 35 to 70mm. In these cases I often include some of the surrounding "habitat" with the subject.

Before I get carried away discussing lenses, equipment and other issues like visual design, a little primer on magnification is probably in order. I could spend a great deal of time discussing magnification

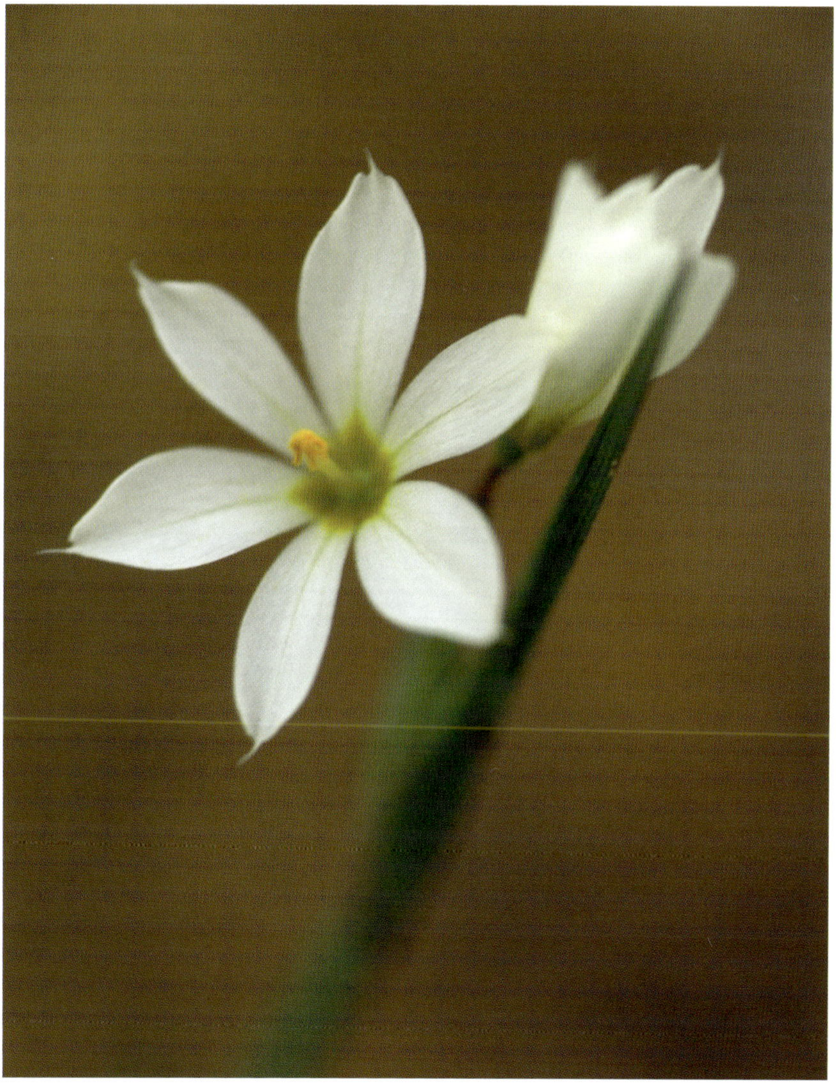

This white blue-eyed grass is three times life-size which means it is about the size of a dime.

rates and making something "life-size" on film, but, in reality, most people aren't all that interested in this technical stuff. In his book, *Closeups in Nature*, John Shaw has an excellent discussion about magnification, and I highly recommend that you read it if you are interested in the technical stuff. Here is the 50-cent tour with pertinent information. In general, when the size of the subject that fills the frame relative to its size in the real world is roughly equal, you have taken a life-size image. Life-size for 35mm system is roughly about the size of a quarter meaning that if you shoot a quarter and fill the frame with the coin, you are shooting at life-size or 1x. Most of the modern zoom lenses that have an M (for macro) focus at about one-quarter X meaning you can fill the frame with a flower the size of a tulip. One of the advantages of using a DSLR with a smaller (non full frame) sensor is that you increase your magnification rate and can get better than life-size reproduction. For instance, a 100mm lens on a Nikon D300 would equate to a 150mm lens, and on a Canon D40 it would be a 160mm lens.

The Basics of Photographing Flowers

The Digital Revolution

The Rare Wildflowers of Kentucky was my last effort in using film for a book project and this is the second book project based on using digital imagery. Most photographers today have switched, or are switching, to digital photography instead of the traditional film-based approach that was in use for many years. Why have folks switched? There are numerous reasons, one being cost, as it is cheaper to shoot on reusable digital media cards compared to film, and it can be more environmentally friendly not having to deal with chemicals in developing, silver residues, etc. Things have changed since the early digital cameras came out, and today the quality of high-end digital cameras may surpass that of film. Because the technology develops so quickly, there is no doubt quality will continue to improve with time.

Other reasons for shooting digitally include being able to 1) change the ISO from one image to the next without having to remove film (as well as the potential for wasting lots of film), 2) change the white balance to match ambient light conditions (or using it creatively for special effects), 3) to "fix" minor problems in the digital darkroom with computers and software, 4) getting instant feedback on the LCD monitor on the back of the camera to learn quickly from your mistakes, even in the field, while the flower is still there and in the same condition 5) make panoramic images without using a panoramic camera (I did this for the Louisville Science Center, and it was a hoot!) and 6) shooting multiple exposures of the same scene and blending those images with software to create more even exposures that appear as you saw them in the field.

Finally, moving to the digital world has allowed my creativity to soar and I find myself trying different approaches because I know that I can easily delete the images in the field or at home if they are not worth saving.

I admit that there are disadvantages, but they are minor. One big issue is image storage on the computer hard drive and the fact that as image quality and file size increase, so does the amount of storage you need in the computer and on external hard drives used to back up the computer if it fails (I have experienced that, and it is not a good feeling to see years of information potentially lost if you do not back up files). Fortunately, storage is becoming cheaper all the time.

Another drawback with digital SLR is dust on the sensor. When you change lenses, particularly in the field, the sensor (which captures the image), is electro statically charged and will attract dust (it can be removed in post-processing, but it is time consuming), which shows up as dark blotches on the image. You must become familiar with, and comfortable with, cleaning that sensor or paying to have someone clean it for you.

Finally, the biggest drawback is it can make people lazy with their photographic techniques because they feel they can always "fix" the image in a program like Photoshop. Let's face it, software and technology are pretty amazing at what they can accomplish, but a soft, fuzzy, out-of-focus image cannot be corrected with software and out-of-focus images are still out of focus. The same goes with exposure. Grossly over- or under-exposed images can be salvaged with some software, but you will not get quality results. Just remember the old adage, "Garbage in, garbage out." The other old saying that I always remember is that I will take technique over technology any day of the week.

How do digital cameras work? Well, pretty much like film cameras in that light enters through the lens, the shutter is tripped, and the scene is captured on the sensor (instead of film), and then stored on a digital media card as pixels (picture elements that have red, green, and blue sub-pixels for color images). These pixels (or tiny dots) are made up of something called bits, and the greater the bits (depth), the more information about color they can hold. An 8-bit image will have 256 different colors or shades of gray represented. This is certainly okay for simple graphics on a computer, but for photographic reproduction you want at least 16-bit color depth with the resulting 65,000 color combinations. A 24-bit or 32-bit image will have millions of color combinations. The upside of all of this is to say that the more pixels arranged on the sensor, the higher the resolution, and, in theory, the quality of the image increases.

However, other design features can also affect pixel quality. What does this mean when you purchase a 6-megapixel camera? It means it has a resolution of 2,000 vertical pixels and 3,000 horizontal pixels, which equals 6,000,000 pixels or 6 megapixels. I will delve into this in a bit (get the pun?) more detail when I discuss selecting a camera. For now, let's get into the business of creating better wildflower photos by setting the stage for more advanced information: How does the system work and what terms do you need to become familiar with? For those who already know this basic stuff, you may pass go (this section), and collect your $200 and get on with playing the photography game.

Photographic Terminology

—Understanding Exposure and Your Camera's Meter and relating it to the Use of Light

For all you readers who are acutely aware of exposure and how the modern SLR system works, you can skip over this section because this is for beginners who want to really elevate their photography to the next level. It is surprising that even with today's modern digital SLR cameras with program modes, I still shoot wildflower images almost exclusively using the manual (I have to set both aperture and shutter speed) or aperture priority (I set the aperture and the camera sets the shutter speed) modes.

What is exposure, and why is it important for you to understand exposure even if you have a point-and-shoot or an automatic, auto-everything camera? To make a long story short; for any given image – flower, scenic, or whatever – there is an optimum or ideal exposure. This means the full range of tones, from light to dark, are present, and the lights aren't too light, and the darks aren't too dark, and the mid-tones are not too bright or too dark. In addition, properly exposed images have excellent color saturation and appropriate contrast. It is impossible to put back detail in either the light or dark of an image, no matter which post-processing software you use. It is better to have a properly exposed image to begin with.

When judging any exposure, you should also assess the contrast of the image. The easiest way to do this in the field is to use the "squint test." This is nothing more than closing your eyes about three-quarters of the way shut and looking at the image to see if the subject can be recognized and stands out against the background. Then look to see where your eyes gravitate to: It should be the subject. Try the squint test for exposure and contrast on the red trillium image at right.

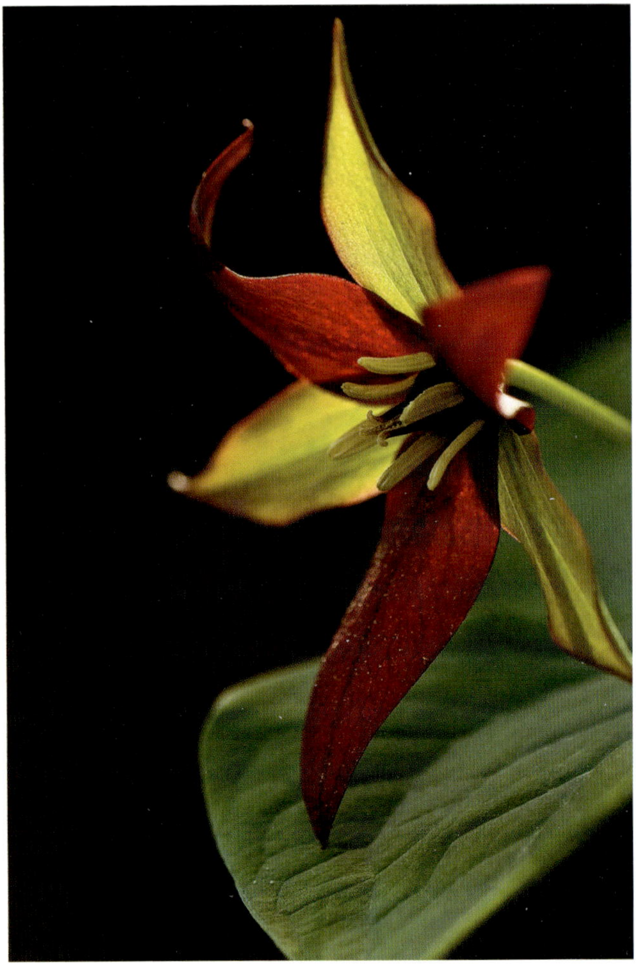

Red Trillium

Exposure is simply a measure of how much light comes through your lens and hits the sensor on the back of the camera much like light hitting film in the old days. Perhaps an example will clarify your thinking here. Let's say the proper exposure for a particular flower is 100 units or photons of light, so if you let in 200 units of light, the image will appear bleached out or overexposed and you will have no detail in the highlights, etc. If you let in 50 units of light, the image will be underexposed or dark, and you will have no details in the shadows.

There are three ways of modifying the amount of light hitting the sensor: changing the aperture, shutter speed, or ISO rating (how sensitive to light the sensor is). In the old days, you could not change the ISO rating on the fly so to speak, and to increase ISO you needed to actually change to a different film that was more sensitive to light. This is a distinct advantage to digital photography because you can select any ISO setting you want. Remember in photography there are trade-offs and in general, as you increase the ISO you also increase the amount of noise in the image. Noise is similar to grain in film, which I will discuss later. However, engineers are amazing and the new cameras coming onto the market do a great job of reducing noise so that, in some cases, you can shoot at ISO of 1600 or more and still get acceptable results. Let's begin by discussing shutter speed.

Shutter Speed

The shutter (a series of blades in front of the sensor that move either up and down or side to side exposing the sensor) controls the length of time light hits the sensor. Shutter speed is measured in seconds or fractions of seconds. Historically because film was so sensitive to light, shutter speed was measured in fractions of a second. A slow shutter speed is typically less than 1/30th of a second and a fast shutter speed might be 1/1000th of a second. If the shutter is open longer, it lets in more light, and if open for a shorter period of time, it lets in less light.

Shutter speed is important because it can be used for creative purposes, but, more importantly if the speed is too slow, the photo will be blurry. The general rule of thumb here is that you can effectively hand-hold a camera at 1/lens length, meaning if you are shooting with a 200mm lens, you could effectively hand hold this at 1/250th of a second. While there are ways of getting around this, such as bracing against a stable object, etc., I have found that often doesn't hold true if you are in the field, have been hiking for awhile, are tired, and are less stable than we used to be when we were younger. For these very reasons, plus all the others I mention in the equipment section, buy a tripod because it allows you to use *all* the shutter speeds, slow and fast, to get the desired type of image you are looking for.

For much wildflower photography, you will want to use faster shutter speeds to stop motion – or then again perhaps you don't, and simply wait out the wind. One interesting, creative use of a slow shutter speed would be to allow the flowers to "blow in the wind," giving an abstract blurred effect. For those who want to do this type of wildflower photography, I highly recommend Tony Sweet's book, *Fine Art Flower Photography: Creative Techniques and the Art of Observation*.

Aperture

The second way of altering the amount of light hitting the sensor is by adjusting the aperture. Aperture is nothing except a fancy term for the hole or opening in the lens. The aperture is made up of a series of blades that fan open to make a hole in the lens larger or smaller. The maximum aperture of any lens is determined by simple physics, but in general it is determined by the size of the primary "element" or outermost piece of glass on the lens and the distance between the front of the lens and the sensor (or focal plane). These measurements (aperture) are called "f stops" (remember the vernacular above about talking in stops – this is where that terminology comes from) and are given a number.

Now here is where they try to confuse you because the *larger* the number (f/22, f/16), the smaller the opening. So a small aperture actually has a big number and lets in less light. In general, the smallest aperture is rated f/64 (although you will find few lenses with this aperture as they are extremely expensive to develop), and this would be a very tiny hole versus a large hole such as f/1.4, f/1.8, f/2.8, which lets in lots of light.

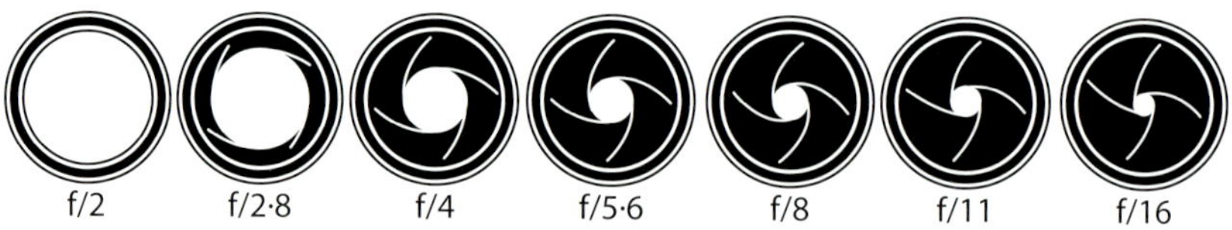

Aperture f stops diagram. Notice how the larger the aperture number the smaller the opening, which means less light will enter through the lens.

Lenses with apertures represented by small numbers are also typically expensive and are often called "fast" lenses because the opening can be so big that they let in more light, and you can use faster shutter speeds. This is why sports and wildlife enthusiasts like long lenses that are fast. For wildflower photography, fast lenses aren't that necessary. Just as with shutter speed, changing one f stop either halves or doubles the amount of light reaching the sensor.

Aperture and its Relationship to Depth of Field

Depth of field is simply the area in front of, around, and in back of the subject that is crisp, clear, and in sharp focus. There are a few factors that you should understand about depth of field because it is a critical part of understanding basic photographic techniques. Two of the biggest factors affecting depth of field are the aperture setting and the focal length of the lens used. Changing the aperture is one of the primary methods used to alter the depth of field of an image. The general rule of thumb is that all factors being equal (image size and distance), the bigger the lens opening (f/1.4, f/2, f/2.8), the less depth of field (shallow). From a wildflower photography perspective, sometimes shallow depth of field using an aperture setting of f/5.6 or f/4 can work for you because it isolates the subject and removes unwanted details from the image. This works particularly well when using a longer (200mm or longer) lens. Conversely, if you want more of the flower in focus, you would need to use a large f stop like f/11 or f/22.

The second factor affecting depth of field is focal distance, not lens length. Technically speaking, if the image size in-camera and

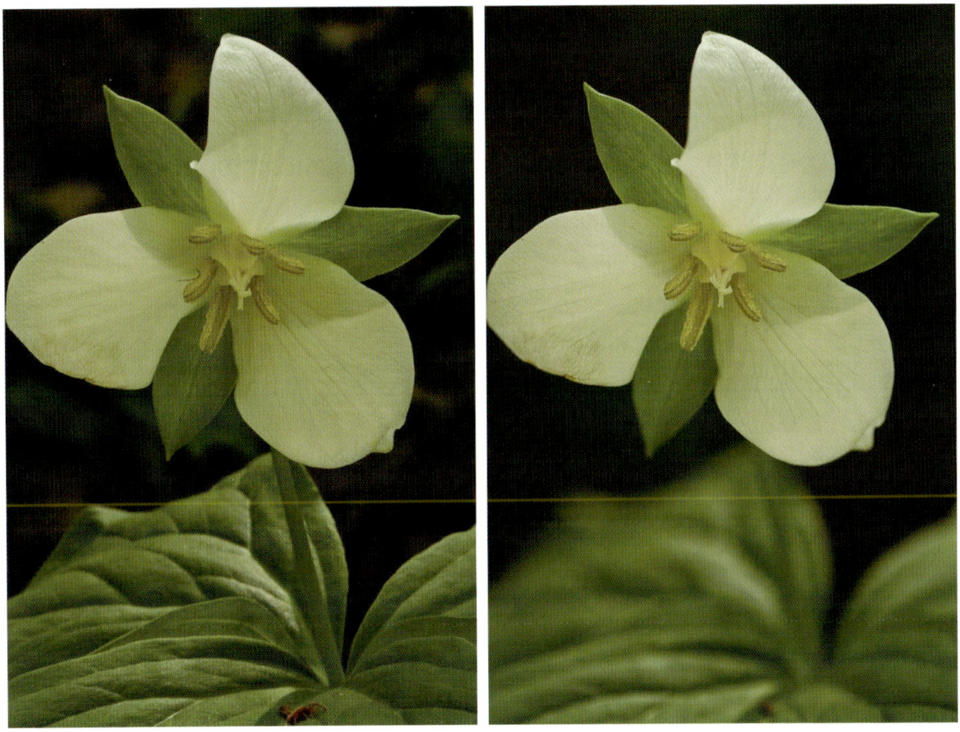

The image on the left was taken at f/22 and has great depth of field. Notice how sharp and in focus the leaves are. Notice that the background has many distracting elements that take away from the subject. The image on the right was taken at f/5.6 with shallow depth of field. Notice the subject (flower) is in focus, but the background and leaves are blurred. I like the image on the right more because there are no distracting elements that take away from the subject.

the f stop are the same for both lenses (say a 50mm vs. 200mm), the depth of field will be identical regardless of lens length. However, it would appear the shorter the lens (35 or 50mm), the deeper the depth of field. Think of it this way, when you stand in the same place and focus on a subject at the same distance, a longer focal length lens will have a shallower depth of field (even though the pictures will show something entirely different) and is an effect due to higher magnification, not focal length. Longer focal lengths also *appear* to have a shallow depth of field because they flatten perspective. This renders a background much larger relative to the foreground – even if no more detail is resolved. Depth of field also appears shallower for SLR cameras than for compact digital cameras, because SLR cameras require a longer focal length to achieve the same field of view.

Finally, distance affects depth of field and it increases as you move farther away from the subject. This is why landscapes have such large depth of field (more about hyper-focal distance later) and macro or shooting close-ups have such little inherent depth of field, which is why focusing and creative aperture use become important concepts to master.

Unfortunately, photography is a two-dimensional media and it is impossible to truly represent depth. But we can create the illusion or perception of the third dimension (depth) within an image. The techniques used to create three-dimensional form include overlapping, changing sizes or placements of objects in the image, linear perspective, the effect of color, and a combination of all the methods mentioned above.

One of the simplest ways to create a sense of depth is to overlap parts of your objects such as in the case of overlapping flowers, leaves or stems. In the photo of jack-in-the-pulpits and yellow violets on the following page, a sense of depth was created by the overlapping leaves and petals. It is easy to identify those with petals in front of the first Jack are closer than those whose petals by the second Jack in the background.

Another easy, and often used technique, is to change the size and placement of an object in the image. This is most often seen in landscape images where a flower or groups of flowers are placed in focus in the front of an image while the remaining forms and shapes appear in the distance and still remain in focus.

The third most commonly used technique to create a sense of depth is to use leading lines or linear perspective. Lines that

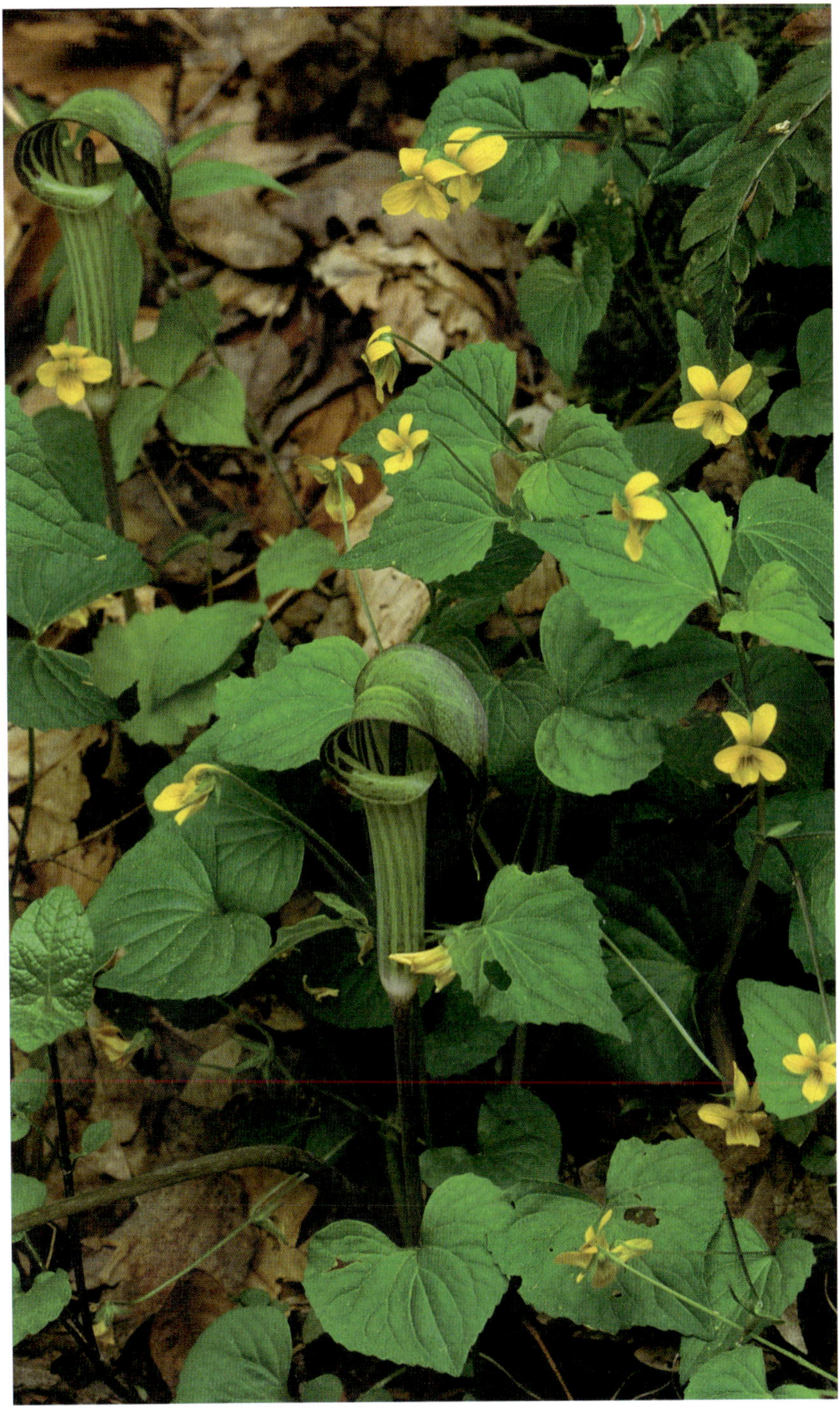

These jack-in-the-pulpits and yellow violets demonstrate the technique of overlapping to create a sense of depth.

converge can imply depth and distance because the illusion is that objects appear smaller and come together to some "point" on the horizon line, either real or imagined.

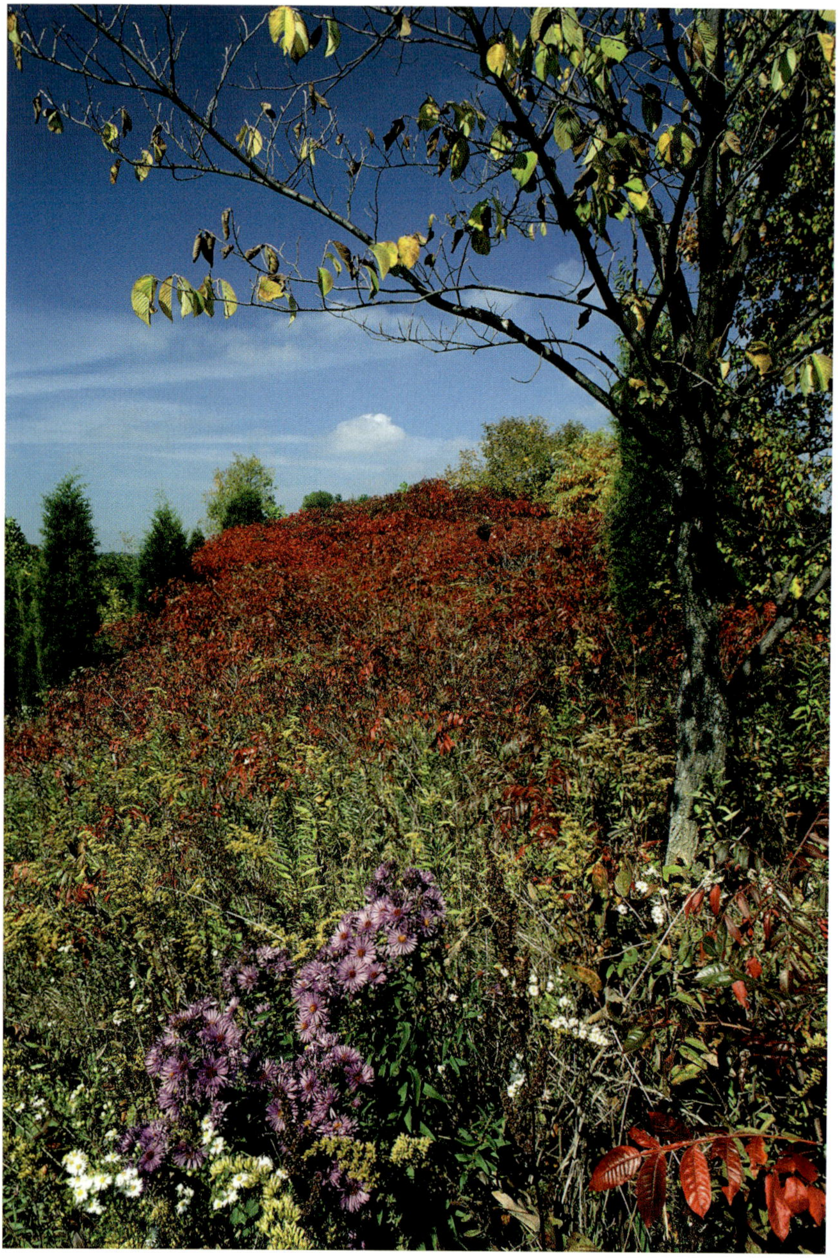

By placing the New England Asters close to the lens and making it appear large within the frame, balanced against the sumac in the distance, is an example of using a large subject in the foreground and keeping the background in focus.

Warm colors like this blue jasmine leatherflower set against a cool background of green is an example of using color to help create a sense of depth.

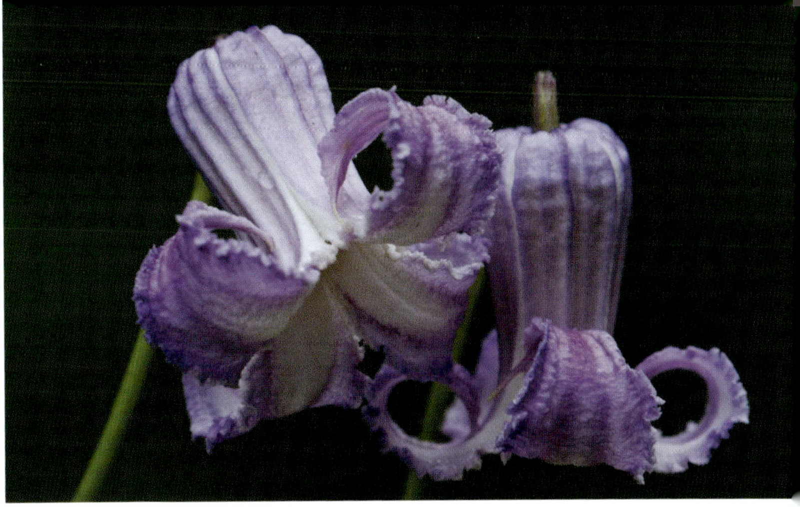

Finally, color can affect depth perception. This concept will be expanded in the color section. In general, warm colors appear closer than do cool colors, and stronger hues (red) come forward more than do less saturated hues (pink).

Perhaps the best way to achieve the perception of depth is to use all of the above techniques in combination with one another to alter how we perceive an image. For instance, light objects come forward, and dark objects recede, and when there is a large amount of contrast, a small area of differing tone will come forward. Where you place the subject and its size is also important. Larger objects come forward, and objects in the lower half of the image come forward, or command more of our attention. One rule of thumb to improve your images is if you can't make it good, make it *big*! Of course, this stuff all sounds good in theory, and you can break every single rule, and still achieve your desired effect. I try to stick to the basics, which usually keeps me out of trouble.

One of the most perplexing questions I am often asked is "How do you get the flowers in the front of the image to be in focus with the distant background?" The answer is a technical one based on physics and using something called the hyper-focal distance. Whenever you are taking an image, there are always parts of the image that are in focus and other parts that are not in focus. The part that is in focus is called the "focal plane." Roughly one-third of the focal plane is in front of the object in focus and two-thirds are behind. So you can cheat in some cases by just focusing on some flowers from about one-third of the way in the image and using maximum aperture settings of f/16 or f/22; everything from that point to infinity will be in focus. Hyper-focal distance works for any lens and the principle remains constant.

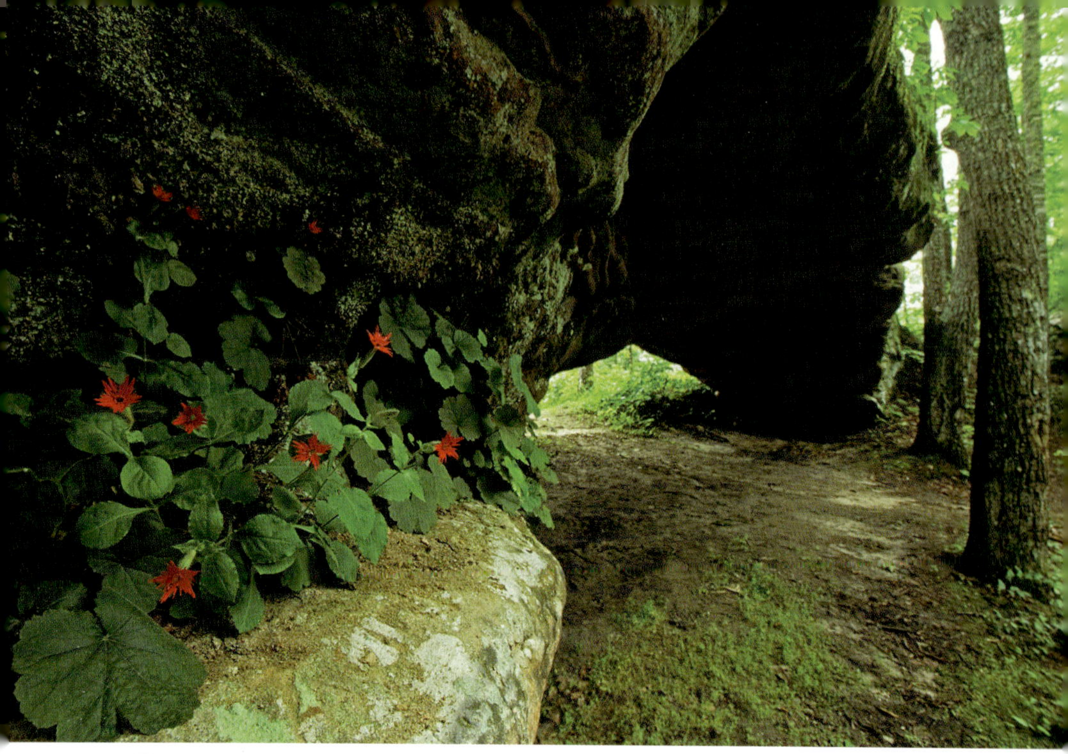

The use of hyper-focal distance was used to keep the catchfly in focus as well as the twin arch.

However, if you want to get the maximum amount of depth of field, you can use a hyper-focal distance chart which does the complicated math for you and gives you how close you can focus at which aperture and have everything in the photo sharp from that point to infinity. For example, let's say you are using a 28mm wide-angle lens. The hyper-focal distance at aperture 2.8 is 30.6 feet, and at f/22 it is 3.9 feet, which means that everything from this distance to infinity will be sharp when the lens is manually focused at 3.9 feet and the aperture is set to f/22.

This is also a useful technique to use when photographing a field of flowers with a longer lens. For example, say you are using a short telephoto lens in the range of 100mm. The hyper-focal distance at f/2.8 is 390 feet and at f/22 it is 30 feet. To use this technique with any lens requires a good tripod because shutter speeds will be slow. Set the camera to manual focus – this is critical – after composing the scene, focus at the set hyper-focal distance. Note, the foreground will appear sharp and the background out of focus, but do not refocus. If you use a depth of field preview button to view the scene, you will notice that everything is sharp and in focus. Once you have focused at the hyper-focal distance, take your exposure reading and

Lens focal length	Hyper-focal & nearest focus	F/1.8	F/2.8	F/4	F/5.6	F/8	F/11	F/16	F/22	F/32
24mm	HF	37' 10"	23' 10"	16' 10"	11' 11"	8' 5"	6'	4' 3"	3'	2' 1"
	NF	18' 11"	11' 11"	8' 5"	6'	4' 3"	3'	2' 1"	1' 6"	1' 1'
35mm	HF	80' 7"	50' 9"	35' 11"	25' 4"	17' 11"	12' 8"	9'	6' 4"	4' 6"
	NF	40' 3"	25' 5"	17' 11"	12' 8"	9'	6' 4"	4' 6"	3' 2"	2' 3"
50mm	HF	164'	103'	73' 3"	51' 9"	36' 7"	25' 11"	18' 4"	12' 11"	9' 2"
	NF	82' 2"	51' 9"	36' 7"	25' 11"	18' 4"	12' 11"	9' 2"	6' 6"	4' 7"
200mm	HF	2630'	1657'	1171'	828'	585'	414'	292'	207'	146'
	NF	1315'	828'	585'	414'	292'	207'	146'	103'	73' 3"

For each focal length of the lens, the HF stands for the focal length distance, or the distance to which you should set the lens to in feet and inches. The NF is the closest distance that will be in focus (about ½ the HF distance) from that point to infinity with 35mm style DSLR. For example, if you have a 35mm lens set to f/16 and set the focusing ring to six feet, four inches, everything from three feet two inches to infinity will be in focus.

begin snapping photos. If your camera has a depth of field preview button you will notice the view finder gets very dark and it is hard to see what is in focus. This is another place where using this chart can help figure out maximum depth of field.

ISO Rating

In the analog world of film, the sensitivity of film was determined and given an exposure rating called ISO or ASA in the past. These acronyms are short for International Standards Association or American Standards Association. The higher the ISO number, the more sensitive the film was to light. Each time the film speed doubled meant that it was twice as sensitive to light. Thus, a film rated 100 ISO would be twice as sensitive to light as a film rated ISO 50. In the same vein, film rated 400 ISO would be eight times as sensitive as a film rated ISO 50.

The advantage of using a film with a lower ISO rating was that the grain (when film was developed it had an optical texture as a result of minute metallic silver particles developed from silver halide) was smaller and not noticeable, whereas if you used a film with ISO 400, it would sometimes have a speckled look where the particles were larger and would appear on enlargements. Nature photographers, who wanted better color saturation, finer grain, and perhaps more stable emulsions, usually selected slow films because the "quality" was better.

The same rules now apply to digital photography, and every time you double the ISO (100 to 200 to 400) it doubles the light sensitivity of the sensor. Fortunately the new electronics and software in digital SLR's allow the selection of "in-between" ISO numbers such as 125, 160, 200, 320, etc. While we do not have to deal with grain issues with digital photography, we do have to deal with "noise" which has the appearance of grain or a speckling effect on the images. Noise can also show up when you use very slow shutter speeds with digital photography. Fortunately, better quality digital SLR cameras have noise filters that help reduce noise and technology has resulted in new digital cameras that can be shot at ISO 1600 to 3200 with little noticeable noise. Finally, there are multiple software programs that can also reduce or remove digital noise.

Obtaining Properly Exposed Images in the Camera

—Understanding Histograms

Now let's put this into perspective to understand getting a good exposure in the camera. One of the really great aspects of the new digital SLR is that you can display a histogram on the back LCD panel (buy a camera with as big an LCD display as possible) which helps eliminate any guesswork as to whether the image is properly exposed and whether you have all the details in the white (highlights) end of the spectrum or the black (shadows) end.

A histogram is basically a graph of 256 vertical bars (squashed together) that represents the tonal qualities in an 8-bit image (16-bit images are condensed to 8-bits). The left end of the histogram represents pure black (equals 0), and the right side represents pure white (equals 255). It is important to pay attention to the two ends and not so much the middle (this has mostly color information in it), which looks like a mountain peak or series of peaks related to grays, greens, browns, etc. The reason to pay attention to the ends is that you do not want to lose important details in either the dark or white end of the exposure. What the middle looks like can vary tremendously, and there is no right or wrong histogram as far as the middle portion goes. In most cases, unless you have an image with a tremendous amount of dark tones, the tails at either end should not "push" up against the edge and should have some

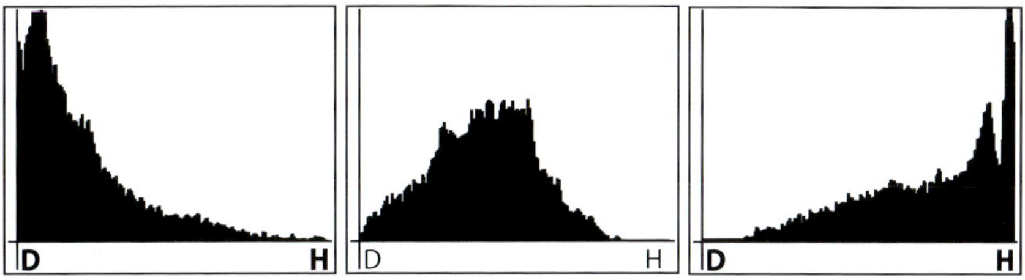

This generally shows three typical histograms indicating exposure that might be under-exposed (left), properly exposed (center), and over-exposed (right).

amount of tail. If either tail is cut off it is called "clipping."

You can get situations where there are tremendous amounts of light or dark in an image, like a background, that can shift the histogram to the left, and the way to ensure that the image is properly exposed is to look to the middle and right to make sure there is a tail. The reverse is also true for images that contain a large amount of white or highlights, although this does not happen often when photographing wildflowers.

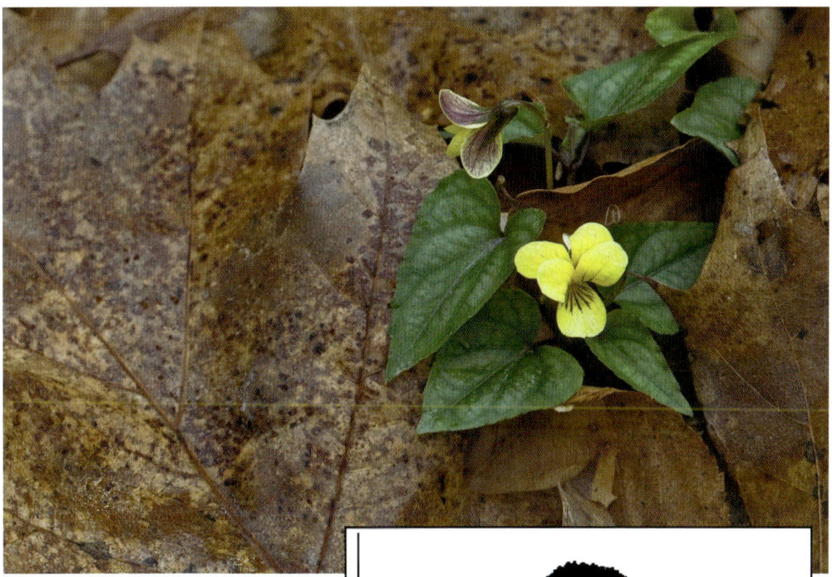

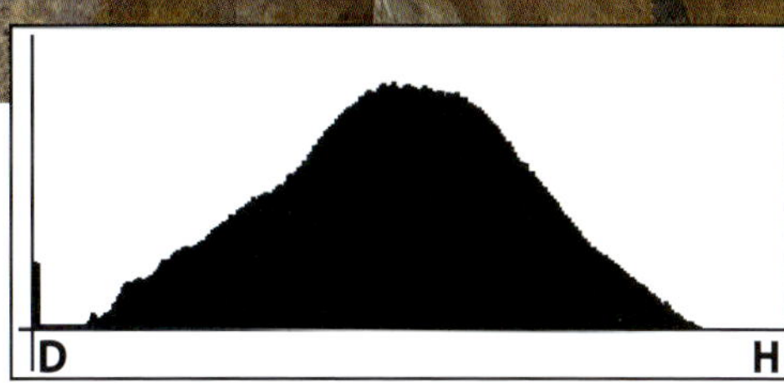

Note on the histogram that this has a tail that extends to the left and to the right with a nice bell-shaped curve in the middle. This is a "standard" histogram for an image like this one of the Halberd violet because there are mostly mid-tones and no really dark areas or strong highlights.

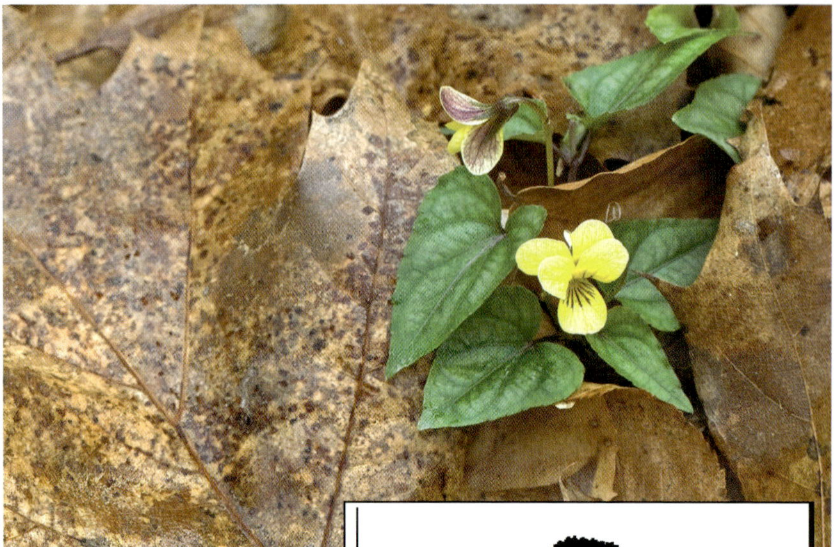

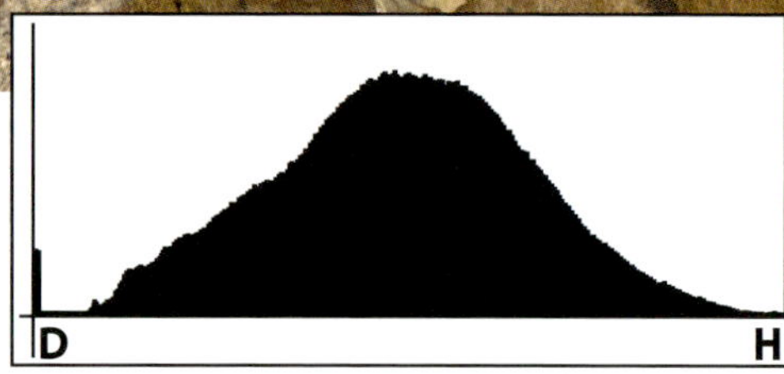

Here is the same image one stop over-exposed. Notice the lack of detail in the highlights, how the histogram has shifted to the right, and how the right side of the graph is going up the side.

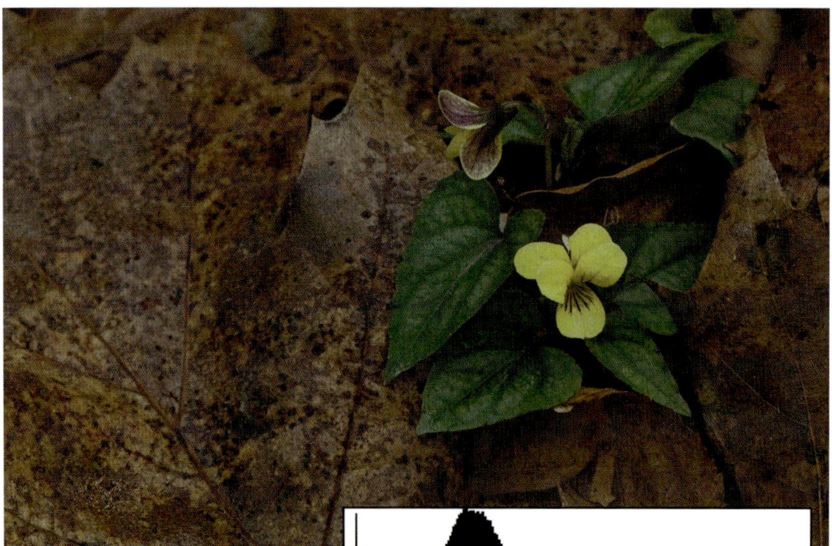

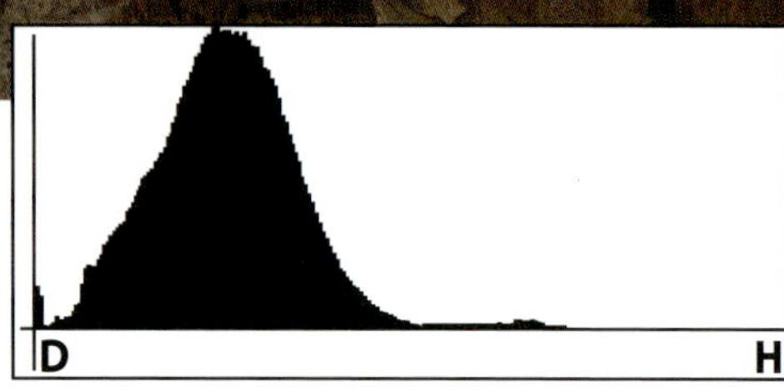

Here is the same image one stop under-exposed. Notice that the histogram shows no highlights and it has shifted too far to the left.

Let me reiterate that the left side of the histogram represents black or shadows and the right side represents white or highlights. Furthermore, there is some optimal or ideal exposure based on technicalities, and then there is the appropriate exposure. Sometimes you can get fooled by the histogram into thinking the image is not properly exposed. The perfect example is taking a white flower against a dark background as shown below. In this case, the histogram is naturally going to be heavy on the left side (and if there are pure blacks it will clip on the left). This is to be expected, and the important point is whether there is clipping on the right side (which means you have lost your details in the whites). If you are going to err on the side of caution, it is better to be heavy on the left side than to lose details in the highlights that cannot be retrieved. Finally, there is no perfect histogram for all images, and the shape depends on the tonal values in the image, and how you decide to capture them. This information is just a primer on getting properly exposed images in the field, and the best way to ensure you are getting well-exposed images is to practice, practice, practice and look at the histograms. There are more histograms with photographs in the visual design section, which shows some challenging lighting conditions.

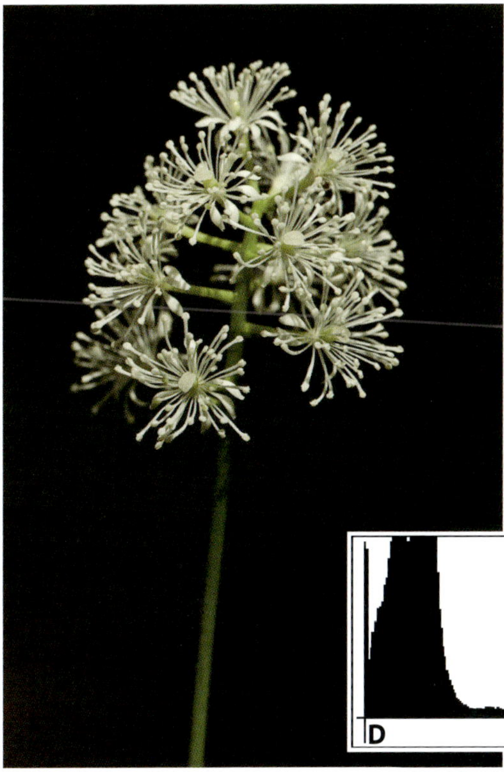

Note on the histogram that it is shifted strongly to the left, which accounts for the large amount of dark in the image. The important feature to notice is that the white extends all the way to the right-hand side, which indicates no details have been lost in the highlights. This is a well-exposed image.

Using Visual Design to Create More Artistic Photographs

Photography is both science and art. With the introduction of digital photography, the scientific and technical aspects of photography can become overwhelming rather quickly. Much is written daily on this side of photography and many people who have technical knowledge of computers and technology, have now entered into digital photography and produce technically excellent photographs. But photography is more than equipment and technique. Many technically excellent photographs lack emotion, vision, creativity, and fail to convey a message. The great landscape photographer Ansel Adams wrote, "photography is more than a medium for factual communications of ideas, it is creative art" and "there is nothing worse than a brilliant image of a fuzzy concept." What Adams was referring to was that photography is more than a technique and is successful only when the images convey a vision and emotion. Stated again for emphasis, there are many technically excellent photographs that say absolutely nothing.

When you look at the work of many of the "great" nature photographers, look at their resumes, and you might likely find that many have degrees in art. There is no shortage of information out in the world about equipment, image processing, and software to use, how to be more efficient with your camera, what works and what doesn't work from a technical standpoint. However, learning about the other aspect of photography, artistic rendering, it appears that far fewer essays are written, far fewer discussions are held, and far fewer tips and helpful pointers are published on the artistic side of photography.

It is for precisely this reason that I have included this section of the book on visual design. Furthermore, most people do not even consider color when photographing flowers and yet it is the color of the bloom or blossom that is what attracted us to the plant in the first place. Color is so critical because it really and truly dictates what wildflower photos are successful and which ones have little impact visually.

Most photographers have little to no training in understanding visual design in comparison to painters, which is unfortunate. Painters are often taught color theory and general visual design principles in year one of their studies because they create the environment for their images and color contributes to the success of their paintings. In contrast, photographers must "find" their environment in nature and color and flowers are almost synonymous. While the following discussion covers the basics of visual design and color theory, I am acutely aware that providing too much information can cause sensory overload and too much of a discussion will make the subject confusing. I have tried to keep the information to a bare minimum while still getting the primary points across. But I truly believe that to be a better photographer you must at least have some rudimentary concept of visual design floating around inside your head. It may be something you develop over time or it may be something innate, but it is important because photography is both science and art.

The three primary areas I hope to provide information on are light, color, and design. We begin with a discussion of understanding color and color theory.

The Effective Use of Color

Why is it so important to cover some basic color theory? Because without this general understanding, particularly with relationship to the psychological and physiological basis of the theory, people who view their photographs may wonder why some flower images "work" or "don't work" and, when queried about why, the photographer just says it is some gut feeling when in fact it might very well be described by understanding how and why color worked in the image.

Let's look at it from a more practical reason. Quite simply, wildflower photos are an explosion of color and color dramatically affects the emotional appeal of the flower and image. Understanding how color affects an image is not an easy task as it requires an understanding of our human perceptions about light and color, the basic physics of color and light, and the biology of how we "see" light and color. Not only that, but when you get into post-processing of images, you will be hit with terminology about color correcting images, hue, intensity, saturation, and other topics that are discussed below which should help you understand the creative side of using color in the digital darkroom.

Remember Kindergarten? Robert Fulghum wrote a wonderful little book, now in its fifteenth edition entitled: *All I Really Need to Know I Learned in Kindergarten*. If you will recall, one of those topics kindergarten kids learn is basic color theory. There is something to be said for remembering some of the basic concepts related to color theory with respect to wildflower photography. Remember the color wheel and primary versus secondary colors? What happens when you combine red and yellow? You get orange. So let's revisit everything you learned about colors from kindergarten and relate it to creating wildflower images.

This section will provide you a little background that you can draw upon when pondering how to photograph any particular flower. It will not make you a painter or artist overnight, nor will it be constantly in your thoughts when you are in the field. Rather it will be lurking somewhere in the dark recess of your mind and give you the insight about what the flower says to you, what you are trying to say about the flower, and how you want the audience to perceive the image.

With just a rudimentary understanding of color theory you will discover that images with mostly warm colors appear relatively stable and come forward or advance in the design. You will also discover that secondary colors are more unstable and tend to recede into the distance. Furthermore, you will learn that saturated or unbroken colors come forward (like red) and lighter or less saturated colors (like pink) recede into the distance. Finally, light color has a tendency to advance and dark colors typically recede (which is why a dark background so often works for wildflowers because the flower comes forward and can give a three dimensional appearance to the image while at the same time making the subject standout from the background). In the end, the goal is to achieve color harmony in the image. Color harmony is achieved when all the colors in the image are visually appealing and work together.

Obviously improving your ability to use color in wildflower photography for greater expression is closely tied to understanding light properties, because the appearance of color is affected by a variety of factors including the time of day the image was taken, the time of year, depth of field, and length of exposure. The importance of

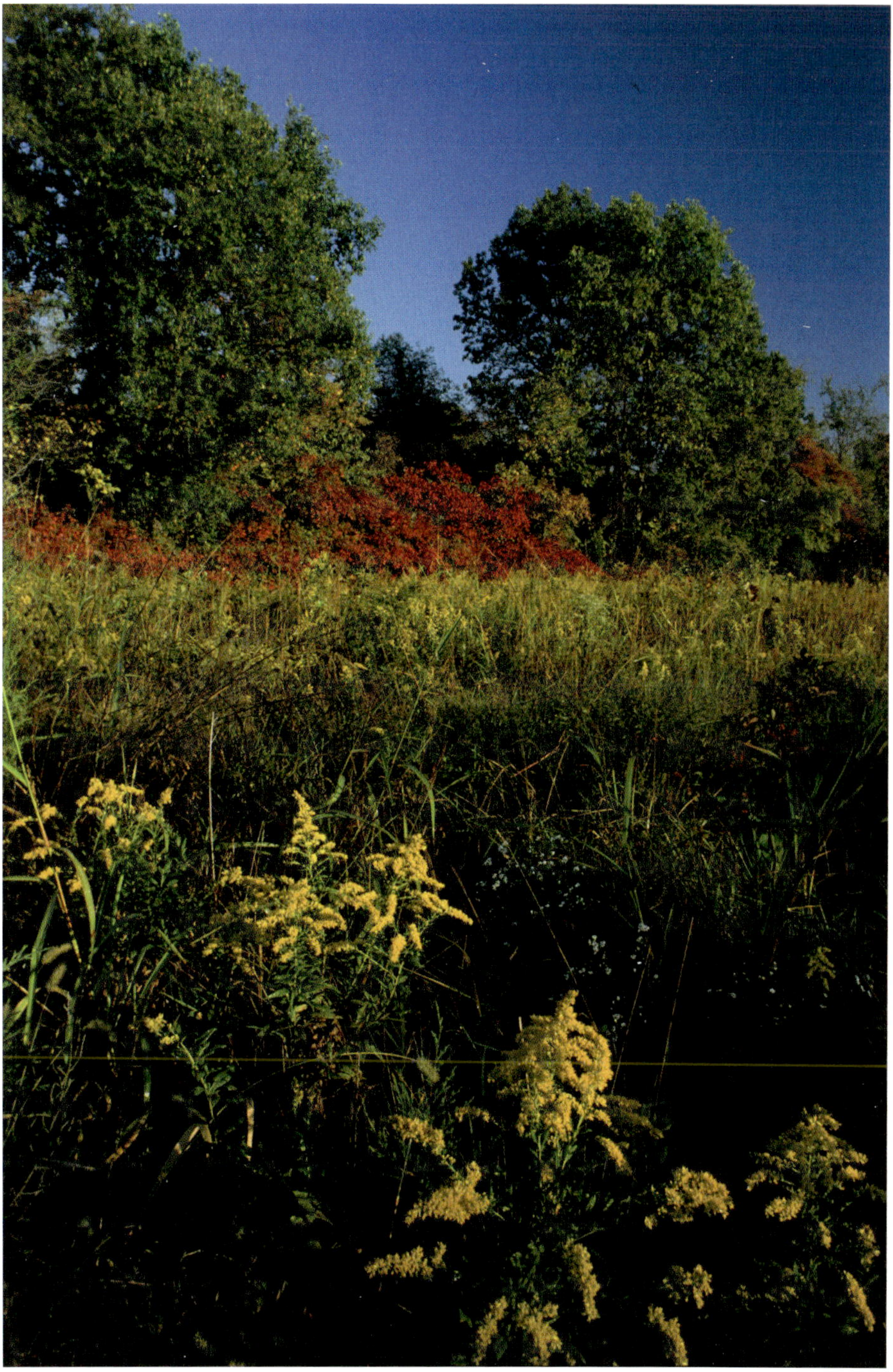

I like the combination of the pure primary colors of red, yellow and blue where the goldenrod flowers are in the "highlight" against a backdrop of neutral green with the red of the sumac and the nice blue sky.

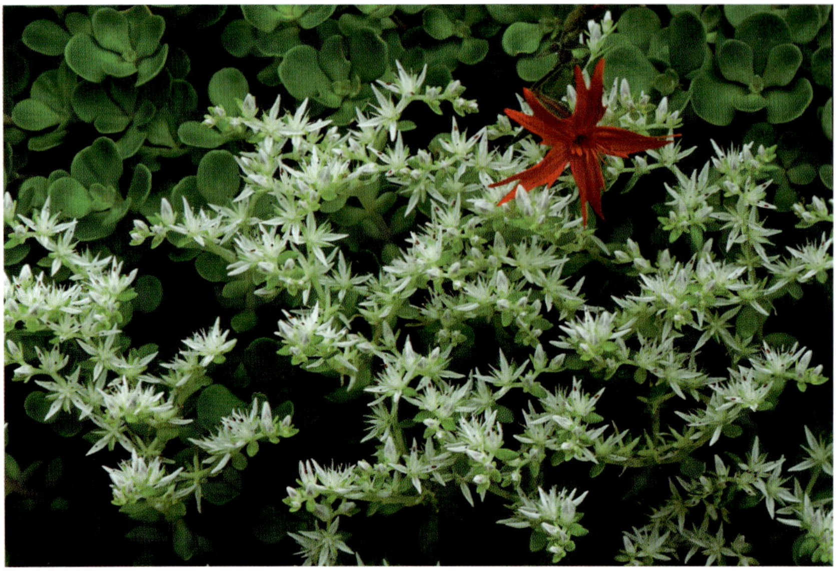

Notice how the red of the fire pink flower stands out against the white stonecrop even though your eyes normally go to the lightest part of an image.

light cannot be under-estimated and I discuss light in detail in the next section. Other factors come into play, including the quality of the ambient light and what other hues are present in the composition. One good piece of advice once given to me by an art instructor was to see how color is used in advertising, interior design, and various other art forms and it will help you develop your own intuitive way of how you perceive color and how you can use it to your advantage.

So let's say you see a beautiful fire pink flower in late spring that is a brilliant, almost pure example of the color red. Just what does this red really mean to us as humans, and what does it say in nature. Red is the universal color in nature that means – "Warning do not eat me! I am toxic!" like the northern red salamander or, in the case of birds, it means, "I am a red berry eat me so that my seeds can be dispersed." In the case of the fire pink, it means, "all you ruby-throated hummingbirds, come and find me and pollinate me so that I may reproduce," because of course, birds can see the color red. Pure, strong red is the color of fire and blood and passion or love. Red is an emotionally intense color and you cannot ignore the color red in a wildflower photo. Consequently, this flower will dominate your attention in the image and will not lend itself to soft, harmonious color compositions.

The Color Wheel

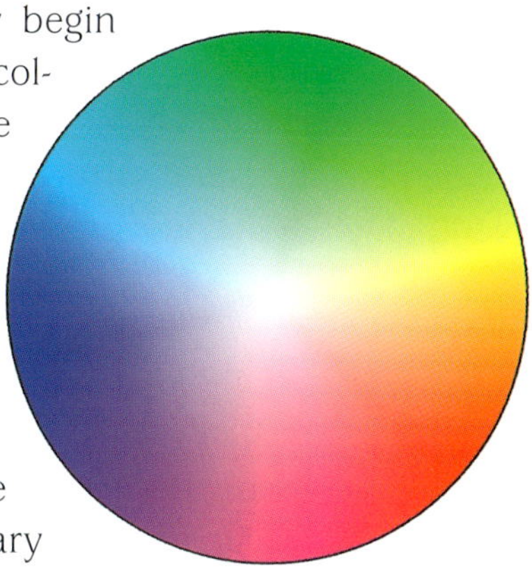

Most discussions of color theory begin with a color wheel with the primary colors of red, yellow, and blue because any color on a color wheel can be made by combining these first-order colors. Green, orange, and violet are second-order colors because they are made by combining two of the primary colors. The tertiary or third-order colors are made by fusion of a primary and secondary color. Black (absent of color with respect to light but with painting it is all the colors combined), white (all colors combined or absence of color with painting), and gray (50 percent black and 50 percent white) are called neutral colors because they are compatible with any color.

Painters and artists call pure, undiluted or unaltered color an unbroken color. This is important because colors can also have a tint. If you add white to a pure color, it makes it lighter such as white and red giving rise to pink. This is called a broken color. Conversely, if you add black, it makes the hue darker and makes red a deep burgundy color. The relative strength or purity of color is often called saturation or intensity. Highly saturated hues have a vivid, intense color, whereas less saturated colors are muted and more grayish and once again are broken colors.

Colors can also be combined to form various schemes including monochromatic, analogous, and complementary. Monochromatic color schemes consist of various tints and intensities of a single color. Monochromatic colors blend well and give a soothing, balanced, and visually appealing look, especially with greens and blues. Working with monochromatic colors is considered "safe" or "boring" because it is difficult to make mistakes with blending and

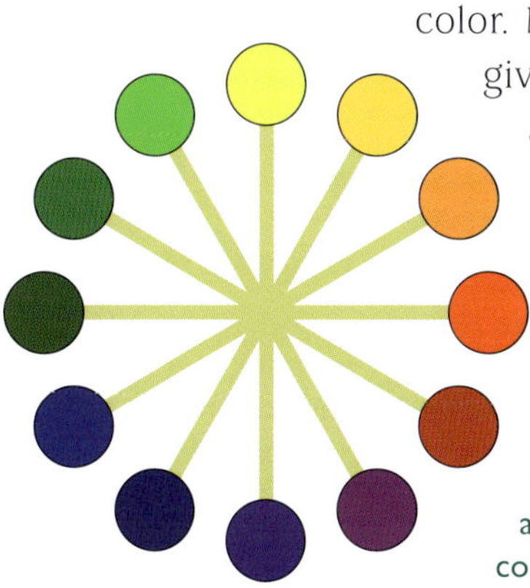

Color hue refers to the intensity of the color and you can use it to create monochromatic color images.

combining colors from other parts of the color wheel. Painters often begin their work with monochromatic designs for this reason.

However, there is little contrast and from a wildflower perspective monochromatic color is difficult to use unless you are trying to create peaceful color harmonies where the subject and background blend together. In my personal experience, working with blue flowers is tough to make the subject stand out because of the color blue.

Analogous color uses hues that are adjacent on the color wheel like green and blue-green, green-blue and blue, and blue and blue-violet. This color scheme has many of the same attributes as the monochromatic scheme but the colors appear richer. Working with analogous color is also considered somewhat safe and you can put more emphasis on the compositional aspects of the photograph because you do not have to worry about color "conflicts."

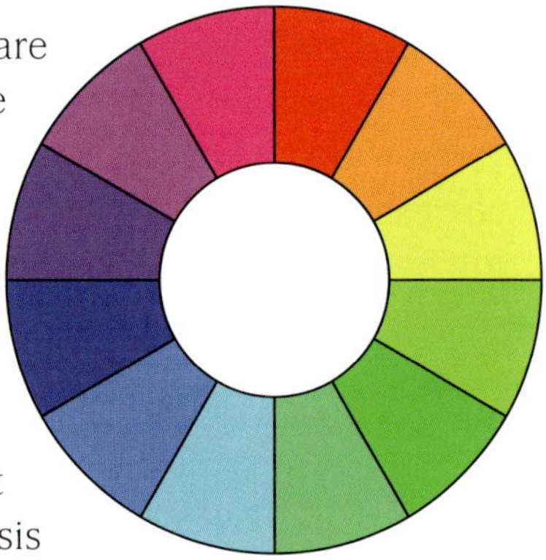

Analogous colors are adjacent on the color wheel. Note the use of analogous colors gives rise to a peaceful color harmony compared to the photo of the blue prairie gentian on the next page.

It also has the disadvantage of lacking contrast like the monochromatic scheme. When using this color scheme you should not use too many hues which will distort or ruin your color harmonies, and you should try not to use warm and cool colors together. Complementary colors are opposite on the color wheel. For example red and green are complementary colors. These complementary colors are about equal in their weight or intensity and are inherently high contrast because when you use complementary colors together it may increase their intensity through a process called simultaneous contrast.

Opposite: The prairie gentian is a difficult flower to photograph because it is such a deep blue color, and it is difficult to get a good background for several reasons such as: the size of the flower; less than optimal light conditions because it only opens during the heat of the day; it grows quite low to the ground dictating a difficult perspective to show the flower actually open; and it flowers in October after most of the prairie grasses are no longer green, but rather a drab brown color, which means you are limited in your selections of background color.

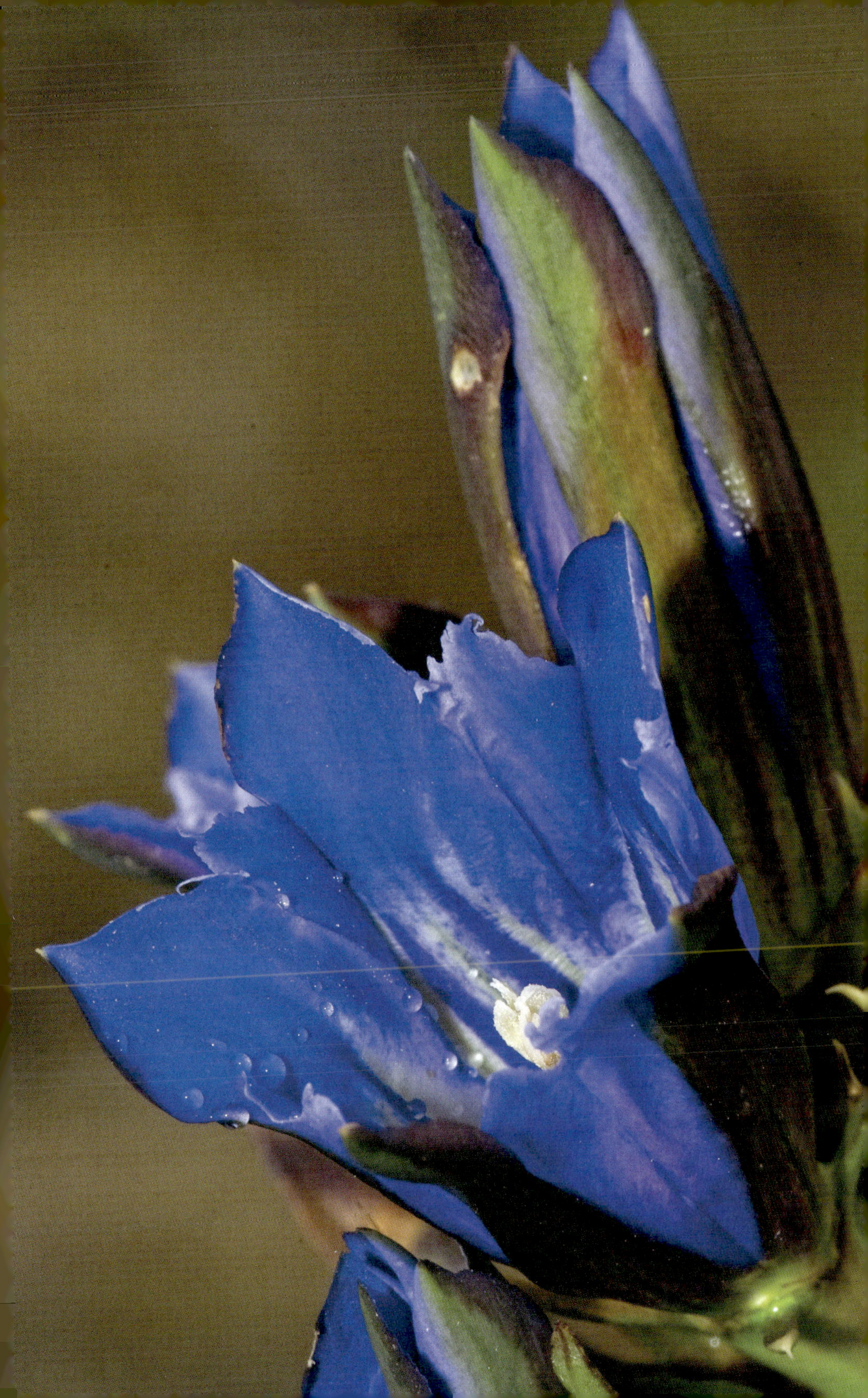

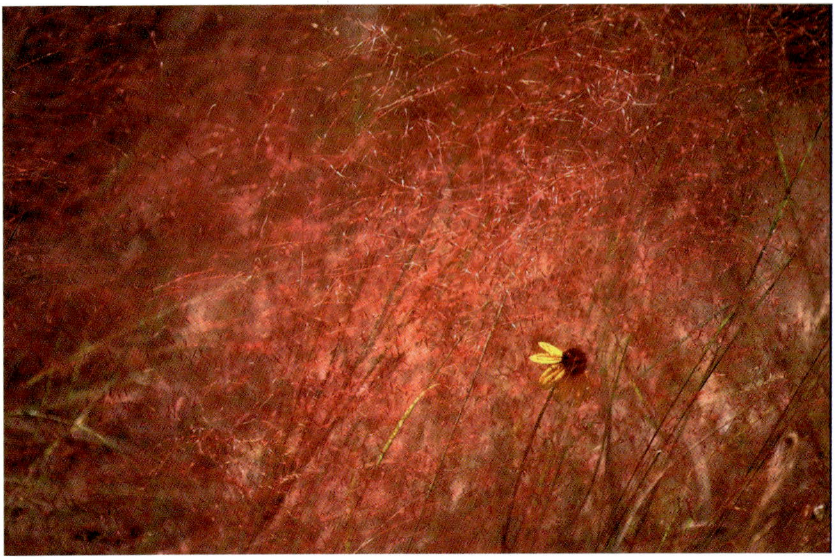

Red and yellow are analogous colors and the yellow really stands out against the red grass and gives a certain "wow" factor because of the colors.

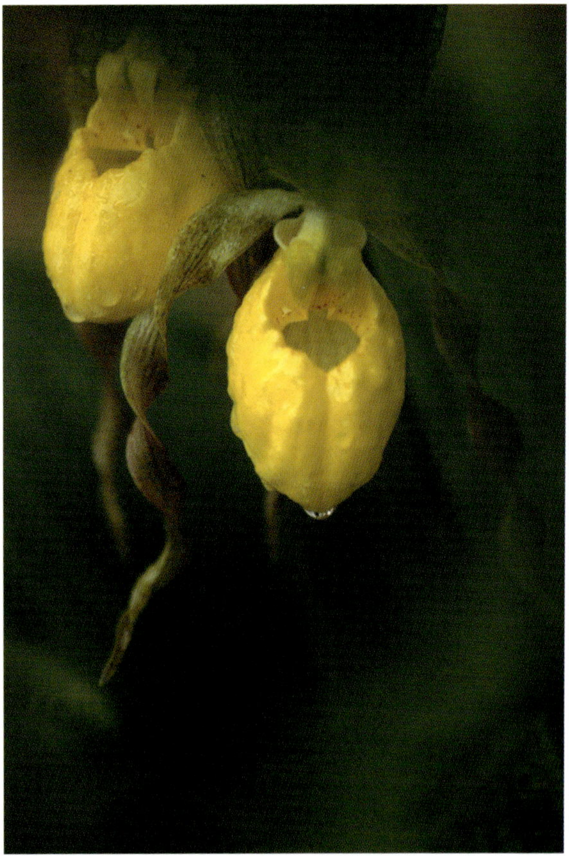

The yellow lady's slipper orchids standout because of the analogous nature of the yellow and green colors. Using a longer focal length lens (200-mm) and shooting through some lady ferns with a wider aperture (f/5.6) draws attention to the flowers and removes any distractions from the foreground and background.

Complementary color is much more difficult to work with because they are opposite on the color wheel, the colors have nothing in common and will therefore "compete" with one another for dominance in the image. For example, pure red (like in the fire pink) is almost impossible to use with pure green because they compete for your attention. How you deal with this situation is to "break" one or both of the colors such that you use a darker or lighter green against the pure red flower.

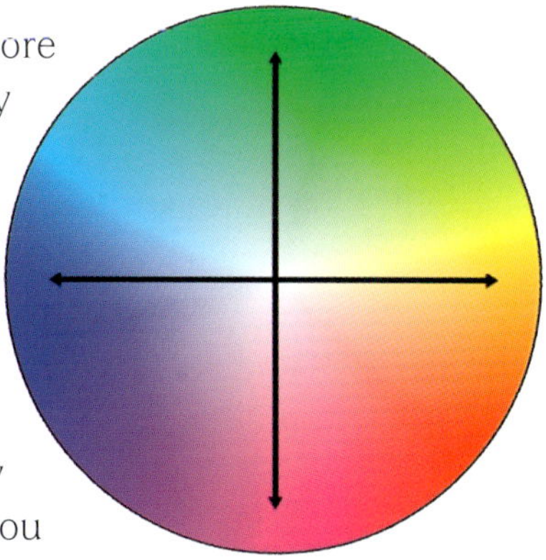

Complementary Colors

Other complementary colors vary in their effect, and

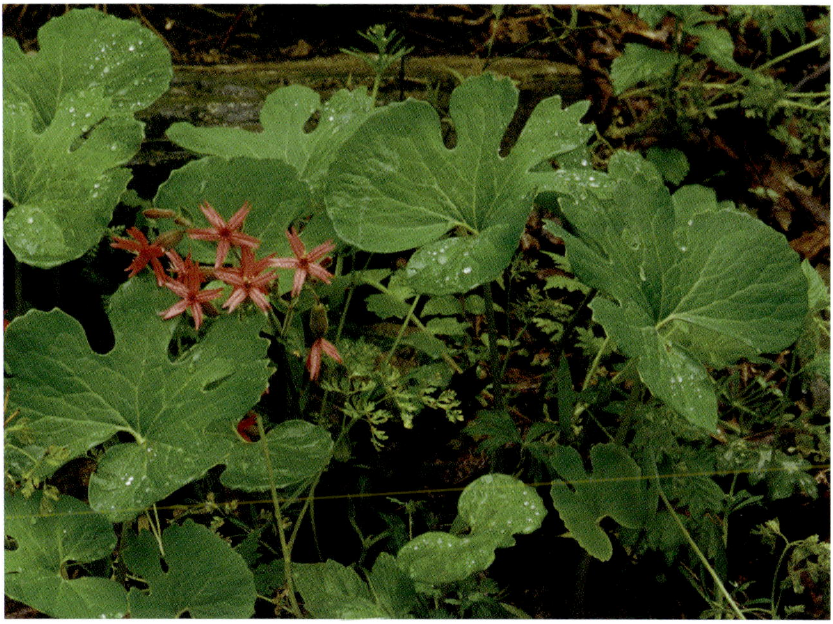

Complementary colors can be difficult to use as shown here because they have nothing in common and both the red and green compete for dominance because they have equal weight. This roughly equal-intensity and unbroken complementary color contribute nothing useful to the composition. One could argue on a positive note, the rule of thirds is employed, there is movement and interest in the lines, shapes, positive/negative space, etc, but there is also no denying the visually annoying relationship of the two complements lying side-by-side. If the red tended a little toward the violet or orange, or if the leaves were slightly yellow, the use of color would be more effective.

complementary colors can compete with one another for our attention. For example, blue and orange will compete with each other when placed next to each other and so orange combines best with blue at a ratio of about three parts orange to about one part blue, or vice versa. The same applies for yellow and violet and about five parts yellow combine best with about one part violet and vice versa.

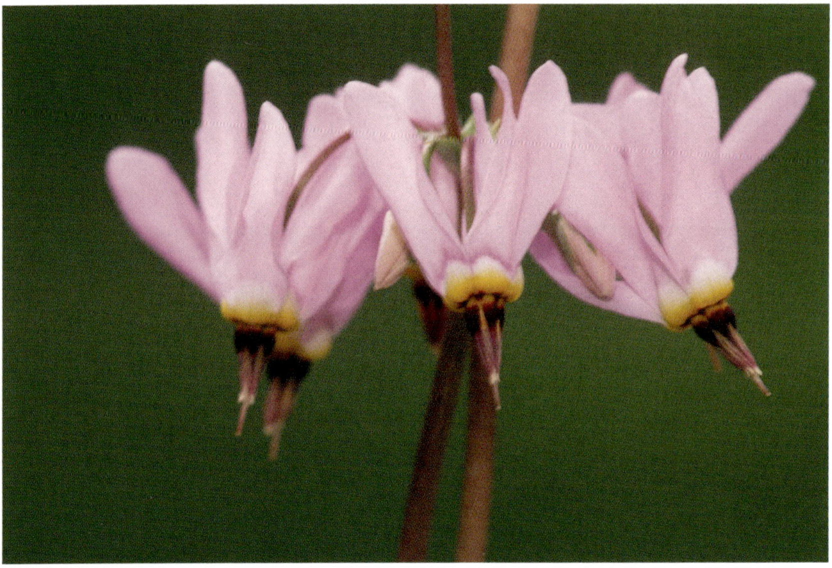

The lavender flowers of the common shooting star work well with the green background, which compliments the flower color. Notice that the colors have been broken, i.e. the red has been muted with white and the green has been darkened with black. This is a much better use of complementary color.

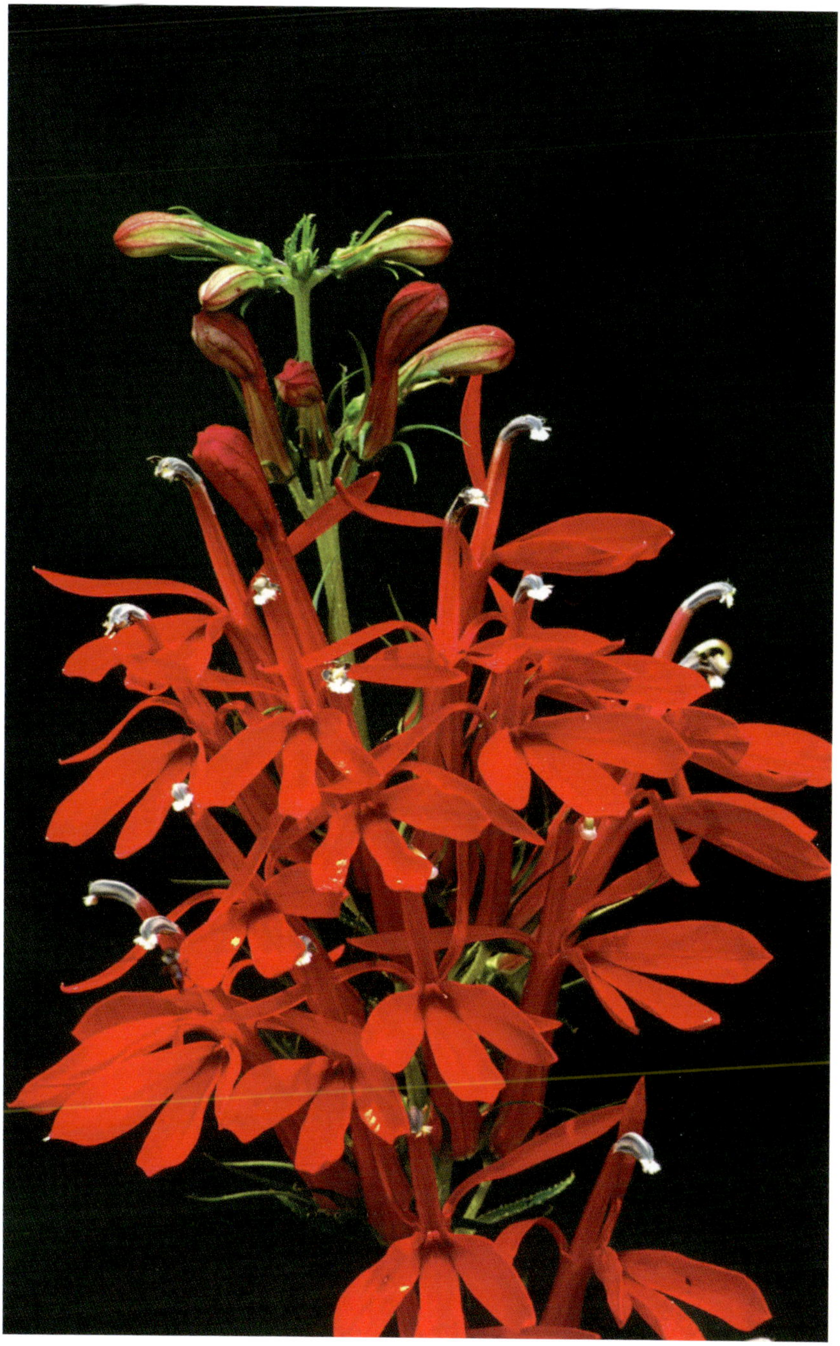

Because red is a high visibility color, it has a tendency to come forward in images and works with high contrast design.

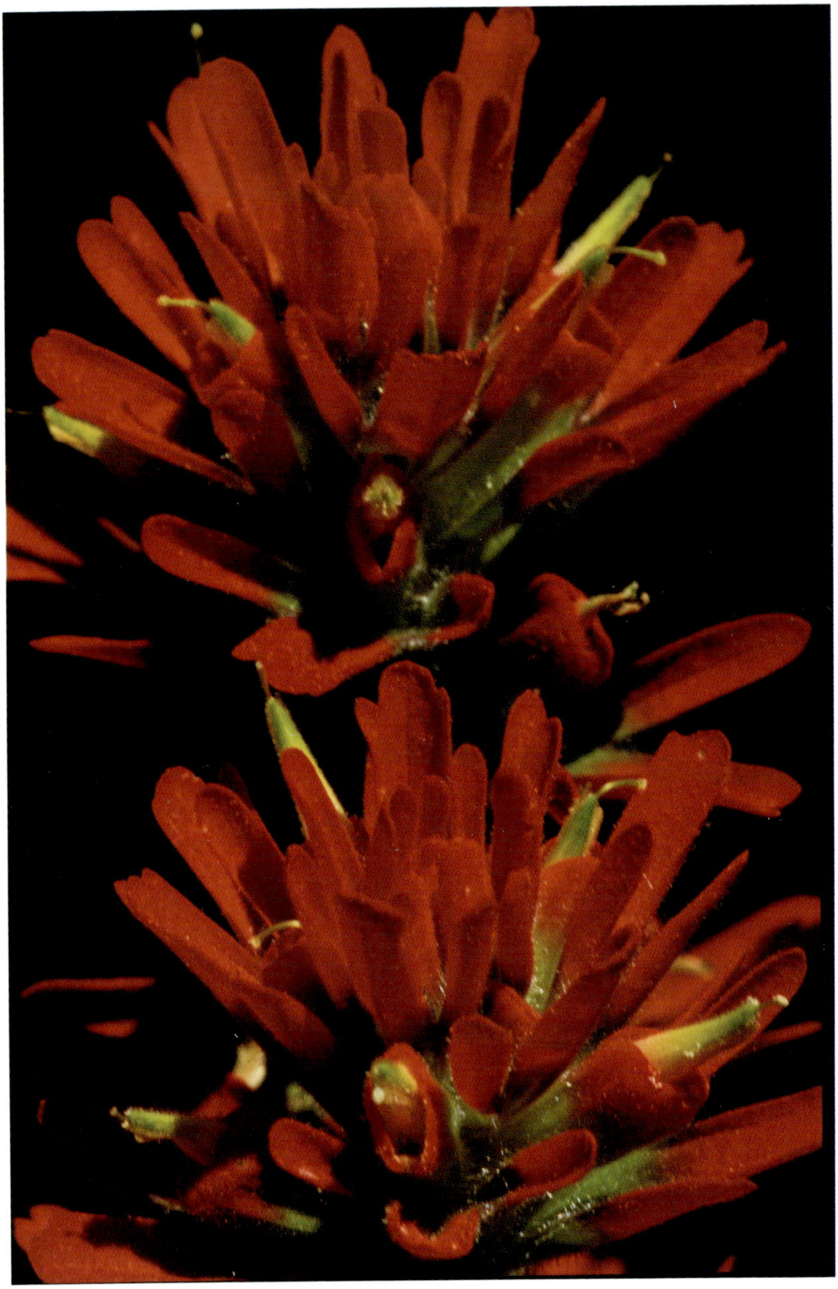

Like red, orange is an intense color and orange objects tend to come forward in the image. It can catch the viewers' attention and be used to bring out highlights in the design.

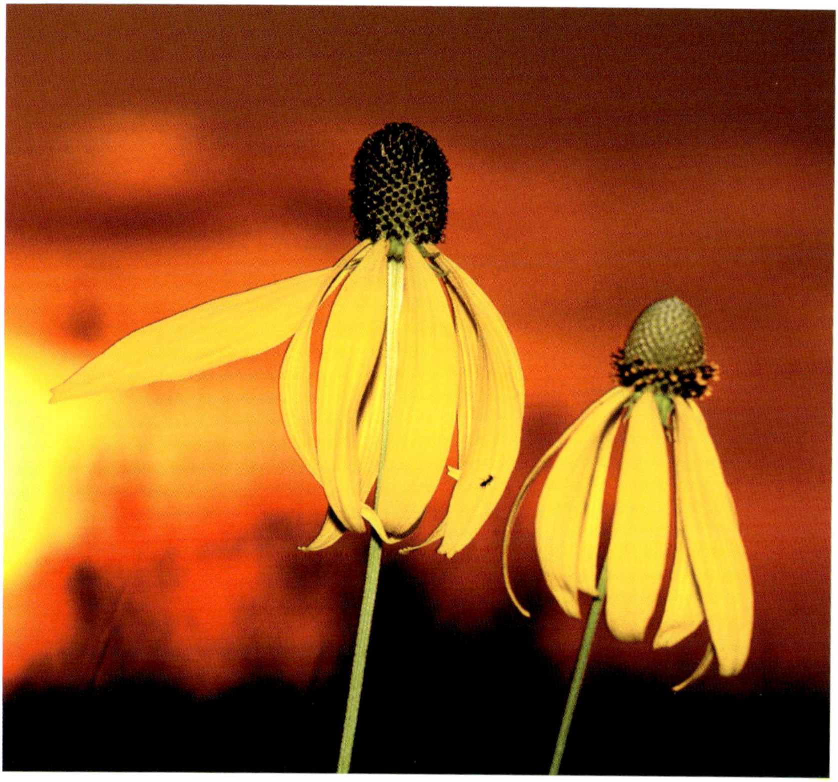

Yellow is also a warm color and is an attention getter. When placed against something black it is the first color recognized.

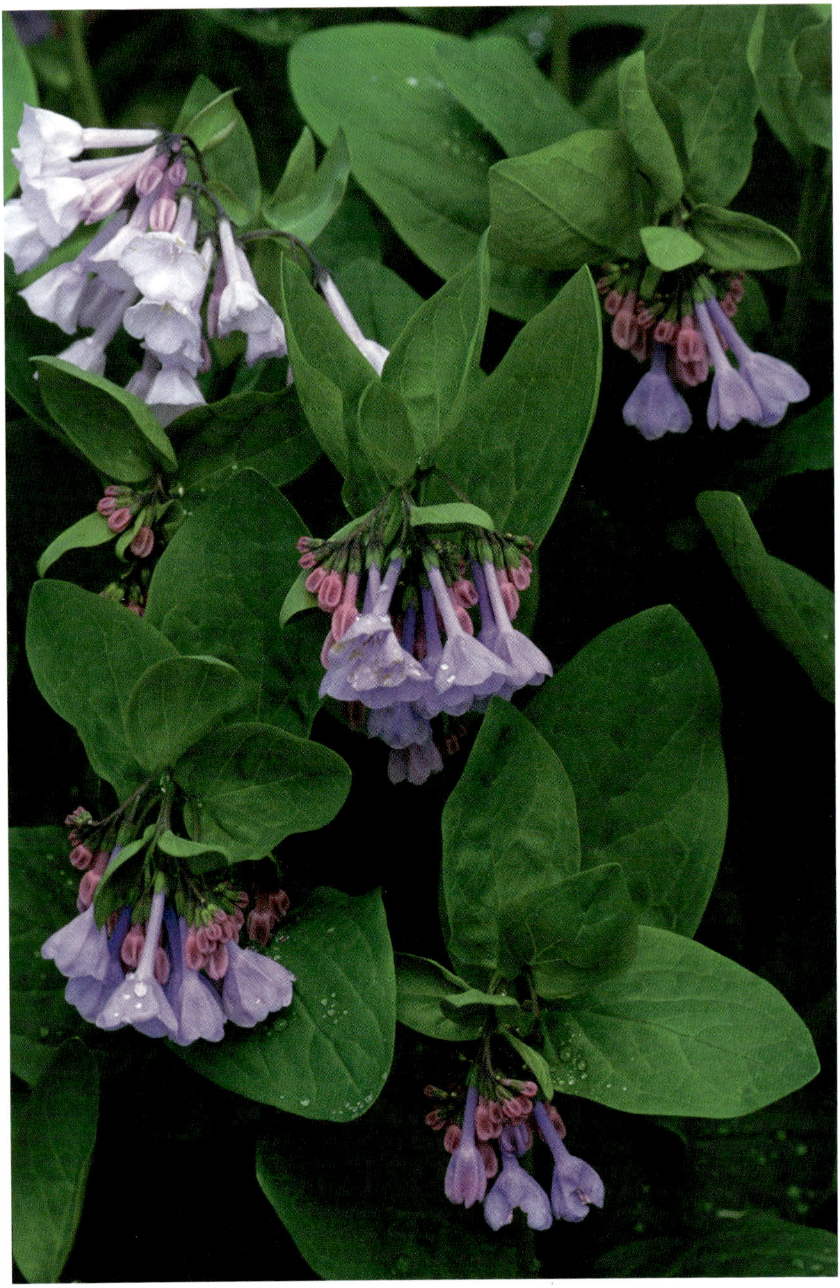

Green is the color of nature and is a restful color that means growth, renewal and the environment. When combined with blue it produces a nice "earthy" harmony.

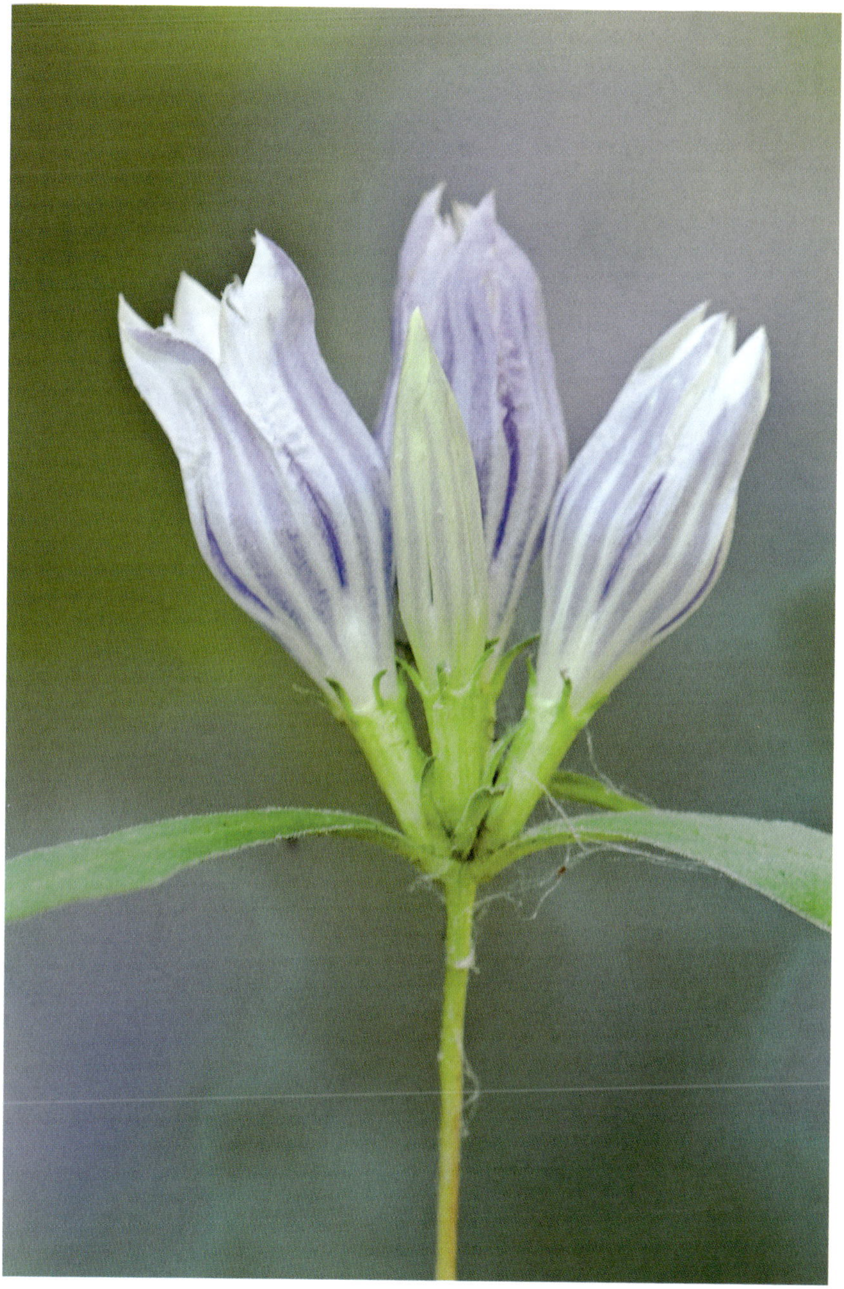

The color blue represents peace and tranquility, stability and reliability and research shows it can have a calming effect on the body.

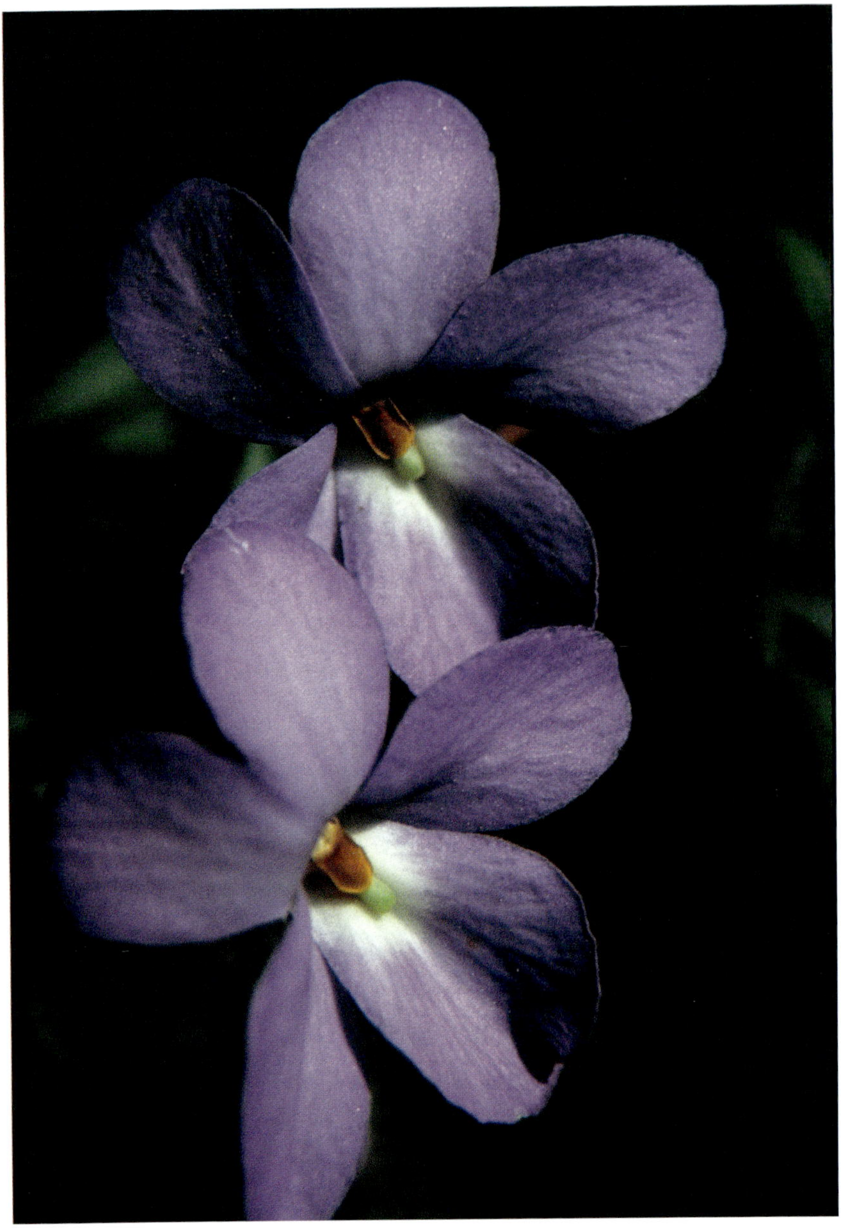

The neutral colors of gray, white, black, beige, and silver make useful backgrounds because they can unify the other bolder colors in the design. These colors serve to tone down colors that can be overpowering or bring together all the colors into balance. Notice how the bold violet color is contrasted to the light green, white and brown center portions of the flower and the darker green leaves around the perimeter. The black serves to unify these colors and the shadows add intrigue. No flash was used for this image to create the dark background, rather it was shaded with a light disc.

Chasing the Light

Photography has been defined as writing with light or painting with light. It follows that light is pretty important for photography, and it can be argued that light is perhaps the most important photographic element you need to understand. Light can be reflected, scattered, transmitted, diffused, refracted, diffracted, polarized or absorbed. All of these affect photography and visual design elements, which ultimately affects the final image.

While three things make any flower photo great – incredible color, outstanding composition, and magic light – it is the light that makes the difference between a merely good photo and an outstanding or exceptional photo. Really good, talented photographers use their knowledge of light to enhance the viewer's emotional response to the image they are looking at. The more we understand light, the more freedom we have to create an image that conveys and communicates our moods, impressions, and interpretation of the subject and its environment. In a sense, we move from being documentary photographers to expressive artists. Understanding light is the vehicle to achieve that expressive art form.

All photography is based on the two basic visual design elements of color and form, and light is an integral component of each design element. Form is actually created by light, which also gives rise to more secondary design principles like shape, texture, line and perspective through the contrast of tones. Using and even controlling light is the most essential design element that you need to understand because it so dramatically affects every other aspect of the image.

Let's look at it from the human portrait photographers' point of view. The standard lighting technique to emphasize the masculinity of a male subject is to use strong, direct side lighting which emphasizes the tonal qualities of the skin and accentuate wrinkles, whiskers, lines, etc. In contrast, soft, diffuse front lighting is typically used for female subjects because it flattens and hides skin imperfections and emphasizes colors and tones, making the subject appear more feminine in appearance.

The same principle applies to nature photography, except we can't precisely control the light with studio lighting. We have to work with the natural environment and the light from the sun and manipulate natural light with reflectors, diffusers, flashes and other light sources.

The first task in using light to accentuate the subject or make it stand out from the background is to understand the language of light. Light is said to have a quality or intensity (hard or soft), direction (front, side, back, or spot), and temperature or color (warm or cool).

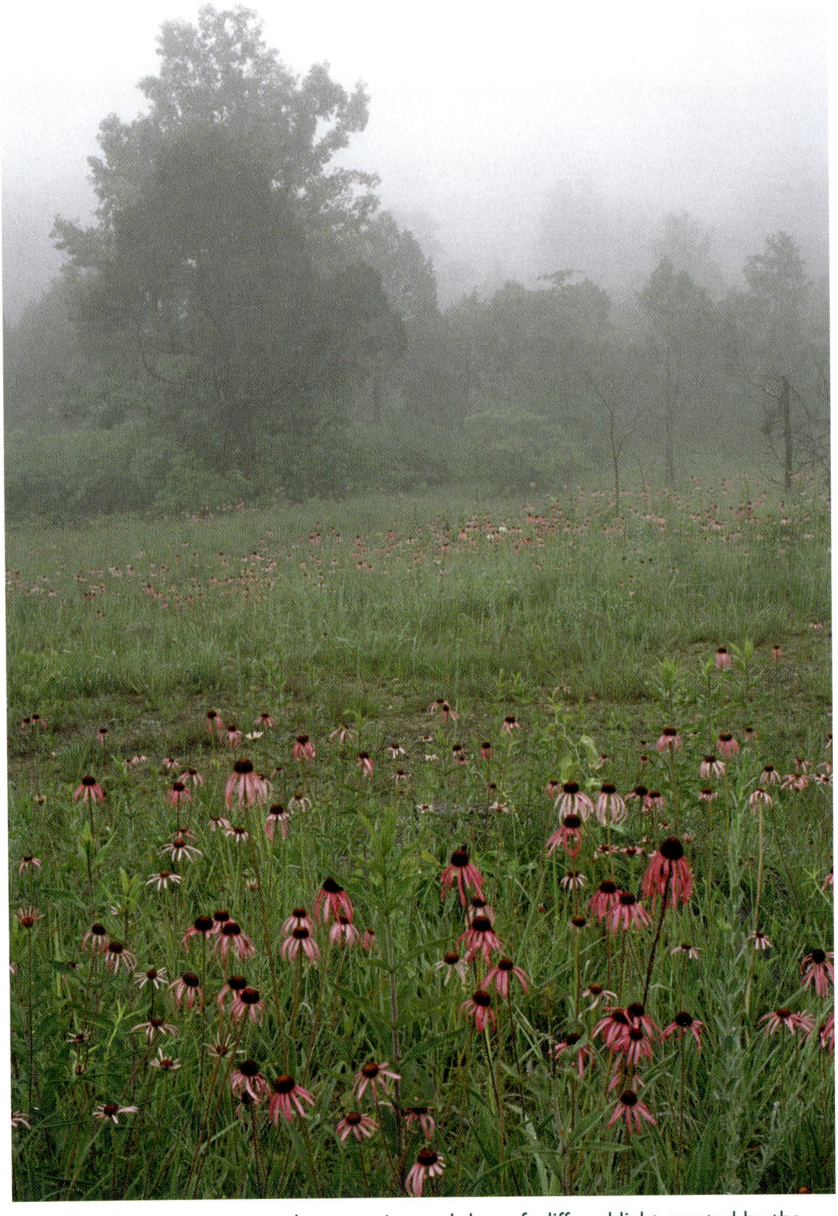

Light can help convey a mood or emotion and the soft diffused light created by the fog on these pale purple coneflowers makes for a more peaceful image.

Light Intensity

Photographers always struggle with contrast (the difference between the light and dark tones) in any particular image. Contrast and subsequent color tonal qualities, to a large extent, are controlled by light. Soft light (or diffuse or indirect light) occurs when the light source is obscured by something (like clouds). The individual particles are not concentrated into a single stream, and the light is scattered before being reflected off the subject. Consider why we use lampshades. We use them to make the light more even or to spread the light particles out so there isn't any particular direction, and everything has a good, even tonal quality with reduced contrast and no harsh shadows. Shapes, lines, and textures may seem less clearly defined, but the color is more saturated, and the variations and subtleties of hues are accentuated. When photographic subjects are lit with this light, they often radiate a luminescence of its own, which is why this is the favored light for photographing wildflowers.

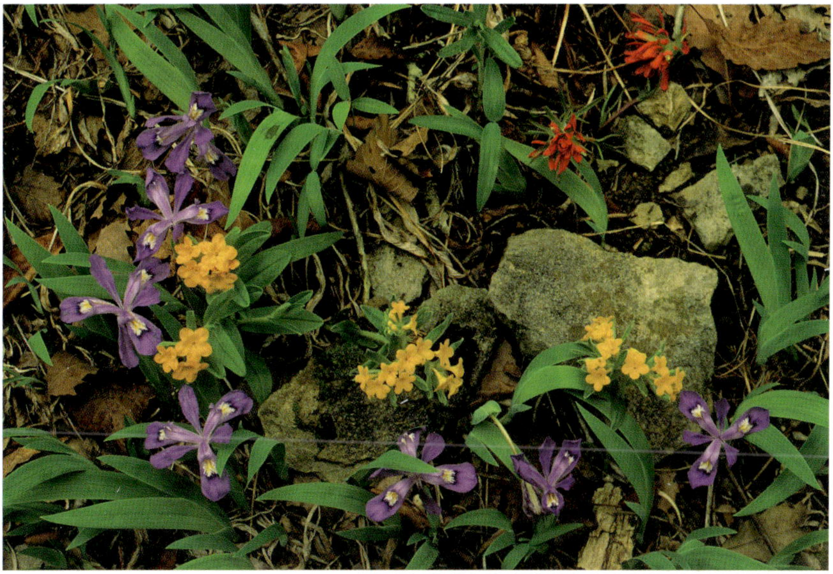

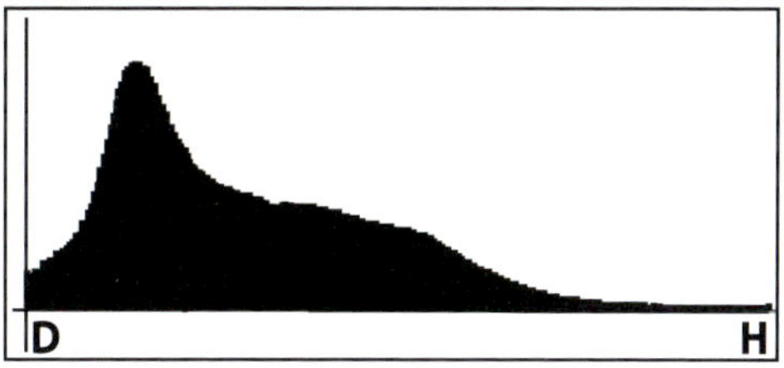

The soft, diffuse light brings out the rich colors of the iris and hoary puccoon and eliminates any harsh shadows. Note the histogram is shifted somewhat left because of the dark tones and shadows and almost clips the top at the left but it doesn't. Also look that the tail on the right extends all the way to the right showing all the highlights have been preserved.

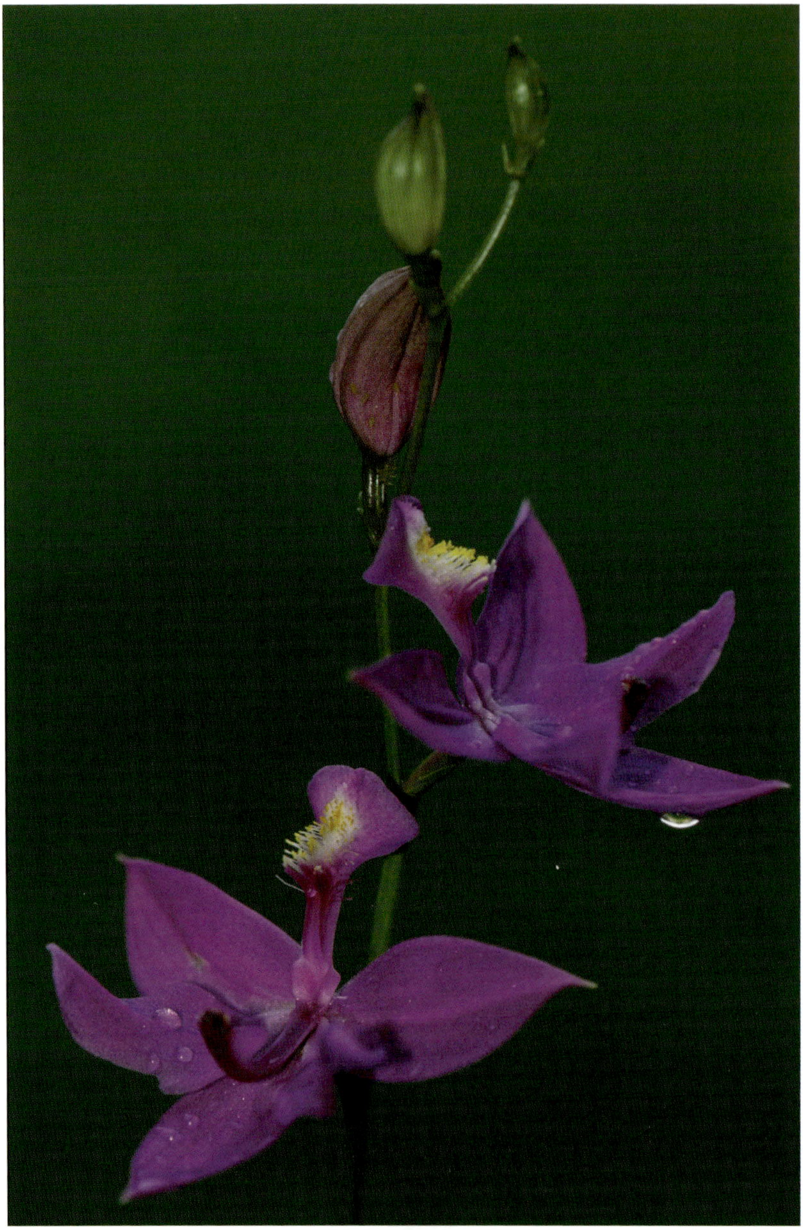

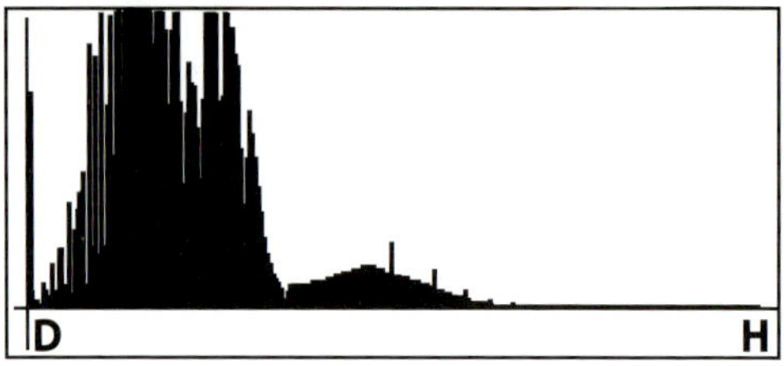

Direct or harsh light can be harnessed and used effectively. In this example, I used a piece of aluminum foil to redirect or bounce back some of the light onto the grass pink flowers so that there were fewer harsh shadows in the flowers. The exposure histogram shows that no shadows or highlights have been lost in the image.

Think about our analogy with the human female portrait and then realize how often flowers are referred to with the feminine gender. As I just mentioned, this light accentuates the female face and hides imperfections, and gives better color tones, etc. Diffuse or soft light occurs on overcast days, at dawn and dusk before the sun illuminates the earth, in the shade on sunny days, and in the fog. You can create this type of light, even on bright sunny days, by diffusing the light with a diffusion umbrella, a collapsible diffuser, or a diffusion tent.

Hard, harsh, or direct light occurs when all the light particles are concentrated into a point source of light, i.e. the sun, and it is unobstructed. Hard light comes from the sun at high noon on a cloudless day, a light bulb, or your camera's flash. This type of light produces hard shadows, limited tonal differentiation, and a stark difference between light and dark tones giving rise to extreme contrast that in some cases may be beyond what the sensor can record. Because this light is so hard to work with and can be dramatic or stark, the first task is to find subject matter that is best expressed with strong contrasts, lines, textures, reflected light, and the appearance of depth. While this light can be harnessed and used creatively to create stark and graphic images, it is extremely difficult to pull off without manipulating or enhancing the light such as using fill flash, reflectors, or a mirror to reduce contrast.

Light Direction

The direction that light hits the subject also dramatically affects the emotional appeal of any wildflower photo. When light hits the front of the subject or hits the subject closest to the camera it is called front lighting. If the light source comes from behind the subject, it is called backlighting, and if it occurs to one side of the subject, it is called side lighting. When a small amount of light hits one particular part of the subject, it is called spotlighting. Each direction produces dramatically different results.

Front lighting is often called boring because it has many of the same characteristics as hard light. However, if you are doing documentary flower photography, it will be the preferred option because it hides shadows (not good for identification in many cases), produces high contrast (this can be good to differentiate the subject from the background for identification purposes), and reduces perspective. From a creative standpoint, front lighting works best for

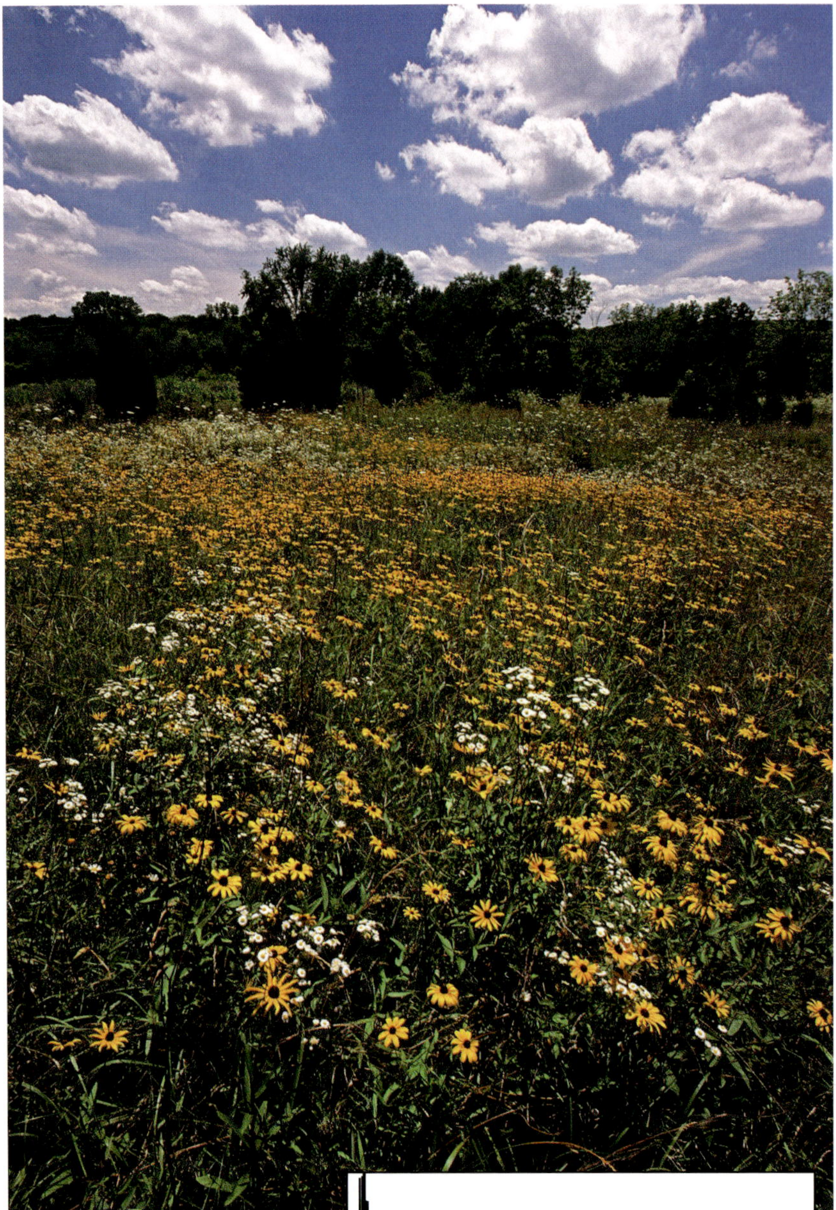

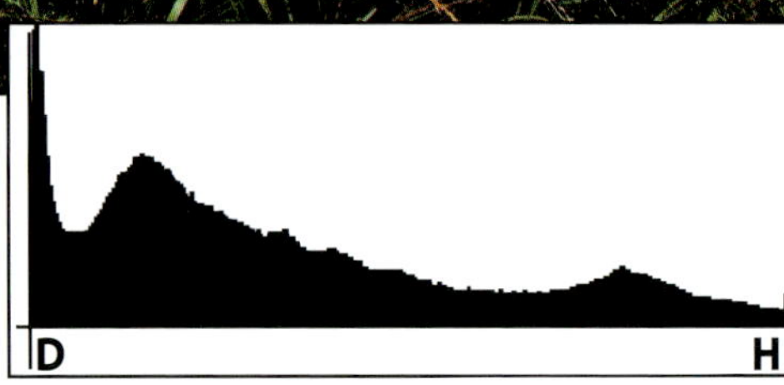

This is what a fairly typical front lighting scene, taken at mid-day would look like and it works because of the color combination. Note that the histogram is fairly flat with no clipping at either end for a proper exposure. If you wanted to spend a great deal of time post-processing, the shadows in the trees could be toned-down and you would not have a spike on the left side of the histogram.

flowers with strong color such as a purple or pink flower against a green backdrop or a yellow flower against a deep blue sky.

Side lighting is usually exciting because the shadows provide contrast and can appear as lines. Side lighting also emphasizes texture, like the wonderful hairs on a stem or leaf. This type of light creates shadows and depth and gives the viewer the opportunity "to feel" what the image might be like. The best sidelight occurs early in the morning and late in the afternoon. Make sure to shade the front of the lens with a lens hood, a hand or hat, or something else to prevent stray light from hitting the front lens element and producing flare.

Back lighting occurs when the light source is in back of the subject. The light illuminates the back of the subject giving rise to dramatic images emphasizing shape and form with often abrupt and extreme contrast. Flower petals become translucent and literally "glow" under this type of light.

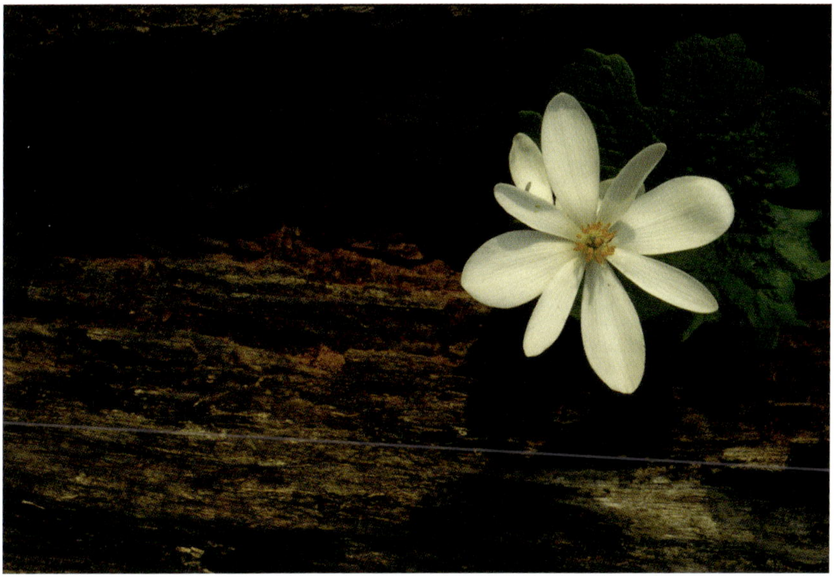

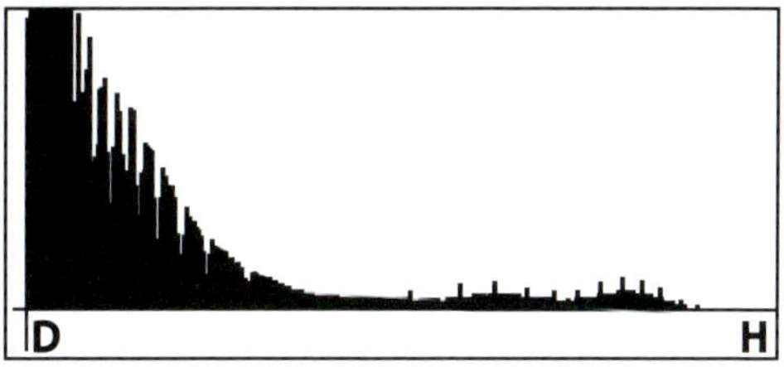

Notice how the early morning sidelight brings out the contrast between the bloodroot flower and the texture of the old, rotting log it was growing out of. Note the histogram shows clipping in the shadows on the left side. This is acceptable for this image because the shadows are part of the image and provide the "feel" or texture and if you brought the details out of the shadows you would lose the texture in the image.

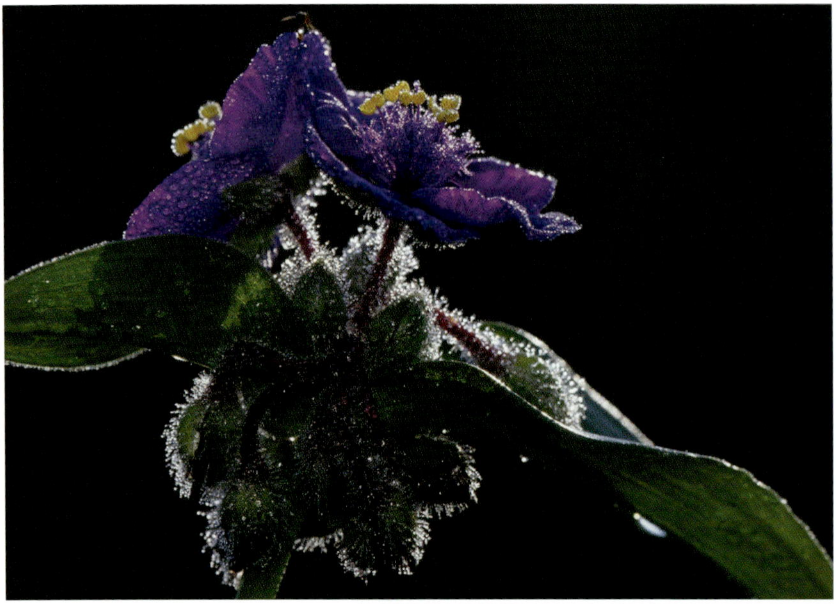

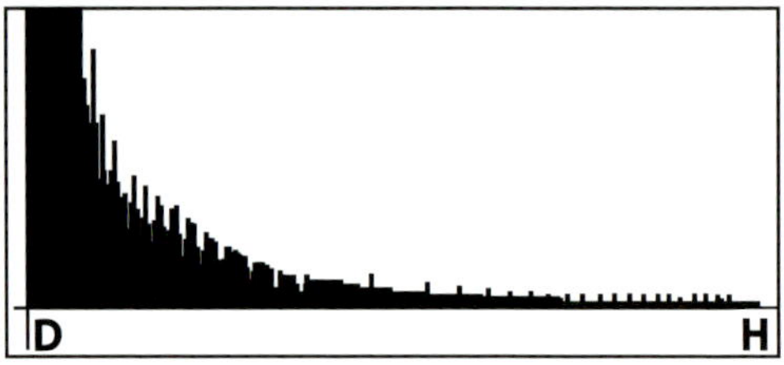

Backlighting helped "highlight" the hairs on this spiderwort and then I bounced some light with a mirror to brighten the flowers in the foreground. As in the image above, the histogram is strongly shifted to the left showing clipping of the shadows, which is okay because you will note that there are no details in the shadow (and if there were they would detract from the subject) and the histogram goes all the way to the right with no clipping of the highlights.

Most people recognize that light is reflected off light colors and that light is absorbed by dark colors. Why mention reflected light now? The simple answer is you may want to reflect light (using a mirror or reflector) onto backlit flower images to brighten the front side while leaving rim lighting (illuminating just the edges of the subject) to alter the emotional appeal of any particular flower.

Another method of producing rim lighting with a backlit flower as the subject is to use electronic flash. To produce this effect simply set your TTL flash unit to under expose by two stops and set it to synchronize at the end of the exposure. Then take your normal exposure and underexpose the subject by one to one and a half stops. This will produce stunning results rendering translucent petals and rim lighting with just enough front exposure to bring out the color of the flower petals.

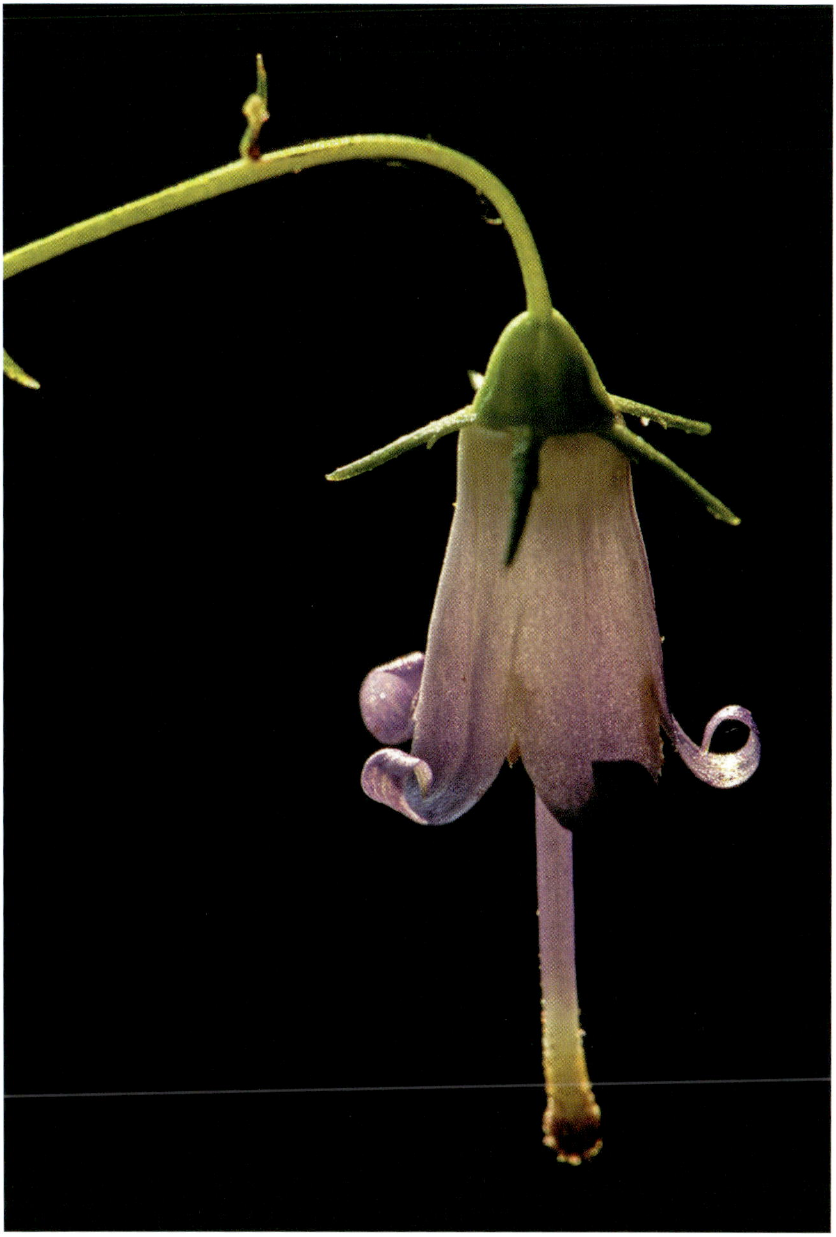

This is another example of how backlighting with a bit of fill flash can make a rather ordinary subject literally come alive. You will notice this histogram looks like the previous two for the same reasons. This effect was created by using fill from a flash using the technique described above.

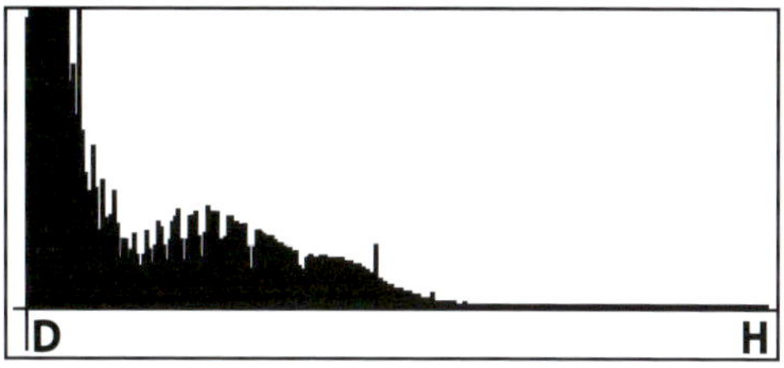

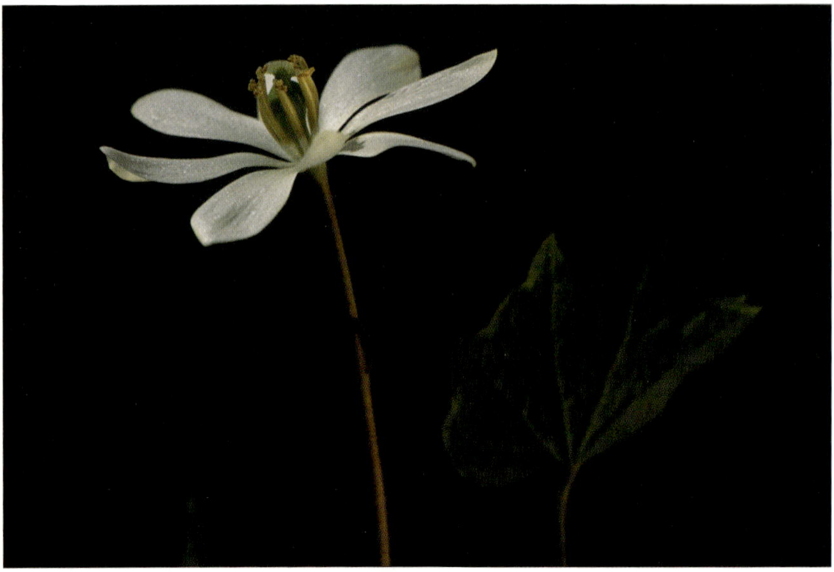

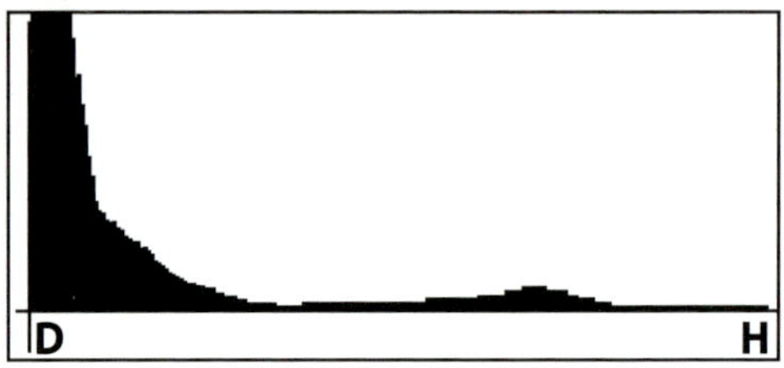

Early in the morning the light hit just the flower and the leaf of this twinleaf giving a spotlight effect. Note this is similar to the last several histograms but what is important is that all the details in the white are present with no highlights missing.

The last type of light used for wildflower photography is called spotlighting. This is where a small portion of the subject receives light and the remainder of the dark areas serves as a frame around that small area of the subject that is lit. This type of light can come from any direction (front, side or back) and the purpose for using it is to make the subject "pop" and give a sense of drama to the image. If your camera has a spot meter this is an excellent time to use this handy little feature.

The Color of Light

Most of us remember from our elementary and secondary school years that white light from the sun is actually light of many different wavelengths or colors that are combined. Each of these colors or wavelengths is associated with a different temperature. Color temperature is measured in Kelvin (K), and temperatures at the lower end of the scale produce light with a yellowish or reddish tint (think of an incandescent light bulb) whereas higher temperatures produce light with a bluish tint (think of a fluorescent light). The "neutral" light in the middle of the day has a temperature of around 5,500 K. In the past, daylight film was balanced to neutral light, and we used filters to correct for the temperature of the light. Because tungsten light was yellowish in color (temperature 3,200 K), we would use a blue filter to "balance" the temperature to make it look like daylight. In the same vein we would place a slight yellowish/orange filter when shooting on an overcast day to make the cool blue light neutral white.

One great advantage of DSLR is that we don't have to worry about filters because we have them built into the camera body. With digital photography you are trying to get to a "neutral" temperature (where whites are white) by either letting the camera make the decision to "balance" the temperature to get to neutral or by setting the temperature yourself and using your creativity to make some

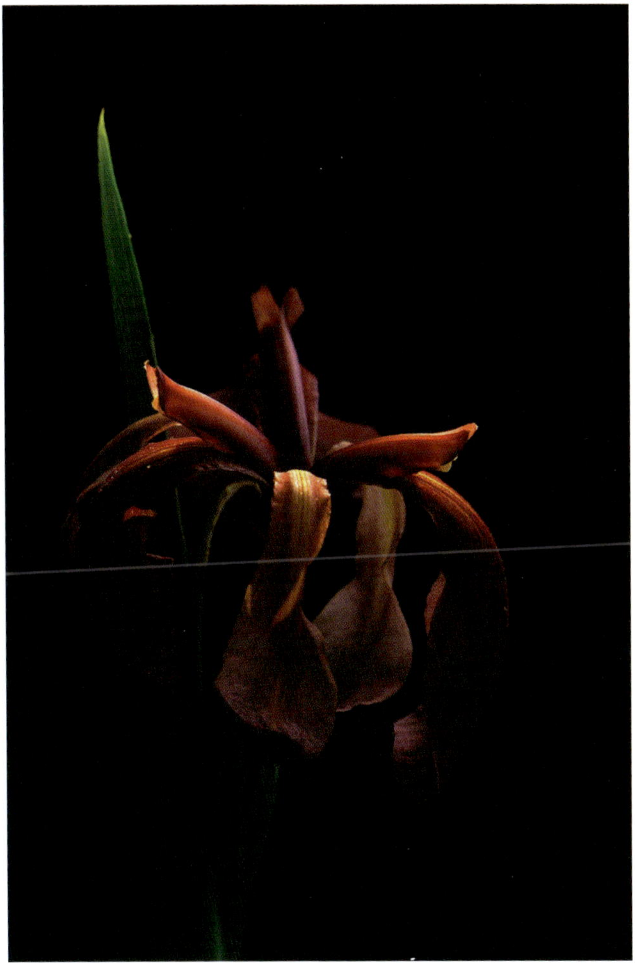

The style arms and tip of the leaf of this copper iris are highlighted with spotlighting from above and behind the flower. This image was taken during the middle of the day but the lighting makes it an effective photograph. Expose for the highlights in this type of image.

decisions. You will notice on your camera body a button or dial that allows you to adjust the "white balance" for the environmental shooting conditions at that time. The settings are usually designated by a symbol that states tungsten, daylight, cloudy, shade, etc. (see diagram).

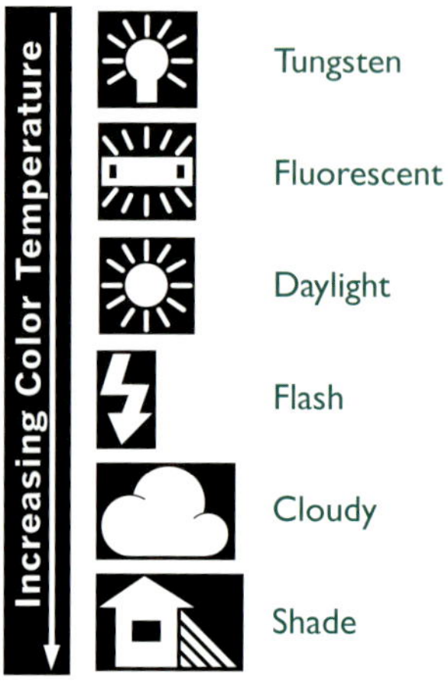

White balance is nothing more than adjusting the camera settings to balance (or correct) the light under which the image was shot. You can allow your camera to do this for you by setting it to the "auto" setting or by setting it to one of the presets mentioned before (daylight, cloudy, etc.). If you really want to fine-tune the white balance, take a light meter; take a reading in degrees K, and simply dial in that number.

Here is a real advantage to shooting in RAW format (discussed in the equipment section). If you are shooting RAW, you can adjust the actual light temperature in degrees K when processing the image after it was shot. You might want to fiddle with the various settings. For example, shooting in the "shade" mode sets the temperature to about 7000 K. One nifty trick to try is to shoot in auto mode, then, if the image looks cool in the LCD on the camera back, you can switch to another setting, or dial in the actual degrees K, and check the image again.

Now, from a creative point of view, here are some things you might want to consider when taking the camera off auto white balance. Tungsten (generally with the image of a light bulb) is yellowish in color. The only time this looks normal is when you are indoors at night. Now if you want to "simulate" night for a plant like evening primrose which flowers in the evening through the dark hours and early in the morning, set the exposure setting to -1 or -2, and put the white balance on the "Tungsten" setting. The resulting image will be bluer than neutral. If you want a warmer appearance when shooting wildflowers, you can set the white balance to "Cloudy" and if you want an even warmer effect set it for "Shade."

Let's explore this concept of color temperature further as it relates to wildflower and nature photography. Often you will hear about the magic times for nature photography, early in the morning and late in the afternoon when the sun is low on the horizon, is somewhat diffuse, and is giving off a golden cast on the subject. This is a great time to take wildflower photographs because of the warm, directional aspects of the light. However, don't limit yourself to these periods because some flowers, particularly forest spring ephemerals, do not open until the sun hits them. This means you would be photographing trout lilies in the middle of the day when they are at their peak of openness. Fortunately, in the spring the sun stays relatively low on the horizon and even midday sun isn't awful and harsh like it can be in the middle of July when the sun is high in the horizon.

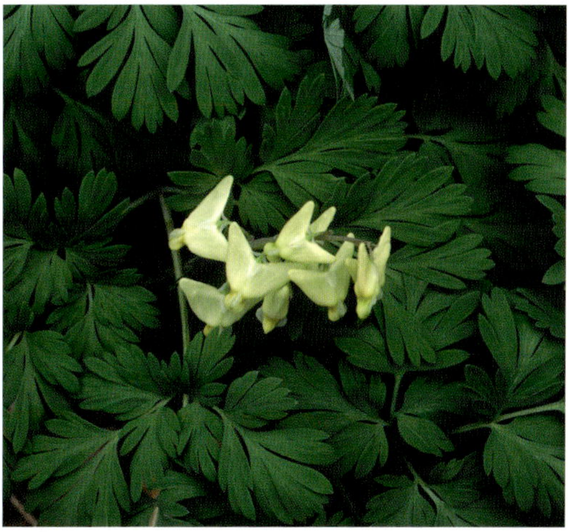

Light temperature can really affect how you "see" color, and this is early morning warm light, whereas the photo below was taken in the shade under cool, blue light and does not give the same emotional feeling as the image taken under warm light.

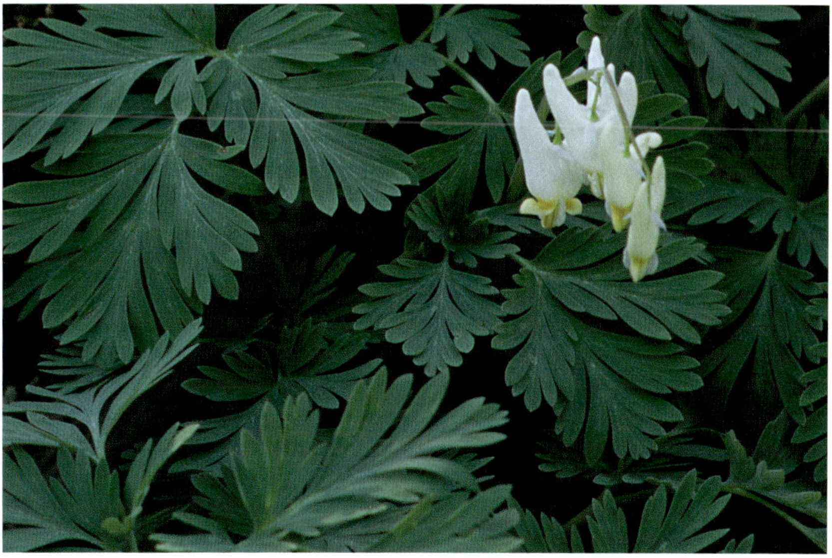

Why do photographers always seem to be up and photographing bright and early or late in the afternoon? It is all about light color or temperature. Because of the curvature of the earth, at sunup and sundown, light waves must travel through more of our atmosphere, which acts like a filter, than they would if coming from directly overhead at noon. As light waves travel through our thick atmosphere, the shorter wavelengths on the cool end of the spectrum get lost in atmospheric dust and water and cannot reach us. This leaves the longer, warmer waves of light to penetrate our atmosphere. As the sun climbs higher into the sky, it shines more directly through our atmosphere, allowing the shorter, cooler wavelengths to reach us, better balancing the color of the light. On a clear day when the sun is directly overhead, it should exhibit no color when cast onto a white surface and should have a neutral tone.

Let's look at it in another way. If you consider "daylight" as normal and then compare this to an incandescent light bulb, it appears yellowish-orange; candlelight may look almost red although our eyes automatically adjust to the changing environment and correct for the change in light temperature. In a similar vein, if you take a photo under shade environments the resulting images look very bluish to bluish green.

Using and Manipulating Natural Light

In the miscellaneous equipment section, I mention that I carry some collapsible diffusers and a small mirror to bounce light. The main reasons I do this is so that I can more effectively control and manipulate the natural light to my advantage. Often times, I use a large (36 inch) diffuser to shade a group of flowers or to darken a background, and I use a smaller diffuser to bounce light up into a flower. The mirror is useful for creating a stronger point source of bounced light into a flower to highlight particular aspects that might be shaded. Most flowers look their best under soft, diffuse lighting and that is why I carry these essential pieces of equipment. However, I often get out of bed early enough so that I don't necessarily need the diffusers except to bounce light into a flower.

In summary, the first and most important photographic element to make a photograph visually stimulating is light. Find the right light that elicits an emotional response from you and the photograph will materialize right before your very own eyes. While it is important to have a basic understanding of what light is and how it affects the

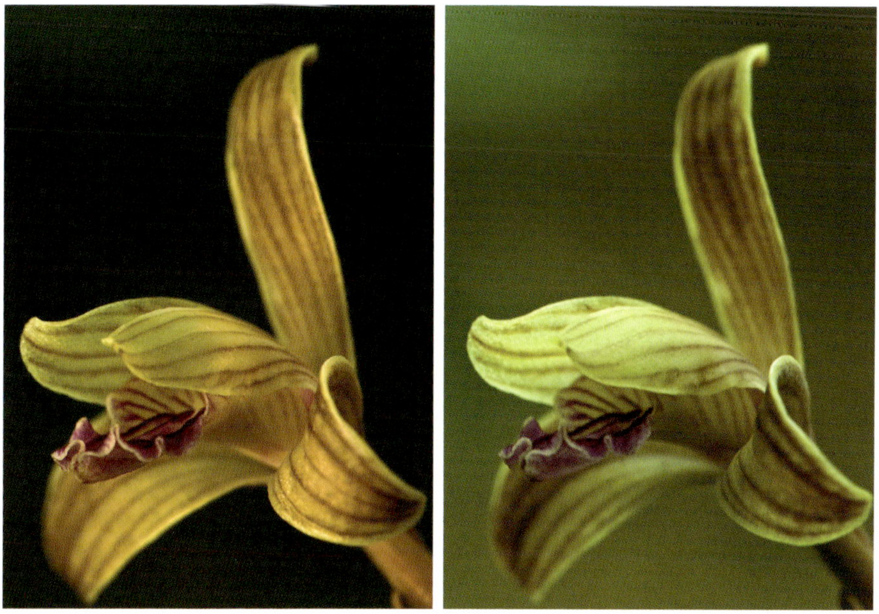

Note the differences in lighting conditions of the crested coral root orchid. The image on the left was taken under natural light conditions, in the shade, with a golden colored light disk that was used to bounce warm light up onto the flower. The second image was taken with no bounced light.

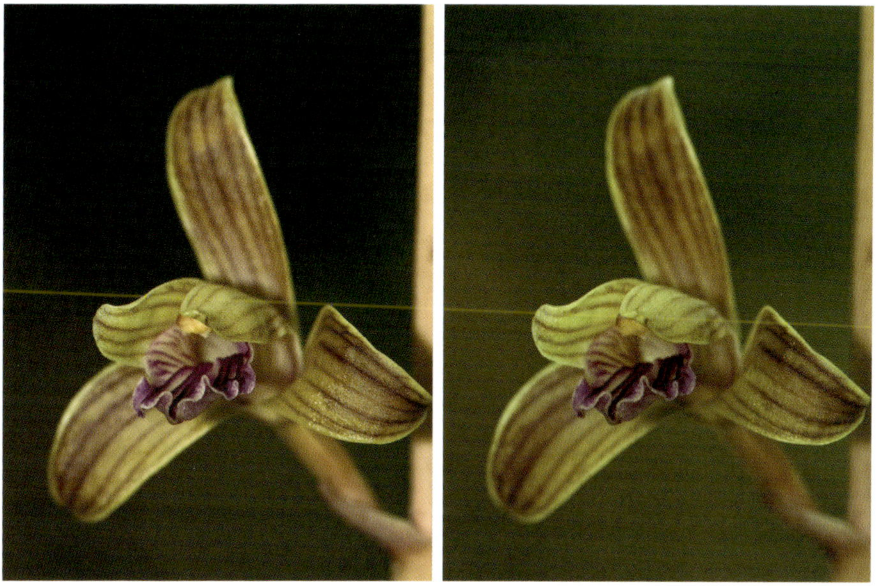

The image on the left was taken with balanced fill flash set to minus two stops with the flash set to rear sync. The image was under-exposed in the camera by two stops. The final image was taken with no balanced fill flash under natural light conditions. Learning to use and manipulate light can mean the difference between good or better in terms of overall visual impact and making your subject stand out.

visual appeal of any image, remember that you are the determining factor and an essential part of the creative process. Also remember technique over technology – understand your camera system and how it reacts to light – and always remember that modern computer chips cannot replace the creative aspects of your mind.

Light and color are important concepts to understand and master because they work together. The temperature of the light affects our moods, sometimes dramatically and sometimes subtly. Cool light, with its bluish tint, is harsh and uninviting, while warm light soothes us. People also respond quickly to bright saturated colors and intensely lit images. People have a more subtle reaction to images done with pastels and soft light.

Visual Design Elements

The human mind is an amazing organ. Put a single dot on a piece of paper, and we intuitively recognize it as a point in space. If you were to place two points on a piece of paper your mind would intuitively draw a line between the points, and if you had three points you would get a triangle. Points in space are linked together to form images or, in the new digital world, we talk about pixels, which are nothing more than dots in space. When you get enough pixels put together, you get an image. When you begin to assemble more and more pixels, an image, or hopefully the subject, of the photograph will begin to emerge.

There is some inherent human process, something I call Gestalt, that moves us to create visual designs. The process is quite similar to how I learn plants. If you look at the plant enough times (either in a book, herbarium specimen, or in the field), at some point you simply "know" that plant, because you pick up on visual clues (botanists have identified these various traits, group plants with similar traits together, and put them in taxonomic keys for those serious about accurate plant identification). The involuntary, innate order that we humans use everyday of our lives forms the basis of the principles of visual design.

Understanding these basic principles will help you improve your composition. It will not guarantee successful images because everyone will view the images based on his or her own life experiences, but it will be a starting point at which you can work with and refine your compositional techniques and improve your images over time.

Line

Line, as stated above, is nothing more than a "path" between two points. In photography, lines are created by changes in tone or color and are usually lighter or darker than the surrounding space in the image, although this is not always true. Lines can either be literal, meaning the line visually exists or is implied (playing mind games here) and our minds fill in between the points (like the horizon of an image). Lines can be used independently for example, in a photograph of a stem or a stick, or it can be combined to form textures and patterns. Not all lines are straight, as some can be curved, and lines can have a position (vertical, horizontal, diagonal, or zigzag). Lines can have direction and are useful in moving the eye subconsciously through an image. They also create shapes, which often become the subject of the wildflower photographer.

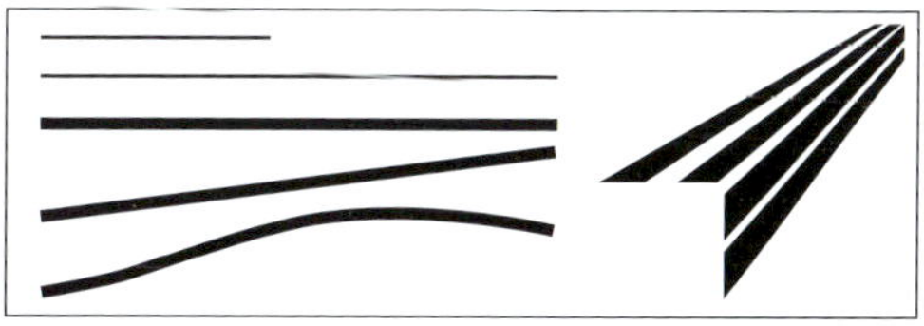

The use of few lines can lead to simple yet dynamic compositions because viewers are not distracted by competing lines drawing their eyes everywhere. In contrast, however, you can use a multiplicity of lines to form patterns and textures if they are used to make some type of unifying composition. For example, many wildflowers have

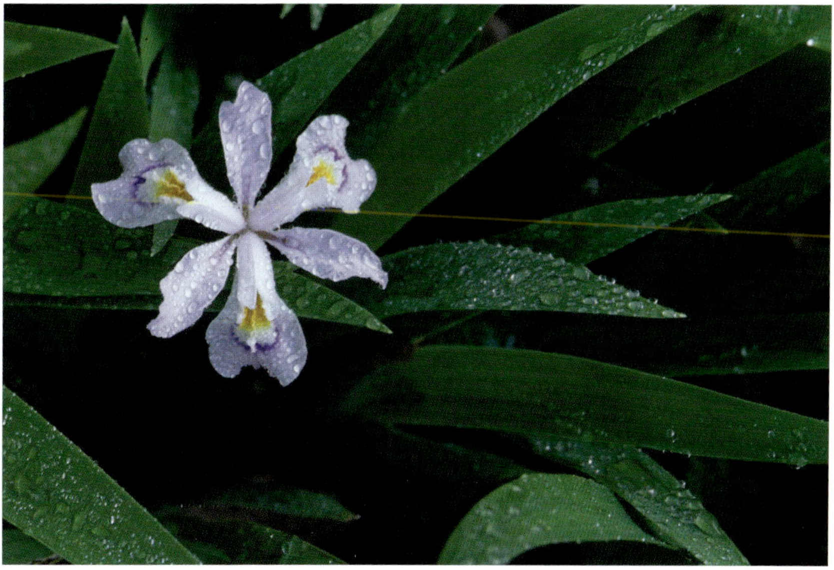

The leaves of this dwarf crested iris are nothing more than lines leading to the main subject which is the flower.

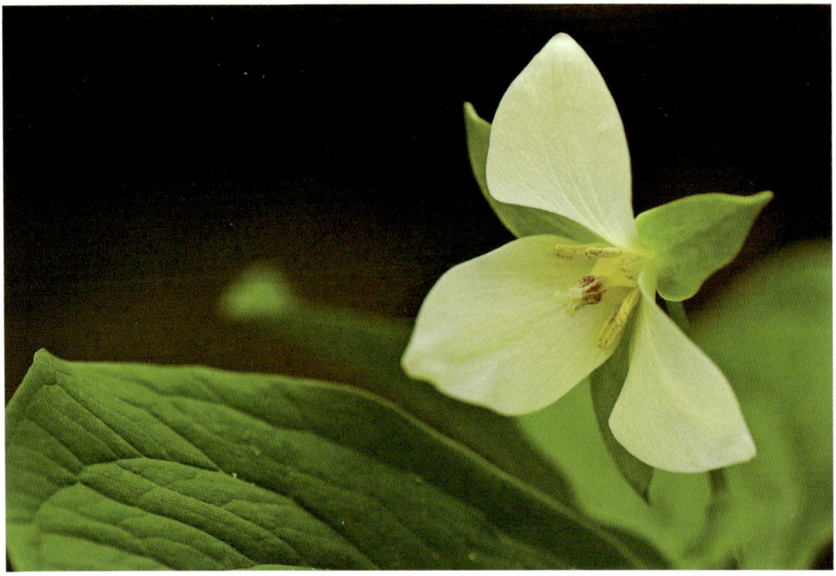

Note the line (leading edge of the leaf) draws your attention to the main subject, the bent trillium flower.

lines that lead the pollinator to the nectar, and you can use those to highlight certain aspects of the flower that you might want to emphasize. When lines converge, they can give the perspective of depth, space, dimension, or scale to an image. A common technique is to use a leading line (fence, road, etc.) that draws you into the image and gives a three-dimensional perspective to a two-dimensional medium.

Just like using color to illicit human emotion to an image, lines can communicate emotion and a state of mind by their character and direction. For example, horizontal lines communicate restfulness, tranquility, or repose because they are parallel to earth's gravity and hence appear more stable. Contrast this to vertical lines that "reach to the heavens" and imply a sense of loftiness, grandeur, strength, and power. When you combine both vertical and horizontal lines, you get stability and solidity because these heavy, dense shapes are in balance with each other and gravity and are not going anywhere. Oblique lines create movement, activity, action or change and these lines create dynamic tension in an image because they are out of balance (being neither vertical nor horizontal) with gravity and in a sense are "in motion."

Finally we have curved lines, those that take us on a gentle stroll, not necessarily in a hurry, around this bend and that and ultimately get us to our destination. Soft, gentle curves give a feeling of comfort, safety, relaxation, calmness, or sensuality. Now you know why landscape designers use curvy lines in garden design. At the other end of the spectrum, hard, brash curves suggest turbulence, frenzy, and confusion and they are difficult to deal with in wildflower photography because you seek the softness and calmness that the weak curves provide for this feminine subject.

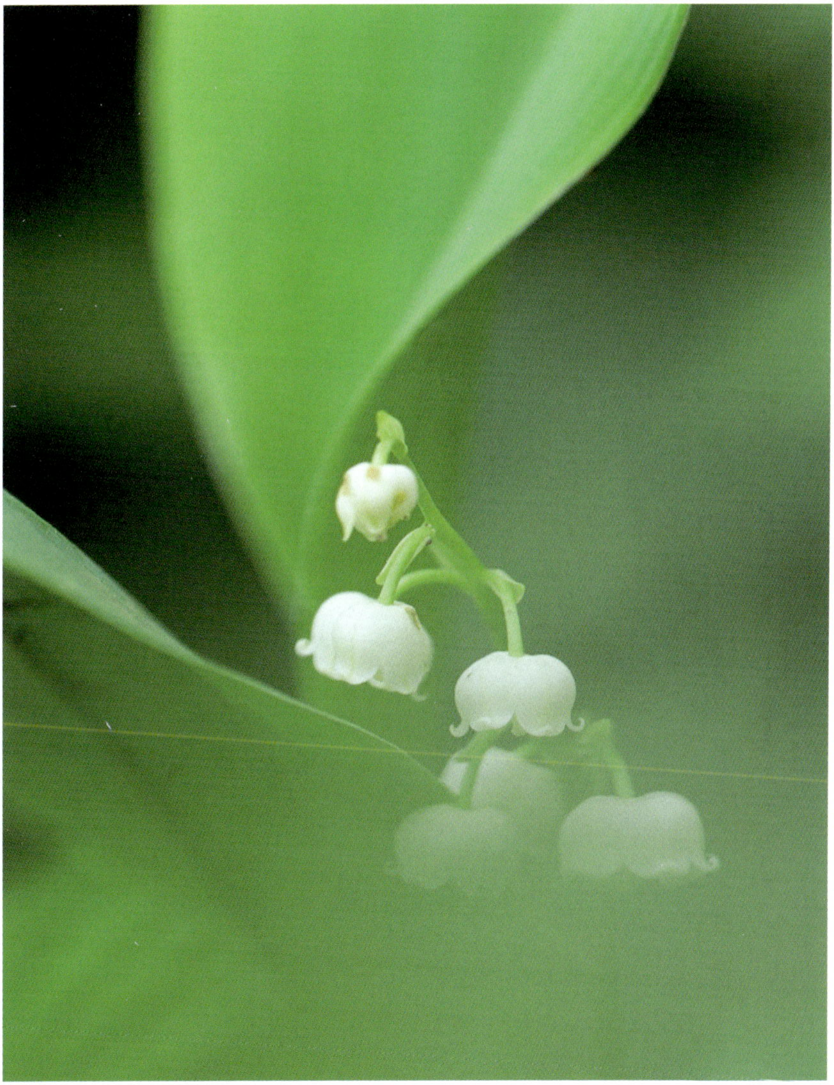

Notice how curved lines draw you into the American lily of the valley flowers. Add to this the soft lighting and soft focus effect and you get a very feminine type of flower image.

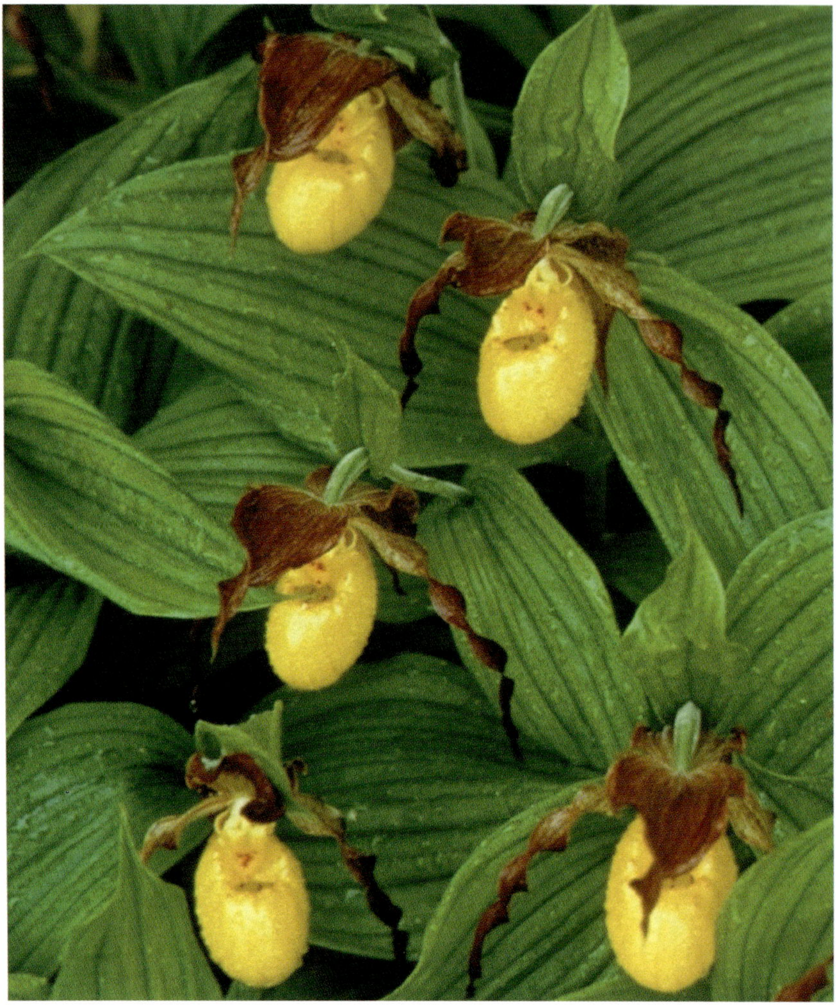

This is a study of diagonal lines and the unique pattern they create, which works by contrasting the green lines with the yellow shapes. Notice this image has a totally different "emotional" feel compared to the lily of the valley flowers above. This is because of the differences in flower color (yellow versus white), simplicity of subject (simple versus complex), and texture (smooth versus not so smooth)

Finally, lines impart a visual language as a result of their quality. This quality definitely affects the "mood" of an image. Look no further than the use of many soft, irregular lines put together to form a black-and-white drawing of a flower versus fewer hard, dark lines that starkly define the subject. To summarize, find and use lines to compose more effective images that draw the attention of the viewer into your subject matter, the glory and beauty of the wildflower.

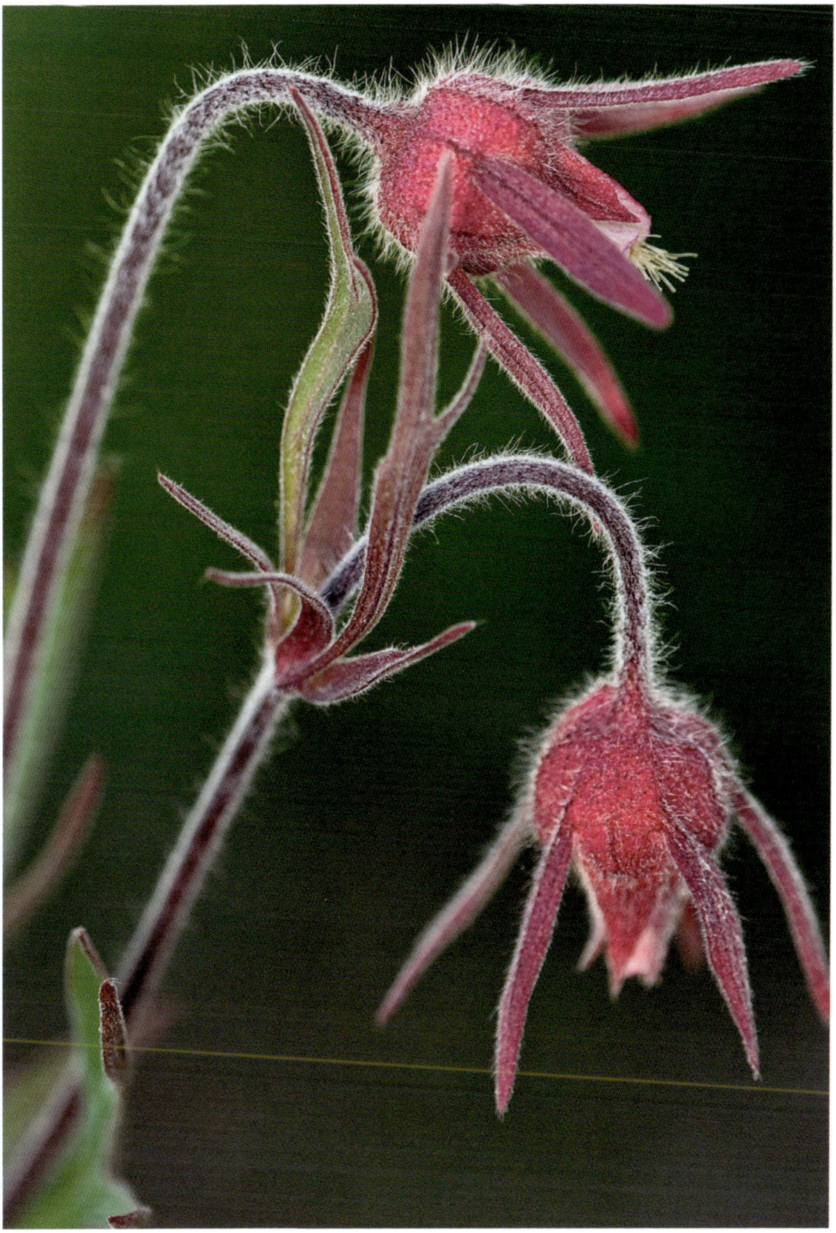

Notice how numerous soft, irregular shaped lines of the stems and flowers of the prairie smoke give this image an emotional appeal.

Form, Shape, and Space

Form and shape are often the subject matter or the center of interest in most wildflower photographs, and mastering these concepts will ultimately increase the quality of any flower image. In a sense, you cannot have form or shape without space because form and shape are masses defined in relationship to the space they exist in. Forms or shapes can either be two-dimensional (height and width) or three-dimensional which includes the extra dimension of depth. In a sense, form or shape can be simply delineated by closed lines (either actual or implied) or changes in color values or intensity (such as light versus dark), or hues or texture or a combination of any of these elements.

Two-dimensional form is the basis for all your composition or organization of design elements in an image. The actual objects or subjects that are delineated by shape or form are referred to as positive space. Contrasted with this is the concept of negative space, which is all the area surrounding the clearly defined form or shape. The most critical aspect of any composition is how the object (positive space) is organized with respect to the negative space.

How we perceive form, shape, and space has a tremendous impact on how effective any composition can be, particularly with respect to visual impact. For instance, the viewpoint from which an image is taken can alter the impact tremendously. Simply moving the camera up or down or to one side or another can turn an ordinary flower into an extraordinary flower, or at least in our perception of the flower. The negative space can serve to attract or focus our attention, or it can distract it. This is why cluttered backgrounds, which serve to diminish the importance of the object or subject, are particularly disturbing for wildflower portraits because the background

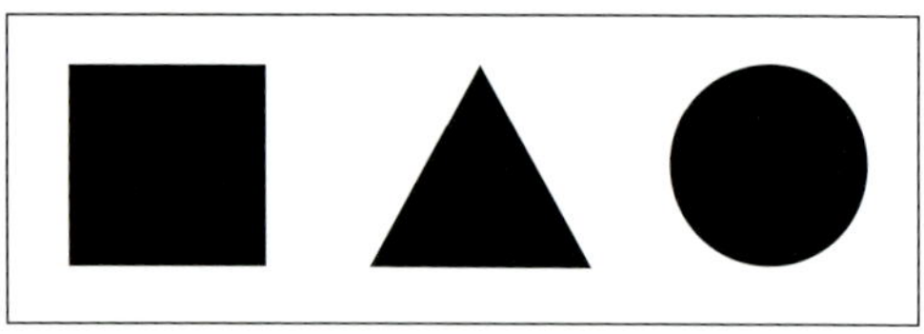

Shapes are variations of squares, triangles, and circles and are usually referred to as the positive space of the image.

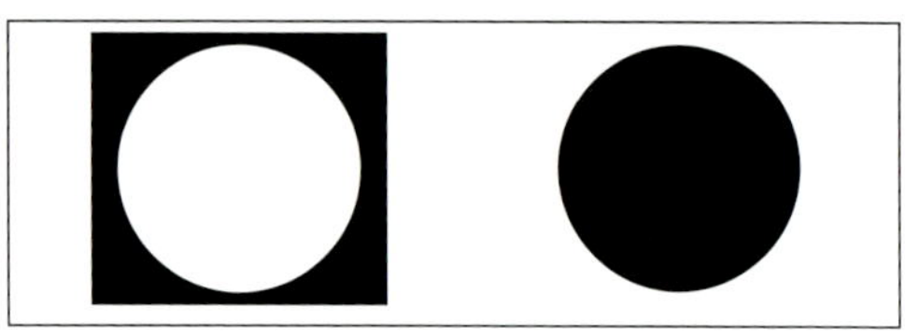

Positive space is denoted by white on the left and negative space is denoted by black indicating a large amount of positive space versus the large amount of negative space (white) surrounding the positive space (black) on the right.

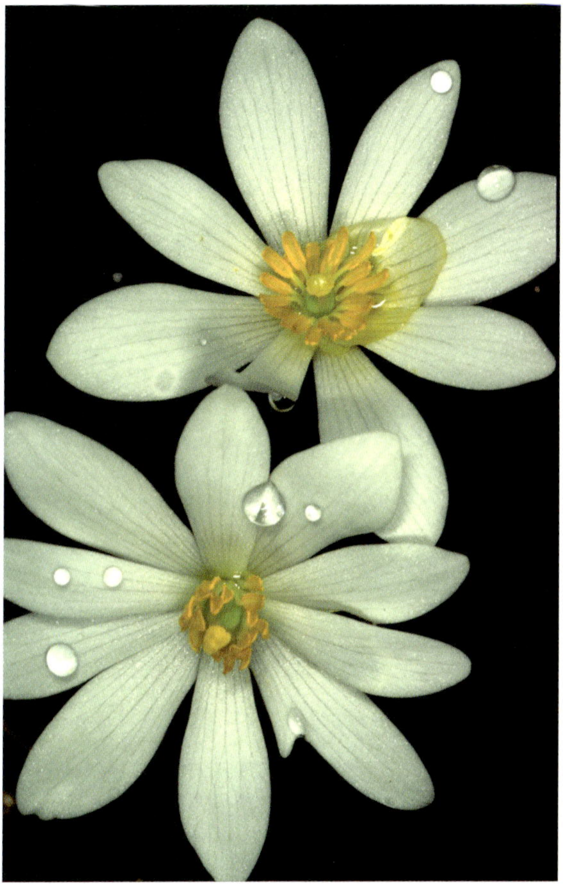

Left:
This is an example of use of a tremendous amount of positive space and little negative space.

Below:
This is an example of the use of negative space and the use of lines (leaves), which draw your attention to the subject, the dwarf iris. Also notice the negative space is dominated by the texture of the fallen pine bark but it is the color of the flower that immediately attracts your attention.

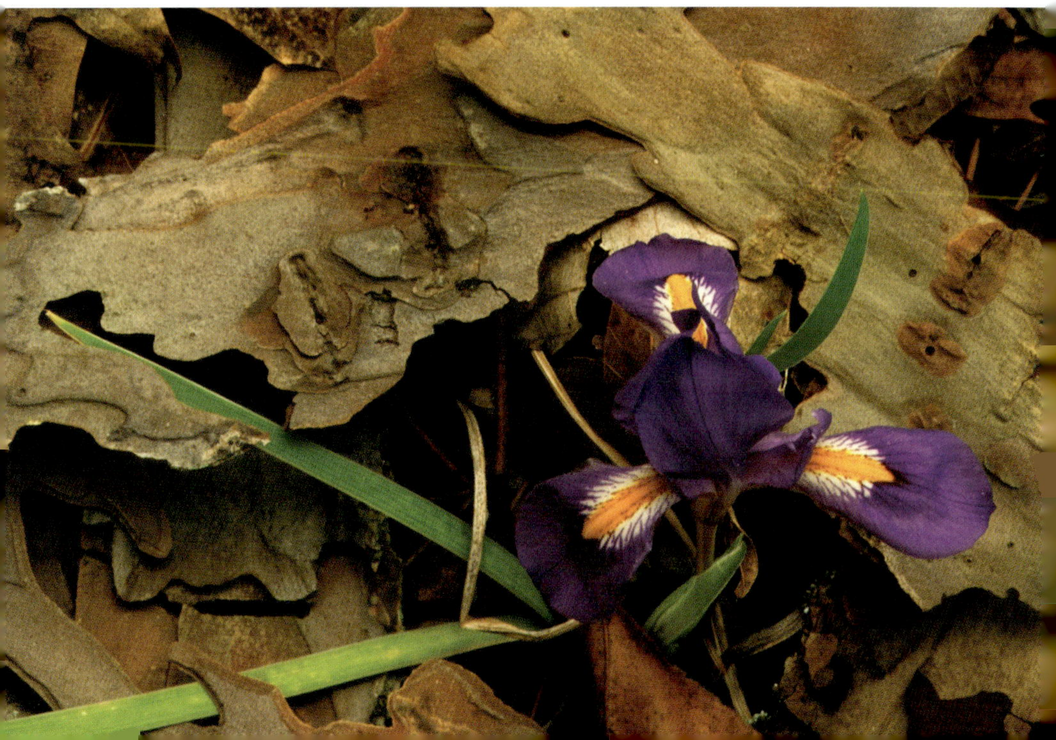

distracts us from the actual object. Conversely, a simple or plain background draws our attention to the subject. The effective use of light (discussed previously) can also affect or define forms, shapes, and space.

Center of Interest (Dominance)

This discussion of form and space obviously leads into a discussion of dominance and the center of interest (or subject). Usually, but not always, any form or object that commands the most amount of attention or influences the composition the most is called the dominant element or center of interest. This is generally the wildflower itself, but it doesn't have to be – and some images may not even have a dominant element. The center of interest is often dominant because of its size, color, placement, its symbolic value in the image, or a combination of all these factors. When I am asked how to improve someone's photography or what is the one most important thing I can improve upon, I always ask them: What is your subject and how can you emphasize your subject in the simplest composition you can think of?

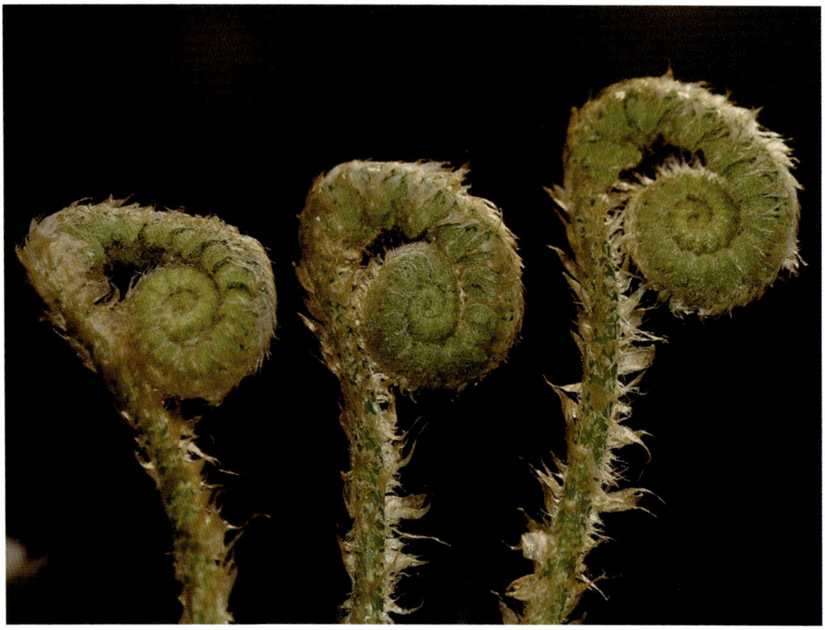

There is no mistaking the center of interest in this image as the three fiddleheads stand out against the dark background. When selecting the center of interest, it is best to work in odd numbers of flowers: one, three, five, etc.

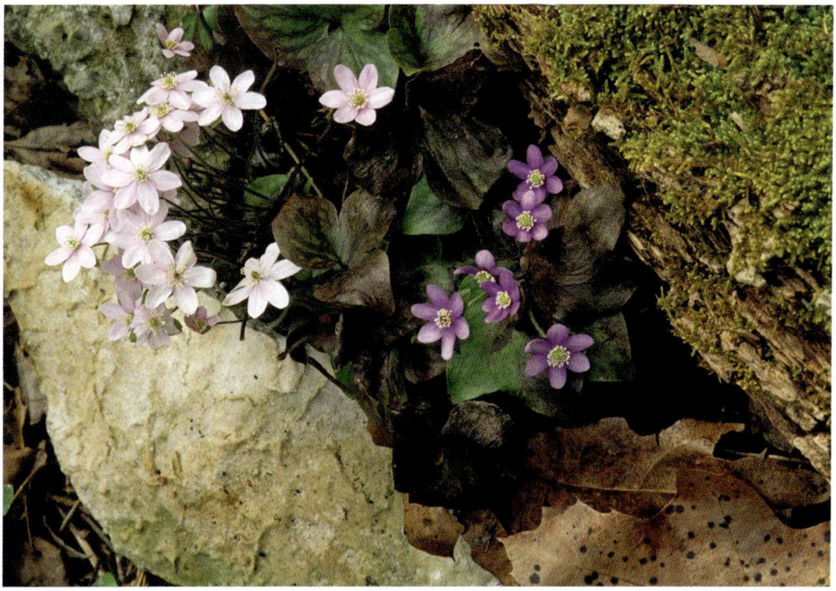

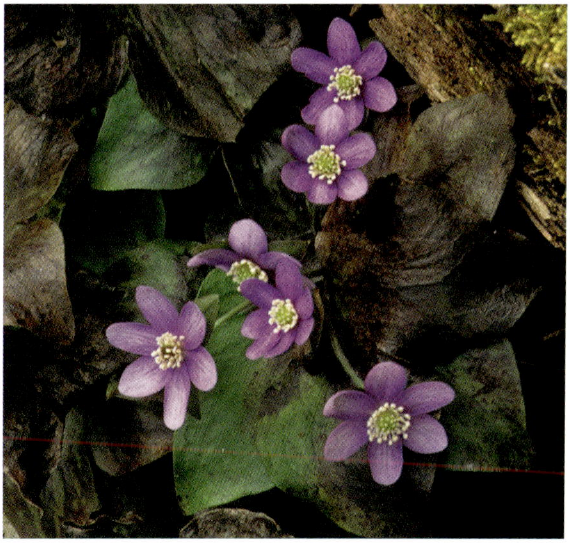

What is going on here? There are multiple problems with the top image. The first problem is that there is no defined center of interest or subject. The second problem is that the light fossil rock is what your eye gravitates to almost immediately (because we see the lightest things first in an image), and the leading line on the right (dead wood) doesn't lead you anywhere.

Remember this rule: "If you can't make it good, make it big." In the second image most of the problems have been cropped out, giving you a true subject that is the dominant part of the image along with leaves that provide an interesting pattern surrounding the flowers.

Pattern and Rhythm

Most of us recognize a pattern instantaneously, and it is nothing more than a repeating shape or form. Rhythm is a method of using a pattern so that the pattern is repeated at regular intervals. The

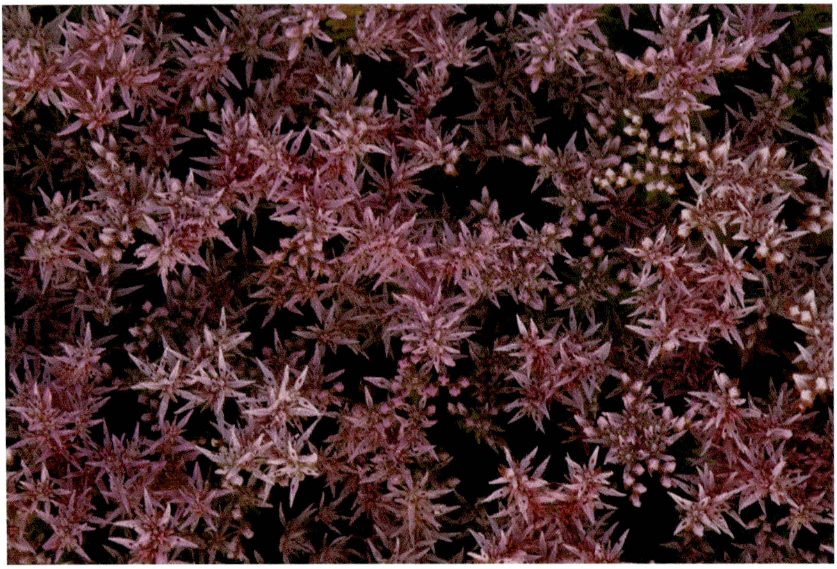

A tight close-up revealed the "pattern" in this group of widow cross flowers.

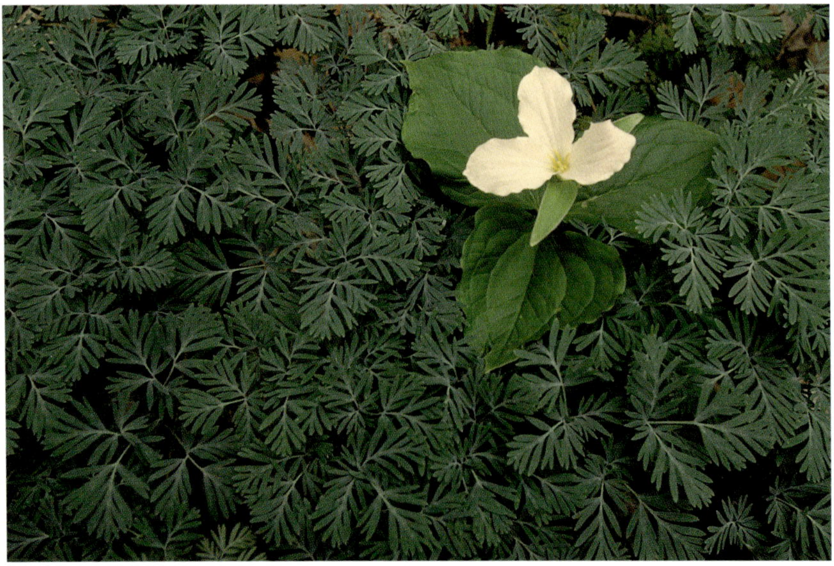

The large flowered white trillium "breaks" the pattern of the squirrel corn leaves and adds visual interest to the image.

best way to think about pattern and rhythm is to borrow the terms from our musically inclined friends and consider how notes are repeated into a pattern and how the patterns of notes are put together to form the rhythm.

For pattern and rhythm to be exciting in a photograph, you should have some variability in the pattern because seeing the same thing over and over has a tendency to get boring. The presence of rhythm in an image gives it a sense of predictability and order.

Texture

Texture refers to the sense of touch. So how do you generate texture in a photograph print? The same way you deal with depth perception. You create the illusion of texture. Textures are related to an object's surface, and all surfaces have textures, from the smoothness of a shiny petal to the roughness of a leaf or stem covered with hairs or bristles.

The best method of creating the illusion of texture is the use of oblique lighting that casts interesting shadows (discussed in the light section).

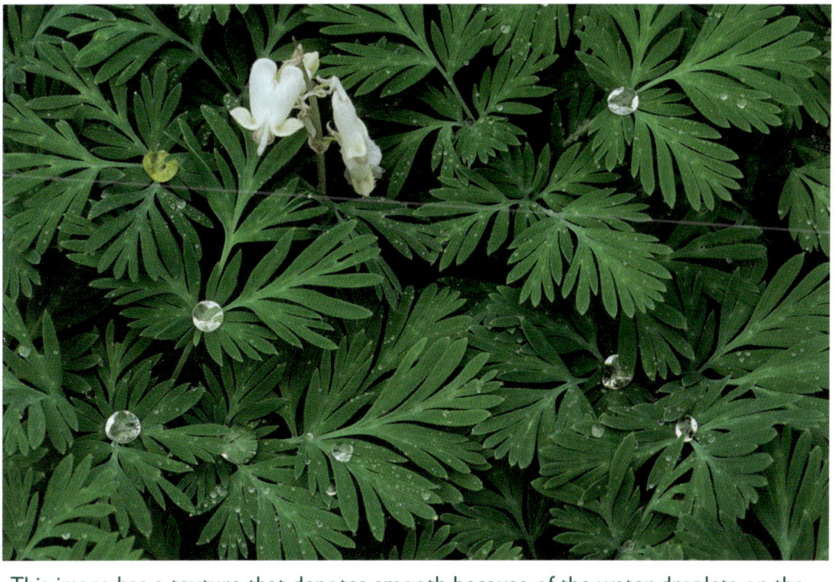

This image has a texture that denotes smooth because of the water droplets on the squirrel corn leaves.

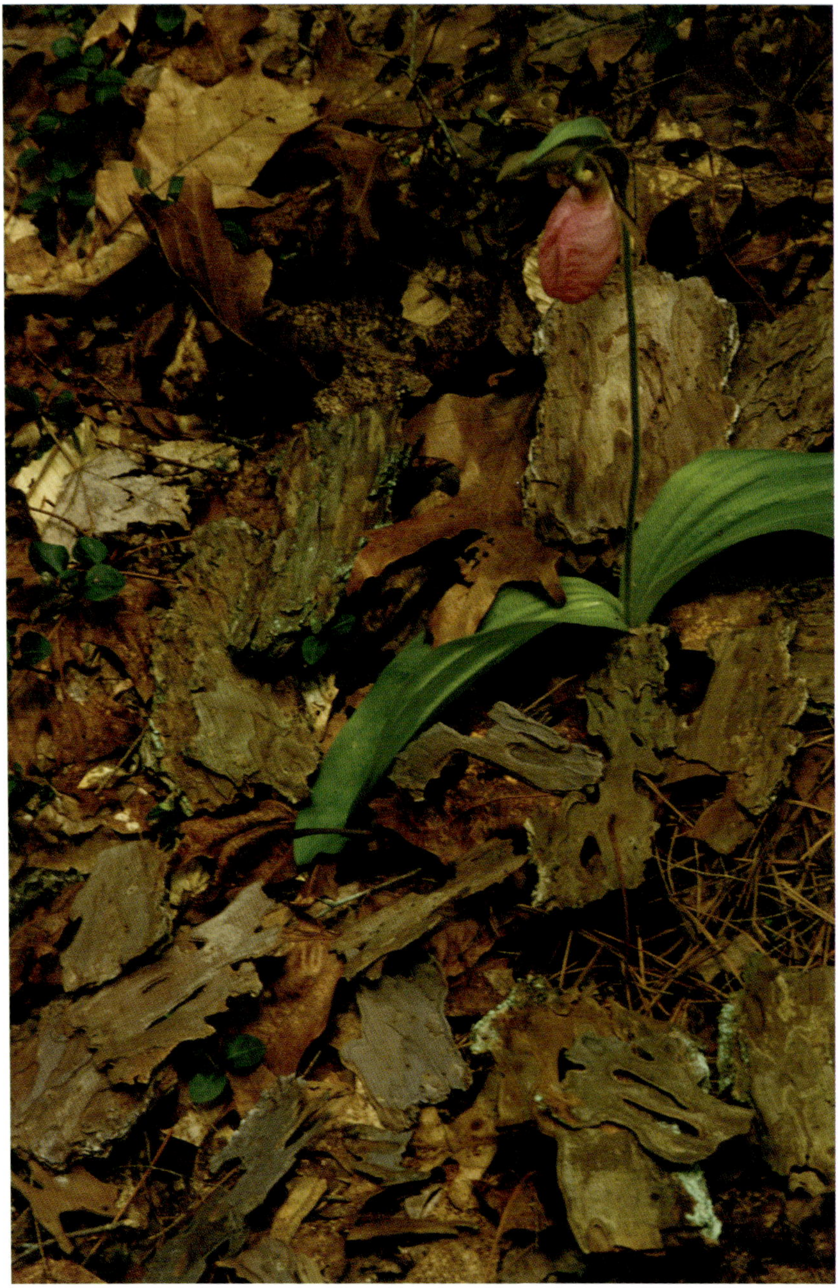

A slight side light from the corner provided just enough light to bring out the texture of smooth leaves contrasted with the rough feel of the shed pine bark.

Using Visual Design to Make Effective Compositions

What is Composition?

Composition is nothing more than arranging and using the different visual elements into a complete or composite whole design. The general theme of any effective wildflower composition often comes down to the KISS principle: "Keep It Simple, Stupid." The Japanese have a better word, shibui, which means simple, subtle, and unobtrusive and yields a highly refined elegance-which sounds more sophisticated than KISS. You have learned a few general design principles and more general rules or guidelines will be presented in this section. But remember, all rules are meant to be broken; however, you can't break the rules effectively until you understand them. The best way to

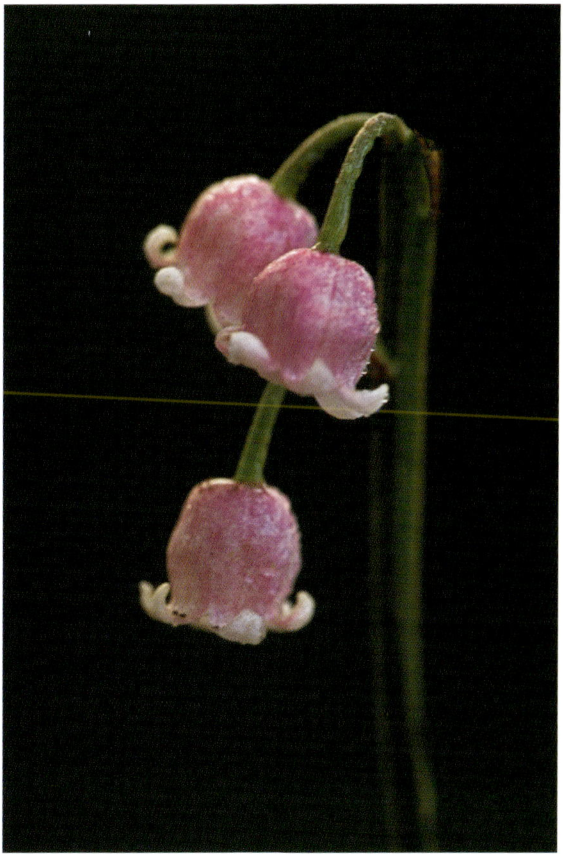

Keep it simple. No distracting elements take away from the pink lily of the valley flowers. Nice diffuse overhead lighting, with a background shaded with a diffuser, and light bounced on the flowers from front make this an effective image.

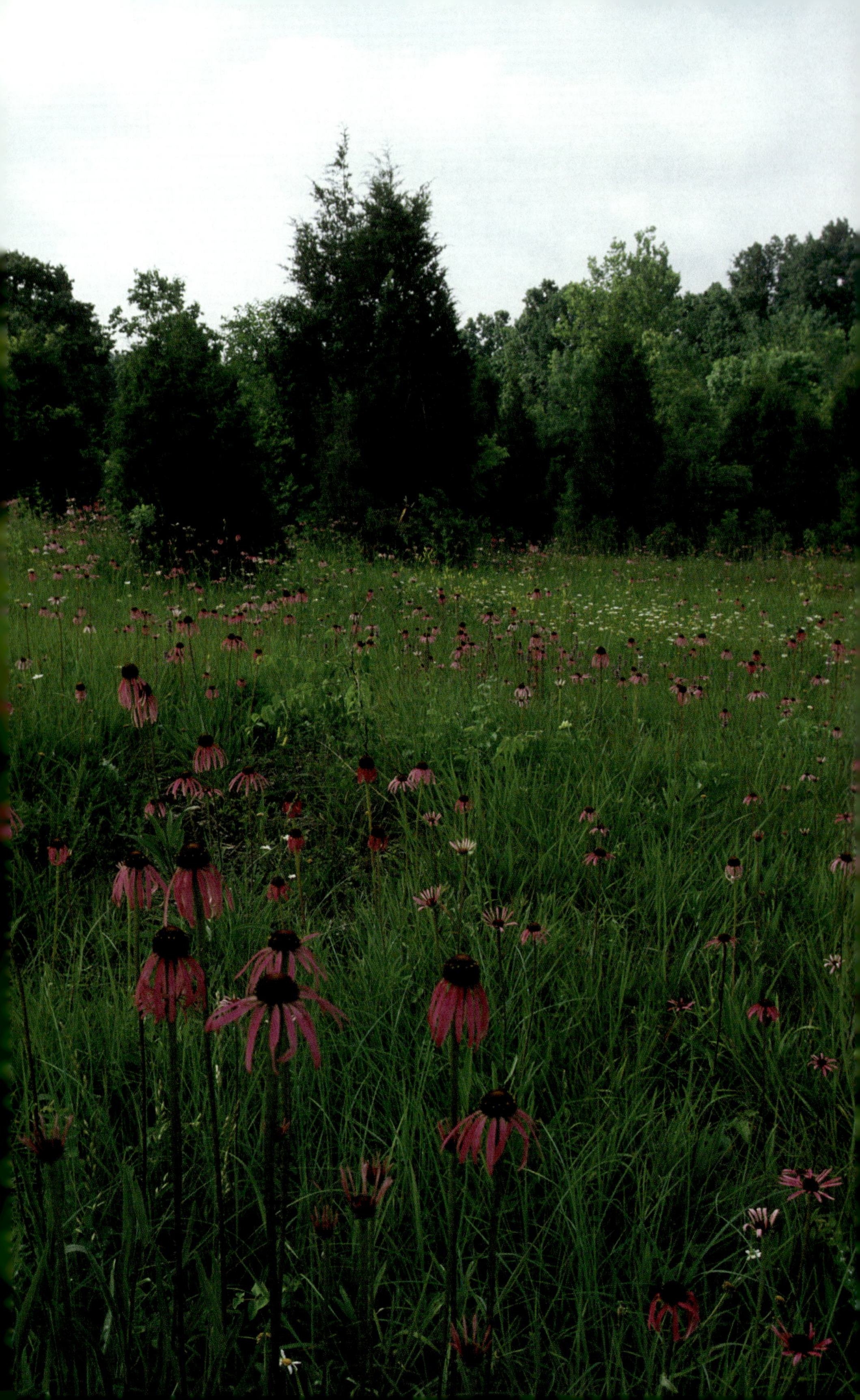

imagine finding effective compositions, and I do mean finding, is to think about painters. They get to add every single visual element they want into a design. You don't have that luxury, and nature is never neat and organized. You must subtract all the unwanted items from the design to make it work for you. Sometimes, I have seen people trying to emulate painters in the field. I watch secretly as they add leaves or something else to their image, and when I wander down to look at what they did, I discover that the composition looks contrived and unnatural.

Working with nature is a balancing act with respect to photography because you have to balance the visual elements with a certain amount of chaos, and this is not an easy task. Fortunately, you now have some of the general ideas about design elements. Now I will discuss how you can put the elements to work for you to create effective compositions.

Balance and Proportion

Think of balance as a form of visual equilibrium that brings stability to an image. All forms or subjects within an image carry a certain amount of "weight" to them as large objects weigh more than small objects and dark objects weigh more than light objects. Closer objects are "heavier" than distant objects. The key to achieving balance is to make sure the weights equalize or come into equilibrium so the image isn't too heavily weighted to one particular form or shape. Think about it this way, you have a flower that has a large, showy bloom (not a technical term here, as it is most likely a cluster of individual flowers) that is elevated on a slim stalk with just leaves at the base of the plant. If you include a large percentage of the stalk in the image, it will appear unbalanced as if the flower is going to topple over.

There are two basic types of balance, symmetrical (formal) and asymmetrical (informal). Symmetrical balance implies that you have equal parts with the same weight. The best analogy to think of is to slice a butterfly in half where each half is the mirror opposite of the other. As humans, we inherently gravitate to symmetrical imagery because our bodies, and much of nature, are in fact symmetrical. Slice us in half, and you discover we are mirror images of ourselves with two eyes, ears, arms, legs, etc. This type of balance gives the appearance of something formal, organized, and orderly, and the image presents a unified image because half of the image is repeated and balanced with the other half. Now, here is the rub; while symmetrical images are quite stable and we are used to seeing this type of design, quite often in commercial advertising, this symmetry has little variety. That brings up the old adage; variety is the spice of life. That is why symmetrical balance is used so much in commercial work, but is used little in the fine arts. In the fine arts, artists want variety to generate interest and the freedom to express themselves more creatively. Hence as I mentioned in the section above about using odd numbers of flowers for your center of interest because they can't be split equally and give an unbalanced composition.

Asymmetrical (informal) balance is much more difficult to pull off visually, and the photographer must have a gut reaction or some internal mechanism that says there is a sense of balance in the image. Most of us can do that because if our eye just wanders all over the place in an even pattern over the image, then it is probably not in balance.

One way to approach asymmetrical balance is to think of the forms or shapes on a balancing beam with a tipping point (fulcrum) somewhere on the beam. A heavy form can be balanced with a lighter form if the heavier form is closer to the fulcrum and the lighter object is a farther distance from the fulcrum. One of the key rules

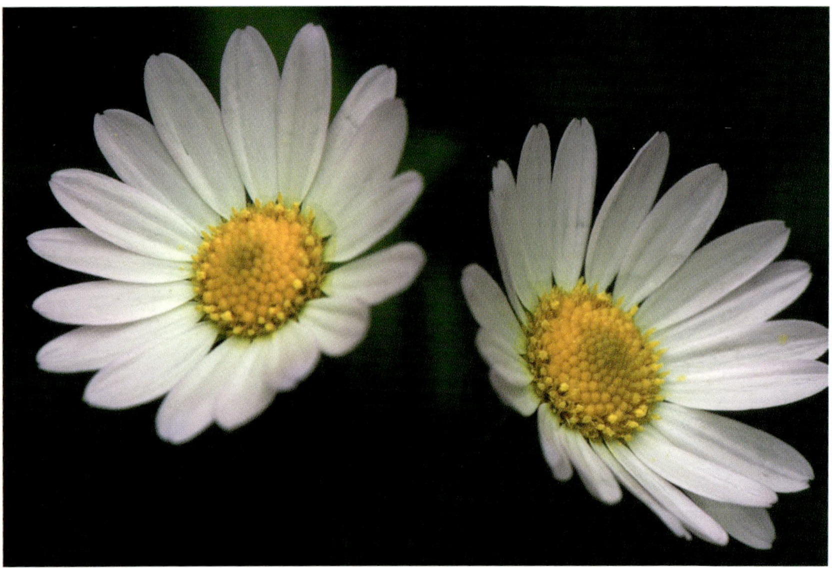

This photo of western daisies is essentially a balanced composition where each side of the image (individual flowers) is nearly identical.

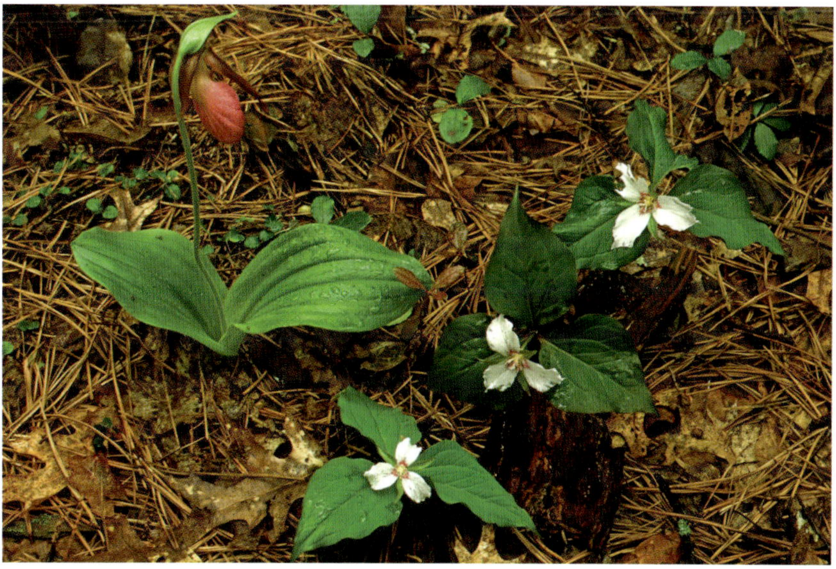

This is an example of an asymmetrical balance composition where the pink lady's slipper balances the three painted trilliums.

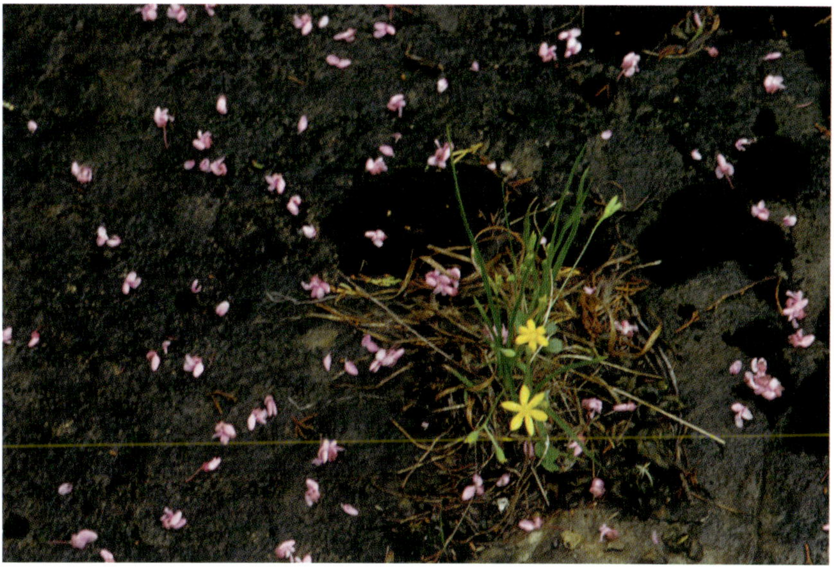

This is an asymmetrical composition with the use of much negative space. The darker moss helps balance the light of the yellow star grass growing out of the dolomitic limestone.

of thumb is not to place your subject or center of interest (flower) in the middle of the image because the central axis will point in all directions. Likewise, try not to line up forms or shapes along these central axes.

Another rule of thumb is not to place the object in the corners, but it should be in the center. One general rule of thumb that photographers use to create asymmetrical balance is to use the rule of thirds, which will be discussed in more detail in the next few paragraphs.

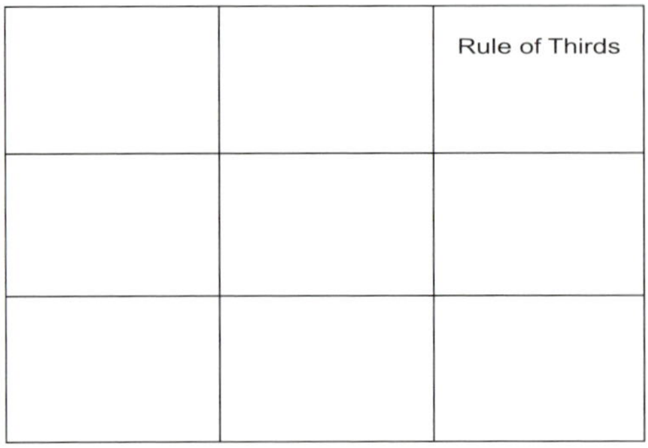

The intersection of each line results in a point that is considered a point of interest in a composition. The key factor to keep in mind is to keep the subject from occupying just the center of the image.

This discussion of balance allows us to transition to the next topic of proportion (the relative size of objects in the image) because balance and proportion are closely linked. Proportion is nothing more than size and the relationship between various objects in the image, their size, and the relationship of their size to each other and the whole image. Some really smart people several hundred years or more ago began to understand how people

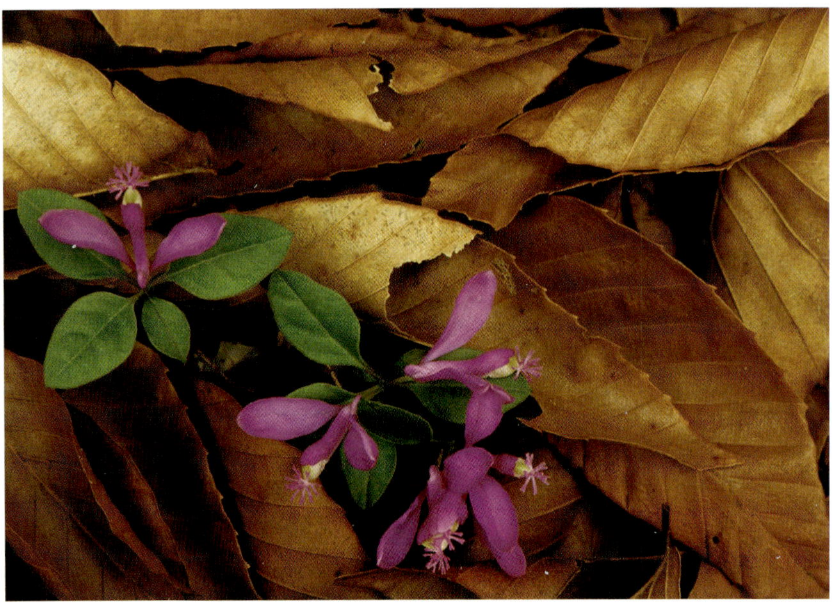

This image of gaywings does not closely adhere to the "rule of thirds" like the trillium and trout lily images shown on the following page but more to the Golden Ratio and Mean which results in an effective composition.

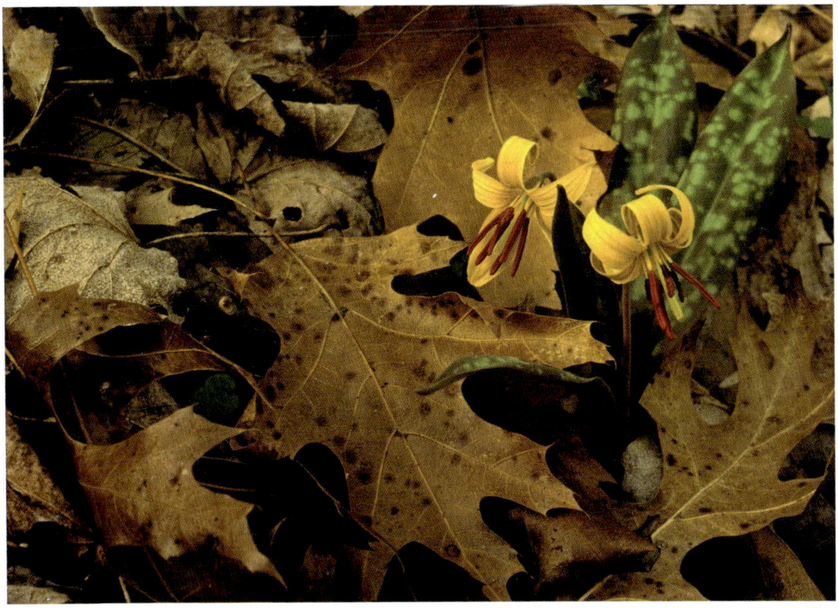

The yellow trout lily flowers have been purposely put in the upper right "third" to draw your attention to them.

respond to proportion in art and came up with a frequently occurring proportion called the Golden Mean based upon the Golden Ratio which photographers have adapted into the "rule of thirds."

The rule of thirds, which is a gross approximation and adaptation of the Golden Ratio and Golden Mean, is about as much as most nature photographers want to deal with. The rule of thirds states that you divide the image into thirds vertically, and horizontally, and at each point of intersection is visually important.

Using the rule of thirds as a guideline, the large flowered white trillium falls into the upper right third quadrant, a point of interest and your attention is immediately drawn to it for this reason and because it breaks the pattern and is the lightest object in the photograph.

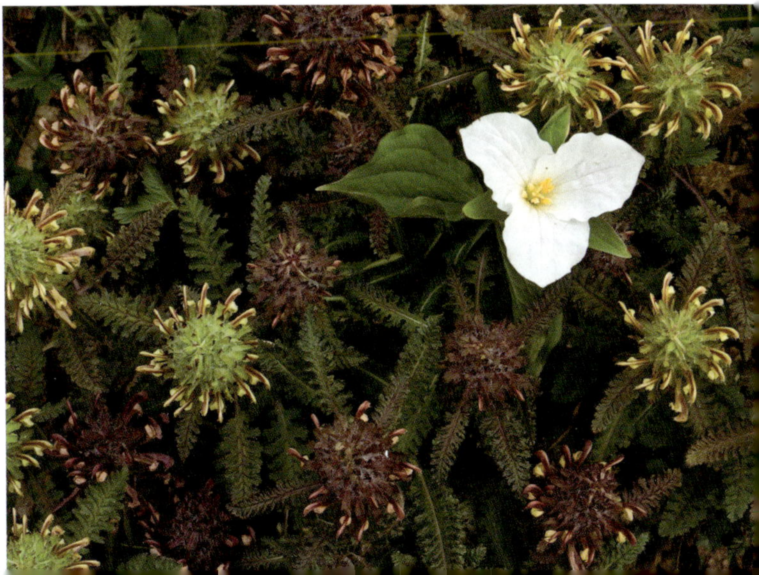

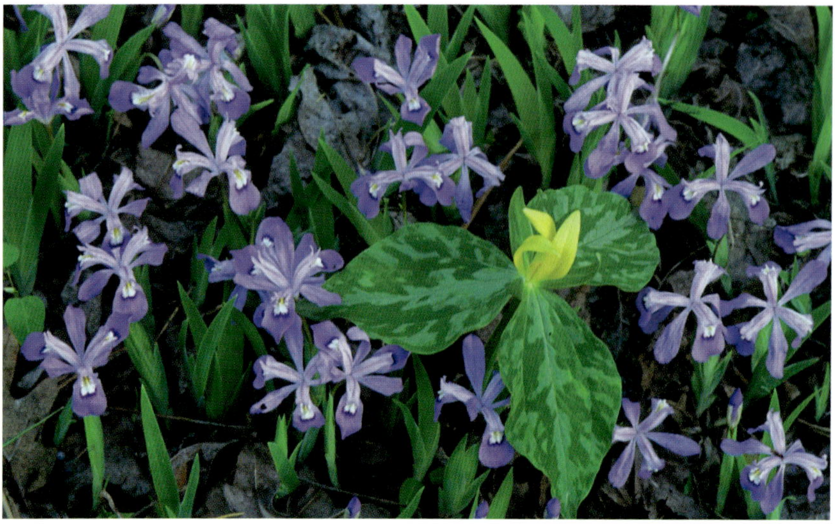

Where is the emphasis in this photograph? The primary emphasis is the yellow trillium which gets that designation because of its size, color, and location in the image. The secondary emphasis is the repeating pattern of dwarf crested iris.

Emphasis and Unity

The two final principles of emphasis and unity will bring us back to the first paragraph in the effective composition section, creating dynamically simple images that bring order from chaos. While simple, highly refined and elegant images are preferred, you must balance this with some amount of chaos because overly simple images fail to keep our interest for very long.

Photographers use emphasis to call attention to something in the image. It could be the center of interest, or they may use emphasis to vary the composition to provide for "visual surprises" as you explore their image. Emphases are those areas that draw the viewer's attention, and there can be a primary emphasis and secondary emphases. Emphasis can be created with repeating visual elements or through contrast of color, texture, shape, size, or position.

Unity is what brings all this together into one whole coherent visual design. Unity is the ordering of all the visual elements so that each contributes to the whole (sum of parts is not greater than the whole in this case) to create visual harmony. And that is the whole purpose for understanding visual design; to create effective photographs that give a sense of purpose and visual harmony.

These images show the evolution of making a creative image of this rare wildflower in Kentucky. The first image of slender marsh pink shows the plant with stems and leaves and two flowers. This

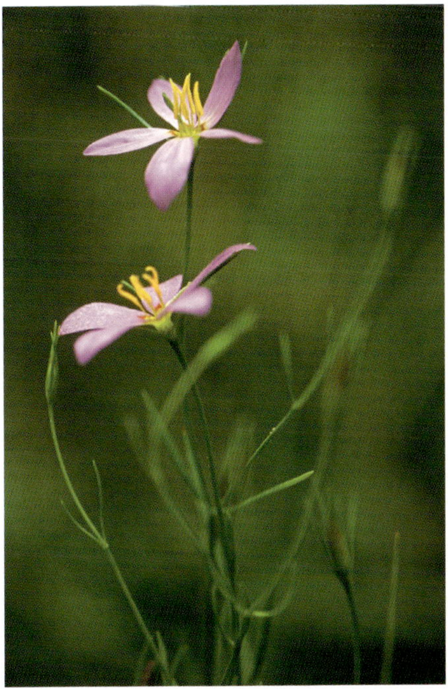

Image one

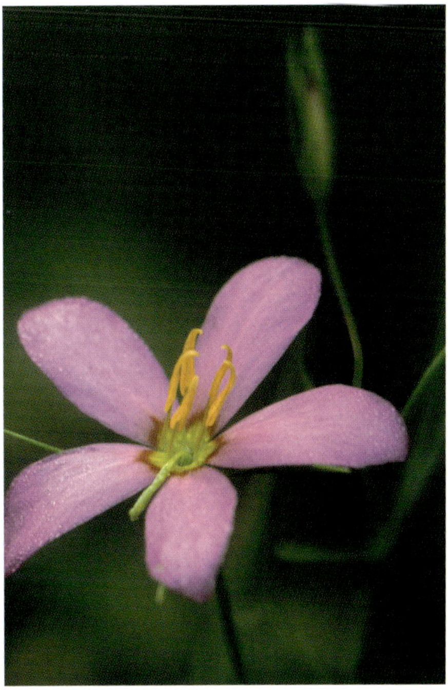

Image two

image lacks unity or harmony because each of the flowers competes for dominance and the varied lines and cluttered background distract from emphasizing the subject.

The second image has solved the problems of distracting stems but the light is more direct, the background more harsh and bi-colored, without a sense of balance.

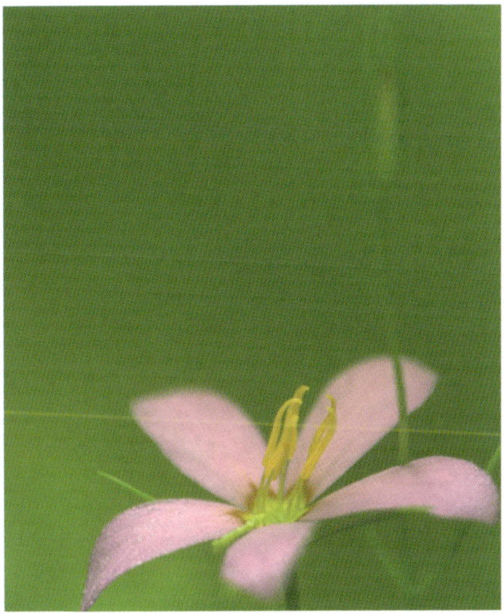

Image three

The final image has simplicity, no distractions from the subject and a sense of balance by using a large amount of negative space, soft-diffuse lighting to emphasize color harmony, and the one out of focus bud at the upper left to balance the heaviness of the flower in the bottom. I spent more than two hours photographing these flowers to get the last image, which was taken when a light fog had moved into the meadow.

Equipment

This equipment section assumes you want to take your wildflower photography to a level beyond taking snapshots or documentary type flower photos. If you are content with the images you are getting and do not want to elevate to a higher quality image, read no further because it is a waste of time. Well, not a complete waste of time. You might take five minutes to read the information about tripods, but then again, most people taking snapshots aren't going to use a tripod anyway, so read no further. For the rest of the reading public, read the entire section on equipment before thinking about going out and investing in a ton of expensive equipment, unless you are an equipment junkie. You probably have perfectly adequate equipment in your bag already and just need to learn a few tips and techniques. Always remember that technology is never a substitute for technique.

Case in point; after I had my second hip replaced, my doctor ordered me not to carry more than 25 pounds, (yeah, right – and not pick up my two-year-old son at the time, or five years later my daughter), I had to rethink the whole concept of carrying a heavy tripod and a backpack with two camera bodies, half a dozen lenses, accessories, film, etc. Actually, I didn't take his advice, and only after I had one of the original hip replacements replaced 13 years later, did I take his advice! Today, I carry only a tripod (6.75 pounds), head (2 pounds), and camera body (1.7 pounds), a wide-angle to normal zoom lens, a macro lens, and flash. It all comes in under the 25-pound limit, and my wildflower photos are just as good as ever. Technology is never a substitute for good technique because it is the photographer who creates the image; the camera sensor just records it.

Tripod

I have heard the complaints about toting a tripod around in the field; too heavy – too awkward and clumsy – slows me down too much – I have a vibration reduction lens and don't need it – I shoot at a high ISO rating and can therefore hand hold my camera – the pictures look great – yada, yada, yada. If any of these comments describe you, don't count on coming back with any high-quality wildflower photos like professionals take because it won't happen without using a tripod. Tripods are necessary for most nature photography and are absolutely essential for close-up work. So, why begin the equipment section with a discussion about tripods and not cameras? The short answer is that ***a tripod is the most important piece of equipment you can own***. It will improve your photography immeasurably no matter which camera you own. Let me repeat myself to ensure you get the message. ***A tripod is not an accessory; it is a mandatory piece of equipment.***

While you may make many compromises in cost versus quality in other photographic equipment, you should not skimp when purchasing a tripod. Why? Here are some pertinent reasons. First and foremost, razor-sharp images are impossible to get hand holding a lens. It is impossible to hand hold a camera steady, even with a vibration reduction lens, at a shutter speed of a half second, or in most cases 1/30th of a second. The general rule of thumb for hand holding is you can safely steady the camera at a shutter speed of 1/lens length. For example, if using a 500mm telephoto lens, you could safely hand hold the camera and lens at 1/500th of a second. However, if the wind is blowing or you are shaking or even the least bit fatigued from hiking on a trail, forget hand holding even at higher speeds.

Even more important than getting razor-sharp images is that the tripod allows you to use the entire range of shutter speeds and apertures your camera has to offer. Let's say you are photographing early in the morning under low light conditions, and you have a beautiful patch of flowers in the foreground with a grand landscape behind those delicate beauties. To get maximum depth of field, you would need to use the smallest aperture opening, f/22, to get that photograph. You then meter the scene, and your meter says you need a shutter speed of 1 second. If you do not use a tripod, it is impossible to get this image. If you open your lens up to f/2.8, which means your shutter speed is 1/60th of a second, it would mean either the flowers or the background would be in focus, but not both.

Another important reason for using a tripod is that it slows you down and allows you the opportunity to fine-tune your compositions. Once you find the right flower and get your equipment set up with just the composition you want, you can then check for depth of field and check the background and edges for distracting elements. It can also enhance your creativity. For example, want some beautiful flowers in front of the waterfall with a milky ethereal feel of flowing water? This is only possible with a slow shutter speed with a camera on a steady tripod. Finally, the tripod frees up your hands to do some selective gardening while looking through the viewfinder or holding an off-camera flash or reflector. It also allows you the opportunity to be ready when the wind stops blowing to quickly click the shutter and get the image.

At this point, don't make the assumption that you will automatically take better photos with a tripod of any type. "Sturdy" and "lightweight" are oxymoronic terms when talking tripods. However, recent technology with carbon fiber tripods has produced sturdy tripods that are about 35 percent lighter than equivalent aluminum tripods. However, carbon tripods are about twice as expensive.

Look for three things when purchasing a tripod. First, how sturdy or stable is it, and how much weight can it support? Second, how low to the ground does it sit? This means heavy-duty tripods with leg braces are out. Finally, when the legs are fully extended, can you look through your camera's viewfinder and not bend over? There was one final consideration I took into account when I purchased my latest tripod, and that was weight. My old standard, the Gitzo 320, was starting to get heavy. As I have aged and my artificial hips have aged as well, weight is of paramount importance to me because of the 25-pound weight limit imposed by my doctor. Consequently, I retired the old Gitzo 320 and upgraded to a new carbon-fiber tripod that cuts the weight by 30 percent or more and I still get the stability I need. These tripods are considerably more expensive than aluminum legs, but if weight is a consideration, they are well worth the investment.

So what do I use, and what are my recommendations about purchasing a tripod? I use a Gitzo G1548 carbon-fiber tripod. Why such a large tripod? First, I wanted one that would support my 500mm f/4 lens. Second, I wanted a set of legs without a center column. Third, weight is an issue and this tripod only weighs 6.75 pounds! Finally, it can be positioned only about five inches off the ground! This tripod is a perfect fit for my photography but a bit on the pricey side at around $700. Several excellent alternatives, and a whole lot more cost effective, are the Manfrotto 055XB Pro series (perhaps the best overall value); the Slik professional tripod, which is a bit pricier but an exceptional value; The Induro adventure series, and finally the Gitzo traveler and systemic series, which are more expensive, but considered the base tripod for many professional photographers.

Now that you have thought about what type of tripod legs you want, the next decision is what type of head to put on the top of those legs. While everyone will give you recommendations about a pan/tilt versus a ball head, in my book there is no place for a pan/tilt head because it is cumbersome, awkward to use at times, and simply not as versatile as a ball head. The big problem with ball-and-socket type heads is most people purchase one that is too small to adequately support the camera and lens. The minimum size ball I recommend is 2 inches and three of the best products on the market today are the Arca-Swiss B1, Kirk B1, and the Really Right Stuff model BH 55. These all have the dovetail-design camera-mounting system that provides for rock-solid support. All three heads are all in the same price range and might seem a bit pricey at around $400, but just like your tripod, this is an area in which you should not scrimp on expense. One of the most important things to think about when purchasing a head is how the camera is attached to the head. The best type is a quick release attachment because you do not want to be screwing your camera on and off the head. All three of the heads I mentioned have a very secure type of dove-tail, Arca-swiss type quick-release system.

Even a sturdy tripod used incorrectly will not ensure better photos. Make sure the tripod is set firmly in the ground, particularly in heavy leaf mold or in sphagnum patches or other spongy soils. Make sure only the largest leg segments are extended if needed (the smallest ones should be extended last – remember the weakest link analogy) and tighten the legs securely.

Finally let me say something about turning the center column upside down to get the camera to ground level. I have owned all the tripods, except the Slik, at one time or another and I actually tried doing this trick. My experience is that it is a whole lot easier to do this in theory than in reality. You would have to be a contortionist to use the equipment in this manner. Better to just cut the center column off (not needed anyway because if you need it to get to your eye level, you have just defeated the purpose of using a tripod because you have a monopod on top of three legs). In my opinion, better to just purchase a set of legs that will get you close to ground level and leave it at that.

Camera Systems

The SLR (single lens reflex) camera body and associated accessories are the very best system, bar none, for wildflower and close-up or macro photography. Note I mentioned system, not camera body, because you are in fact investing in a system. It is the associated lenses, flashes, and other accessories that allow you almost unlimited options for creating unique images of some of the most beautiful subjects on the entire planet, flowers. Most of the current SLR-type digital cameras (DSLR) on the market are more than adequate for wildflower photography, but there are a few features that will take you to a higher level.

At this point, you may ask yourself, "Why should I invest hundreds of dollars into a digital single lens reflex (DSLR) when my point-and-shoot has macro capability, has a 10x digital zoom to bring objects in closer, and I can take photos in either jpeg or raw?" Here are a few quick reasons to think about moving up in quality. Number one is that point-and-shoot cameras have smaller sensors (even though they may have 8 or 10 megapixels) that simply do not provide the opportunities for the highest quality image, especially when it is dark or in low light situations because they produce an excessive amount of noise. This can also be an issue when you try to make large prints from the files. The second reason is that you do not have the same optical quality in the lens, and you do not have the opportunity to change lenses to provide for maximum quality images. Third is that most compact cameras "react" slowly when you push the shutter release (called shutter lag), which means that you can sometimes "miss" the shot, particularly if there is motion involved. Finally, it seems that the flash is only good to about 10 feet or so. That is because most compact cameras have relatively weak flashes, and you do not have the opportunity to place an external flash on the camera body. These are just a few of the reasons to move up to the DSLR.

Before I continue further, I should explain that photographers can generally be grouped into two broad or general categories at the extremes along a wide continuum with respect to equipment. There are equipment junkies, those that like equipment, any and all equipment, gadgets and gizmos, and the latest this and the latest that. At the other end of the continuum are those photographers who are minimalists and use only a limited amount of equipment. The important thing to remember is that just having lots of equipment and gadgets doesn't ensure good wildflower photos. I will take technique over technology any time, any place. There is simply no good substitute for good technique. However, having some basic equipment can make the difference between getting a shot and watching the image "blowin in the wind," so to speak.

For example, wind is a constant problem when shooting wildflower portraits or habitat shots. One excellent piece of equipment I invested in was an 85-mm tilt/shift close-up lens that allows me to tilt the front of the lens so that it is parallel to the film plane and allows me to obtain critical focus at a smaller f stop with the concomitant increase in shutter speed. These lenses aren't cheap and can cost more than $1,000. When I was working on *The Wildflowers and Ferns of Kentucky* this proved to be an invaluable piece of equipment because I had one opportunity to get photographs of any one particular species since most perennials don't stay in flower much longer than a week or so, and returning to the exact flower and location (not to mention the time and travel involved) wasn't practical. On windy days, or on days during the middle of the day when the breeze typically picks up, this lens allowed me to get the image. It was nice to have that piece of insurance in my camera bag. That said, not everyone, unless you are making a living at this stuff, can go out and purchase one of these specialty lenses.

Think of this analogy when contemplating equipment purchases. Much like a painter creates unique artistic impressions with a canvas, paint, and brushes, the photographic equipment you select and use becomes your essential "tools" for creating unique wildflower impressions. It is your vision and creativity, combined with good technique that conceive the composition, understand the light, etc., which makes the actual photograph. The camera is just a machine to expose the medium and record it for posterity.

Technology has given us excellent equipment choices today compared to even five or 10 years ago. Recent advances in digital technology are changing the face of photography forever and many of the simplest "point-and-shoot" digital cameras have some ability to close focus and take wildflower photos that will amaze you. However, if you desire to elevate your ability to take magazine-quality wildflower images, you will need to "upgrade" your camera equipment to a digital SLR type camera with associated lenses and accessories. This is not to say that you should make some rash judgment or hasty decision based on what you read below, but you can get an amazing DSLR for less than $700 today which will get you started taking quality wildflower photos.

Always remember that almost everything about photography involves compromise, and this is certainly true with respect to photographic equipment. Also remember that in general with photographic equipment, the better the quality, the higher the price. For instance, a high-quality camera manufacturer's brand macro lens will probably set you back any where from $500 to more than $1,400. Your budget may not be able to handle that kind of expenditure and you may wish to select a lens that is not made by the same company that manufactured your camera. In this case, a similar lens may cost half that much, and there are advantages and disadvantages to using these lenses. Only you are in the position to determine your own personal trade-offs and what your budget will allow. The best advice I can give is to purchase the absolute best equipment you can afford.

I am going to reinforce that there is no question that a DSLR camera is the best equipment for wildflower photography. The ability to use interchangeable lenses and other accessories allows you maximum flexibility to solve any situation encountered in the field. A recent informal survey by the North American Nature Photographers Association found that Canon and Nikon are by far the most preferred DSLR used by nature photographers.

While most of the major camera manufacturers make excellent cameras and lenses, there are really several features that you should consider when purchasing a body. In the past, a film camera was just a box that allowed you to expose an image on film and then move the film so another image could be created and stored on the film. The particular brand of camera wasn't all that important; rather the film and lens quality were the critical choices for determining, to a large part, the quality of any particular wildflower photograph. Ah, to bring back analog, as this was something we could inherently understand but this is not necessarily the case with the digital revolution. Confusion, confusion, and more confusion.

The short answer of the very long complicated and extremely technical questions about digital photography is that it is now very important to select a good camera body. Why? Not only do you invest in a total system of lenses and other accessories, but the image sensor, which has replaced film in the capturing of the image, has much to do with the quality of the final product. Here is where it can get complex rather quickly because there are a tremendous number of factors that determine image quality such as what size the sensor is (bigger is often better, but not always), what type of sensor (CCD – Charged Coupled Device or CMOS – complementary metal oxide semiconductor), how many megapixels (generally more pixels is better, all other factors being equal – such as pixel size), the quality of the megapixels (generally speaking, bigger pixels are better), how much noise (similar to the grain in film), and the tonal qualities and color quality inherent in the sensor. Finally, you have to pay more attention to lens quality with digital photography. So, it is important to select a good camera body because purchasing the entry level of DSLR for this type of work is going to cost you hundreds if not thousands of dollars.

Here is a quick look at the important issues surrounding sensors and digital cameras. First, how big is the sensor? Compact or point-and-shoot type digital cameras typically have an image sensor size that is 11mm diagonal or smaller which, when set at highest-quality levels, will give you a decent 8.5 x 11 inch print. Many DSLR cameras have a 4/3 sensor that measures 22 to 27mm diagonally and have between 6 and 12 megapixels. Because these sensors range from one-half to two-thirds the size of 35mm film, they have a "focal length multiplier" between 1.5 and 2, which means your 200mm lens for film is a 300mm on your DSLR with this sensor. The final sensor size is generally called full frame because it measures close to the size of 35mm film diagonally which is 24 x 36 mm. These sensors have up 24 or more megapixels which approach the resolution of a medium-format camera. Finally, there are medium-format sensors but these tend to be very pricey. In general, the larger the sensor the better the quality, but the trade off is expense. Cameras with full frame sensors are typically more expensive because they are using CMOS chips, which have higher development costs and require greater on-chip integration than CCD sensor based cameras.

So here are some really important things to keep in mind when purchasing a digital camera body.

- Does it have a depth of field preview button?
- Can the mirror be locked up?
- How slow does the shutter speed go to (not how fast – that is not an issue here)?
- Can the camera be operated manually?

- Does it have different metering systems that include a spot meter?
- Does it have a noise reduction filter?
- Does it have a big LCD monitor on the back?
- Does it have the ability to display the histogram in the LCD?
- How good is the flash system for balancing available light and fill flash?

The depth of field preview button has been one of those features that many camera manufacturers have eliminated in order to save a few bucks on the cost of the camera. Too bad, because this little button is invaluable for figuring out how much of the flower subject is in focus and more often than not, what the background looks like. This is particularly critical for portraits where you don't want something distracting in the background. There have been so many times when I pushed the depth of field preview button only to find a

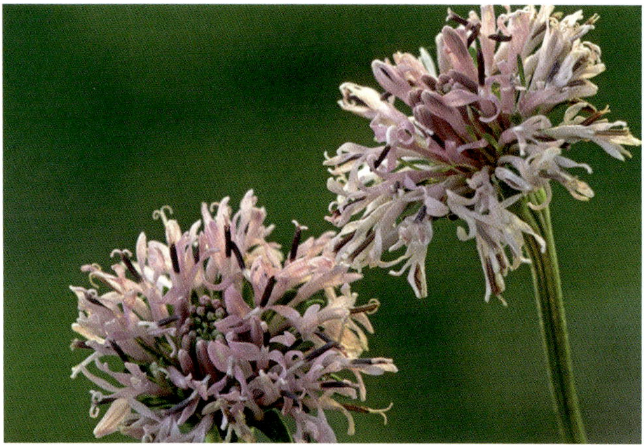

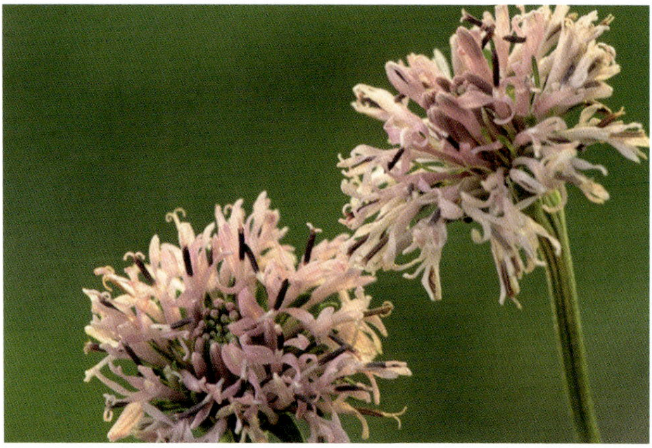

Notice the subtle difference in how much of the background is in focus and distracting in the first image, which was taken at f/11 compared to the lower image, which was taken at f/5.6. Pressing the depth of field preview button showed I could get the Barbara's button flowers in focus and have a cleaner background with the larger aperture opening, which resulted in the use of a faster shutter speed.

"white" or light stick in the background that I hadn't noticed before that would be horribly distracting in the final shot. There have been other times when I discovered, particularly when using a longer lens, that I didn't need to use f/22 to get the flower sharp, only f/11 and the background appeared much nicer and softer.

Here is how the button works. When you look through the lens you are looking at the image with the widest opening of the lens, which lets in more light so you can focus and see the brightest possible image. When the camera actually takes the image, it closes the aperture in the lens to the desired f stop, reducing the amount of light entering through the lens to get the appropriate exposure. When you push the depth of field preview button, it closes the aperture to the selected opening and shows you what the image will look like in its final form. So if at all possible, look for a depth of field preview button on the camera body.

New camera bodies have all kinds of bells and whistles: auto-focus, auto-exposure, auto-everything. However, remember that you, and your brain, are the creative part of wildflower photography. Even though I have automated camera bodies, mine is set on either aperture priority (I set the aperture and the camera sets the shutter speed) or manual almost all of the time. This allows you to control every aspect of taking the image.

Most camera bodies today have a full range of shutter speeds ranging from 1/1000th or more down to 1 second or more. The important range of shutter speeds for wildflower photography is on the slow end, and if you can find a camera body with shutter speeds down to 20 or 30 seconds, you will use that more than a fast speed of 1/4000th of a second. The reason is, to get the depth of field you need with low ISO ratings, you will need that lens open a longer time. Many of the photos in my book, *The Wildflowers and Ferns of Kentucky*, had exposure times of two to 10 seconds. In fact, that was more the rule than the exception. Of course, this means you need to use a tripod for all your shots. One of the nice features of more expensive DSLR cameras is they have a noise reduction filter that reduces the amount of "grain" or distortions in the image when using very slow shutter speeds.

Shake, rattle, and roll. All cameras do it, some more than others. All DSLR cameras have a mirror that must swing up before light and images can be recorded on the sensor. When this happens, there is a small amount of vibration that occurs and can lead to less than

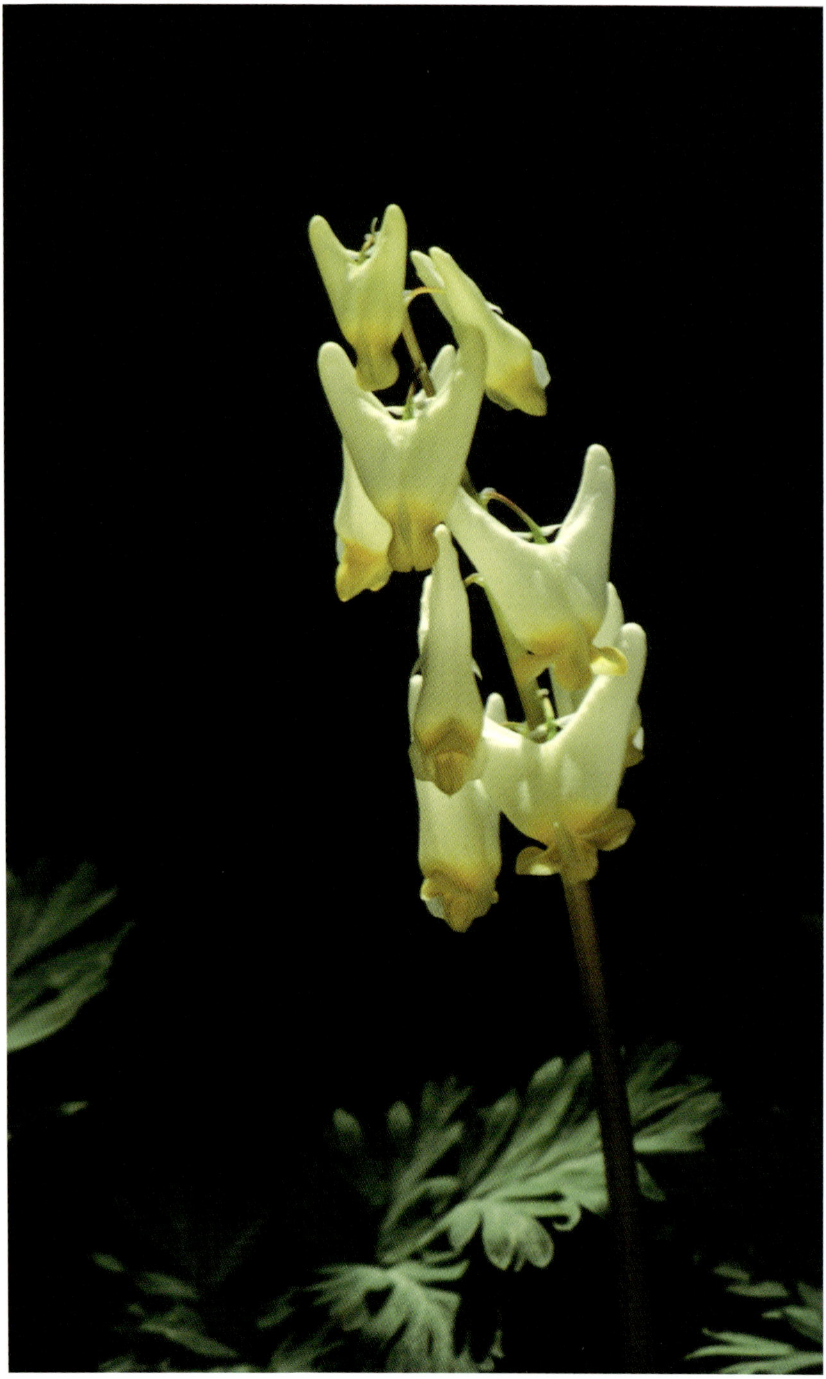

In order to get the entire plant in focus I needed to use a small aperture, f/16, which meant the shutter speed was set to two seconds for this image. It would be impossible to get this type of image without using a tripod and a DSLR that allows a full range of aperture and shutter options.

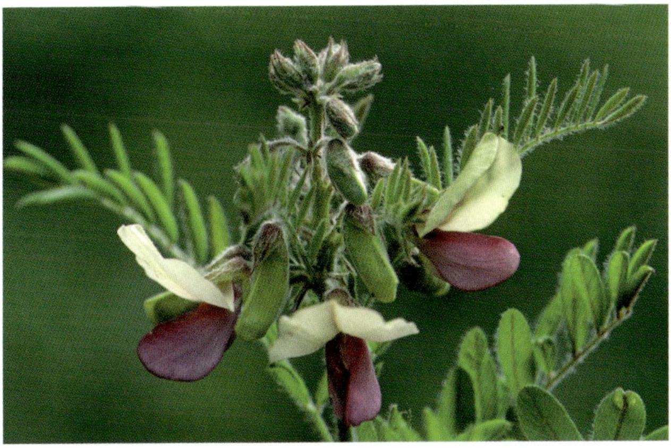

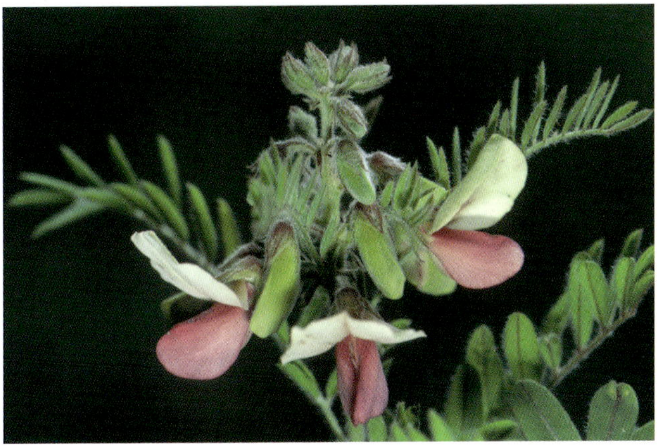

Notice the difference in the emotional appeal of the goats rue flower taken with natural light on top and with balanced fill flash on the bottom. The color has shifted because of the light temperature of the flash, and the background has become a very dark green color, which makes the plant stand out more, but you lose the soft-textured nature of the leaves, which shows up with the image taken under natural light conditions. In my opinion, the one without the use of fill flash is a more creative image, but the lower image probably has more accurate color reproduction.

tack-sharp images. The **mirror lock** is a method of manually moving the mirror up and out of the way prior to tripping the shutter. This is another of those features many camera manufacturers have removed to save money. I generally find that I use this primarily for exposures in the 1/15th to 1 second range where camera vibration seems to be the worst. If you can find a body that has this feature it is definitely worth the investment.

However, if you can't find one or can't afford this feature, don't stress out and keep in mind most vibration comes in the one-quarter to 1/30th of a second range. Use a cable release, and live and let live. The best option for keeping your hands off the camera is to use a **cable release,** which is nothing more than a method of using a cord that attaches to the shutter release and a trigger mechanism at the other end (my camera uses an electronic cable release, but the idea is the same – cord attached to shutter so the photographer can trip the shutter from a distance).

This is an excellent use of balanced fill flash on this native dayflower. The fill flash makes the flower stand out from the background by darkening the background and adding just a touch of light to the flower, yet you can see no discernable use of the flash from the camera.

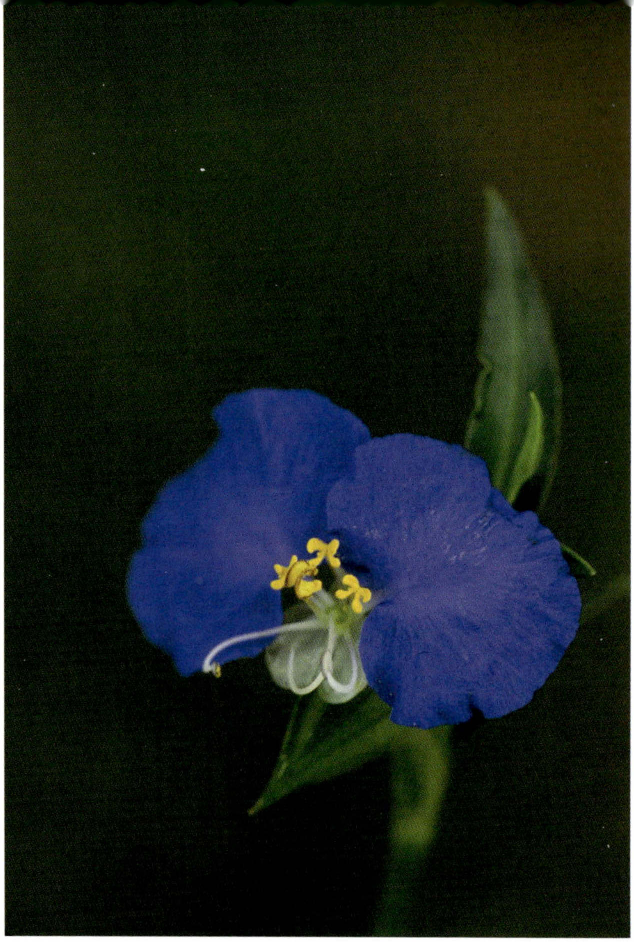

Remember the importance of looking at the histogram on LCD monitor on the camera back? One essential item for your camera is a large LCD monitor (two inches or larger, if possible) so that you can actually see the histogram (and make sure your camera has built-in software to accomplish this task – because it is critical) in the field. Generally speaking, the bigger the LCD monitor, the better.

While I like to do wildflower photography primarily with natural light, there are times when having a bit of fill flash can be the difference between a good and a great photo. When looking at camera systems, look at the flash options available to you. Does the flash have TTL (through the lens) metering using one, two, or even three flashes? Can those flashes be set to different exposures? Do they have built-in slave units (so you don't need a cord attached to each one from the main flash)?

One nifty little feature I use on the more advanced cameras is a spot meter. Let's say you have a dark background with a very light flower. How do you determine the correct exposure with matrix or center-weighted metering? The answer might be to shoot at a variety of exposures, check the exposure on the back of the camera (histogram), and if it isn't correct, delete the image and start over. Or if your camera has a built-in spot meter, you can spot meter the darkest area closest to black and step down two stops, or meter the white or lightest area and open up 1 to 1.5 stops. If the flower or greenery is close to neutral gray, spot meter the flower, and your exposure is perfect.

The final tip on purchasing a camera system is to look at durability issues. This is a really big one for me because I have a tendency to be hard on equipment. Field work is just that, field work. You will be subjected to dust, moisture, rugged terrain, and all sorts of other issues when working in the field. I saw someone once take a low-end, largely plastic 35-mm SLR into the woods and drop it inadvertently. Not a hard drop but nonetheless a drop into the leaves. Guess what? The camera became inoperable and when it was sent in for repair, it could not be fixed. Plastic is great for reducing weight but not so good for a Timex moment where it "takes a licking and keeps on ticking." On the other hand, I am not going to tell you how many times my cameras have taken a beating. The reason they can withstand field conditions is that they are professionally

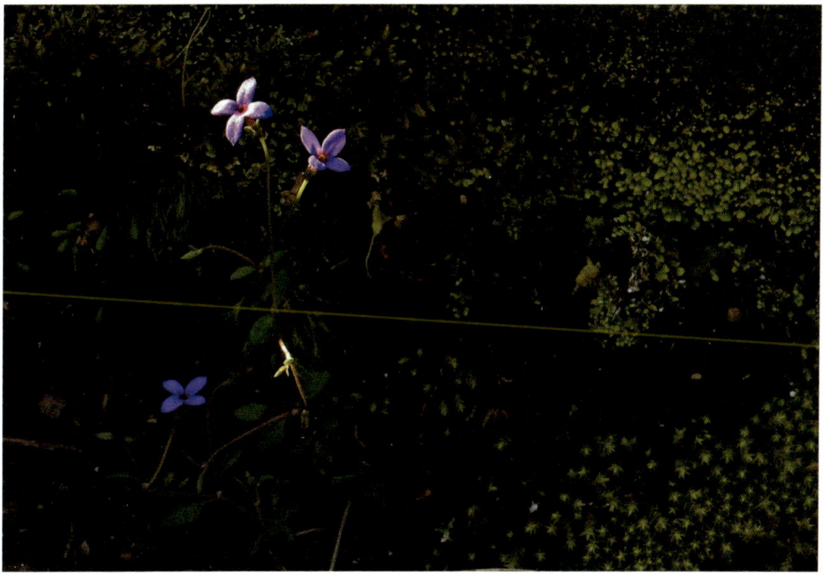

This is the perfect opportunity where a spot meter works wonders. If you relied on matrix or center-weighted metering, this image would appear with the flowers too bright because it would average all the light intensity in the image and the better exposure is that this would be -2 stops using this method. By using the spot meter on the bright flowers and setting the exposure manually, I was able to obtain the proper exposure with one shot.

built, sturdy cameras. Questions you might want to ask include: How sturdy is the camera? How many parts are plastic, and how many metal? What is the reputation of the brand, and what kind of support is there for getting equipment repaired?

Most folks do not have unlimited budgets, and if you are just entering photography as a hobby, just remember when you select your camera that you are in some sense of the word getting married. Getting married! What does that mean, getting married? Unless you have an unlimited budget and can switch from camera brand to camera brand as new technology improves bodies, lenses, and other photographic accessories, your initial selection (which in the digital realm can cost five grand or more for a body!) will determine which manufacturer's system you will be using for a long time. So pick your camera body with care, because most likely you will be married to it for a long time. Before purchasing a camera system, consider:

- What types of lenses are available?
- Possible upgrade systems,
- What accessories are available?
- Durability issues (this is especially critical because you are going to be in the field, and it should stand up to the rigors of field work in less than ideal conditions),
- What features are on the body?
- What the sales person says, (take it for what it is worth-remember they are trying to sell you something),
- What the field tests in photography magazines report,
- And, what people who use this particular camera system say about their experiences, likes and dislikes.

Lenses

Choices, choices, choices. There are so many choices when it comes to selecting lenses for wildflower photography. Do you get a fixed focal length lens or a zoom? Do you get a special macro lens? Are the new vibration reduction or image stabilization lenses worth the extra money? Do you purchase a lens made by the camera manufacturer or an independent brand like Sigma, Tokina, Tamron or Vivitar? As I mentioned before there is always a tradeoff between cost and quality. Furthermore, both camera manufacturers and independent manufacturers make excellent lenses and lemons.

Remembering this, also remember that the sharpness, color rendition, and clarity of any photograph are only as good as the lens that made it and the technique used to produce it (emphasis here on technique!). Also remember that you have more options with higher-quality equipment in that a sharp lens can be made to "soften" images but an inherently soft lens can never be sharpened. Finally, there are "amateur" and "professional" grade lenses made by both camera manufacturers and independent lens manufacturers. In a perfect world, you would use professional lenses made by the manufacturer of your camera. Why? Because they were engineered to work with your camera, have outstanding optical qualities, are well sealed from dust, dirt and moisture, and are built "combat-ready" to withstand rugged use in difficult conditions. That is not to say that independent brands do not have good lenses.

Ultimately, as a wise consumer, you should do your homework and read the independent tests in magazines or online prior to purchasing any particular lens. Also remember that what a salesperson in a camera store recommends is not necessarily the best fit for you because he or she has a vested interest in marketing some brands more than others because they get a higher commission. So purchase the best lenses possible for your budget.

Macro Lenses

While I use both extension tubes and close-up diopters, I, like most advanced amateur and professional photographers, ultimately decided on purchasing a macro lens

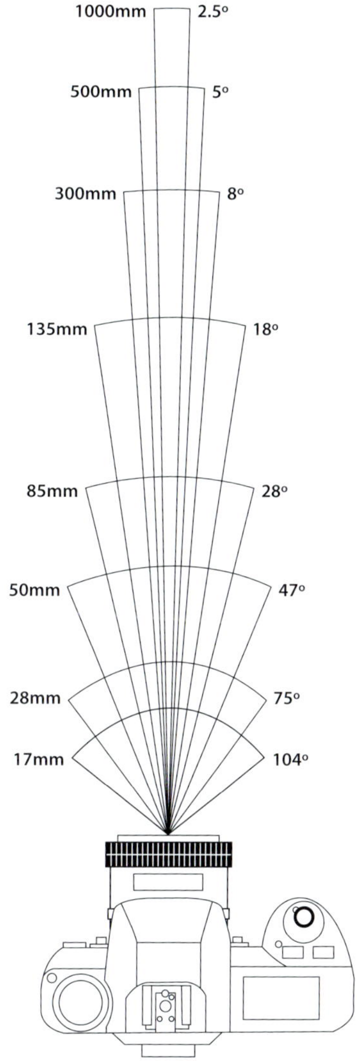

Notice how the angle of view gets narrower as the focal length of the lens gets longer. Using the longer lenses allows you to be more selective in your choice of background and provides for more "working distance" so you do not need to be as close to the subject, such as butterflies, to get small images big on the sensor.

EQUIPMENT

for wildflower portraiture. Macro lenses come in a variety of focal lengths ranging from 50 to 200mm. My first true macro lens was a 105mm followed by a 200mm macro, which has become the primary lens I use for wildflower photography. I selected a 200mm macro for the following reasons: it allows me more opportunity to edit out background clutter and select the background tonality so that the subject stands out against the background, and it gives me more working distance between the front of the camera lens and the subject.

When using a shorter focal length macro (50 to 60mm range) you get a wider angle of view and are likely to get distracting backgrounds. The angle of view is the angle that the lens "sees" from one side to another. The shorter the lens, the wider the angle of view, which means if shooting a portrait against a field of flowers, you are likely to get some sky and even bright spots of varying colors from different flowers in the field. Using a longer focal length lens allows you to eliminate those distractions because the angle of view is narrower and you cover less of the background.

By covering less of the background, a longer focal length lens allows you to select a differing background to bring out or emphasize your subject. By modifying your vantage point in some cases mere inches, you can completely change the appearance and mood of a portrait. To obtain a darker background, you can move so there is dark shade from a tree or a distant juniper versus the green of field or forest. I will discuss more about backgrounds and color later.

Finally, longer focal length lenses allow you more distance between the front of the lens and your subject. For instance, you can keep the size of the subject the same in the frame using any macro lens, but using a 100mm macro moves you twice as far from the subject as a 50mm macro and using a 200mm macro moves you four times as far from the subject. I consider this lens almost a necessity if shooting smallish animals like butterflies on flowers because you can maintain a sufficient distance between the butterfly and your camera lens and the critters don't seem intimidated.

Opposite:
I used a lens in the "normal" range around 50 to 75mm to capture this bouquet of black-eyed Susan, meadow phlox, and Queen Anne's lace.

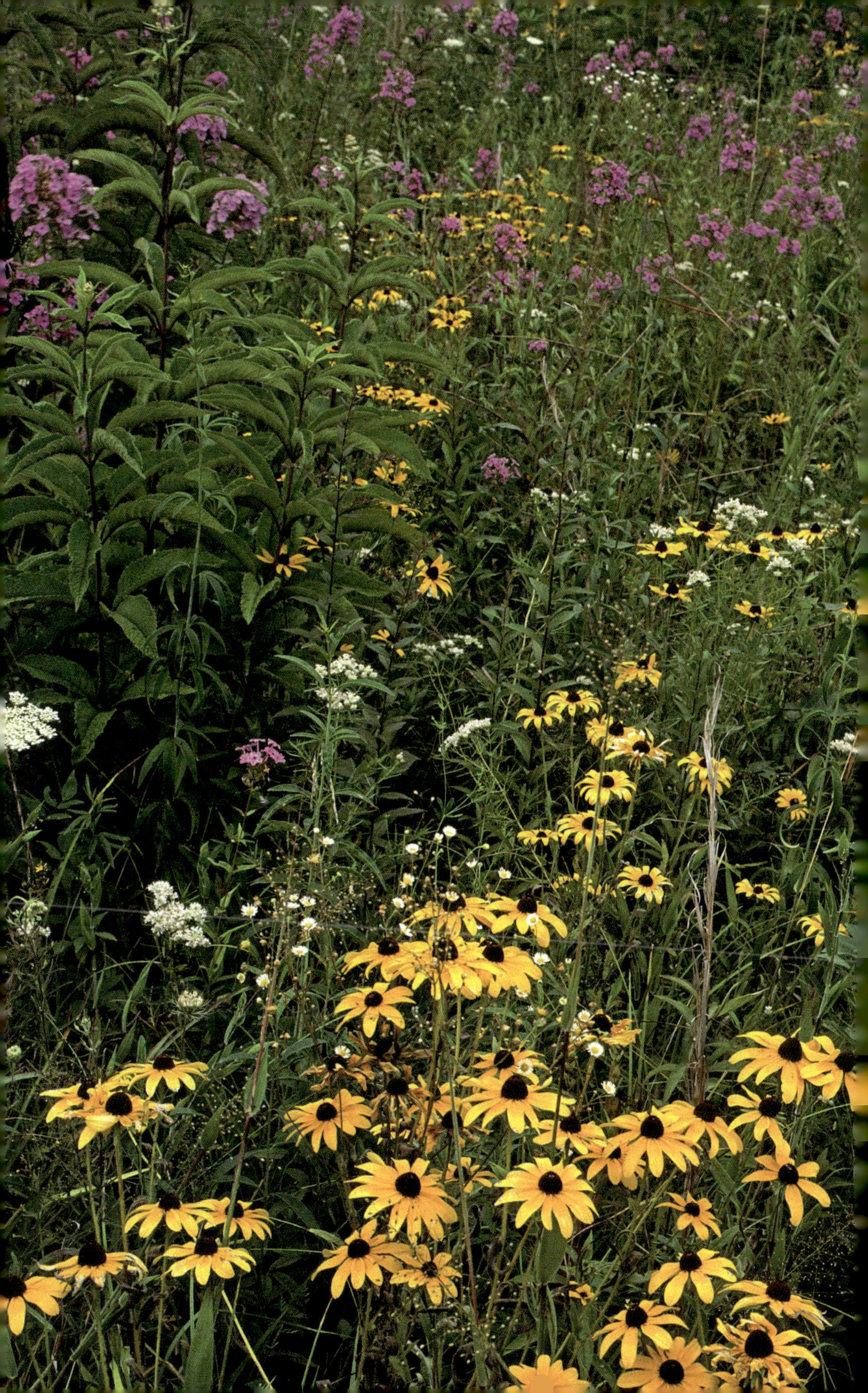

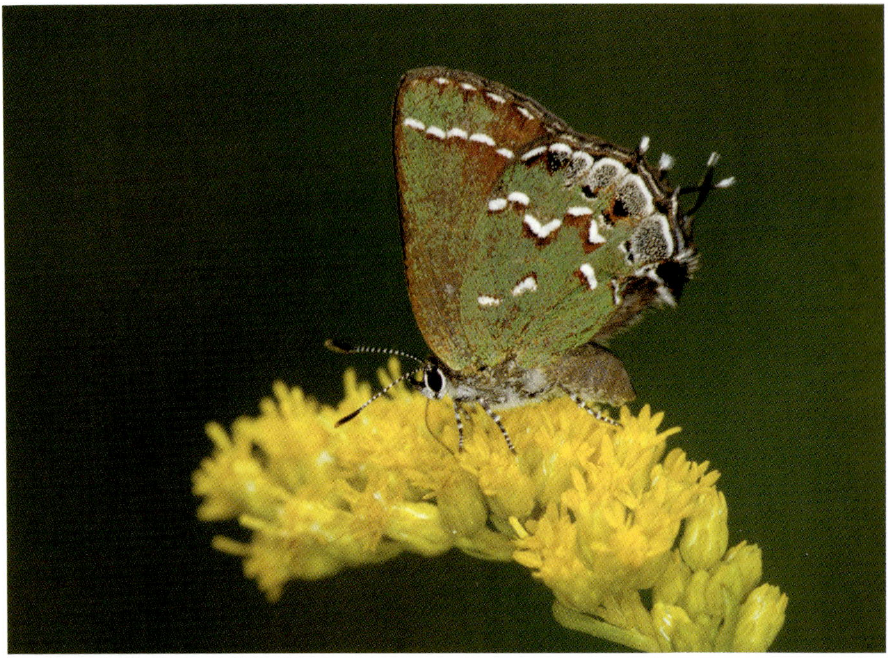

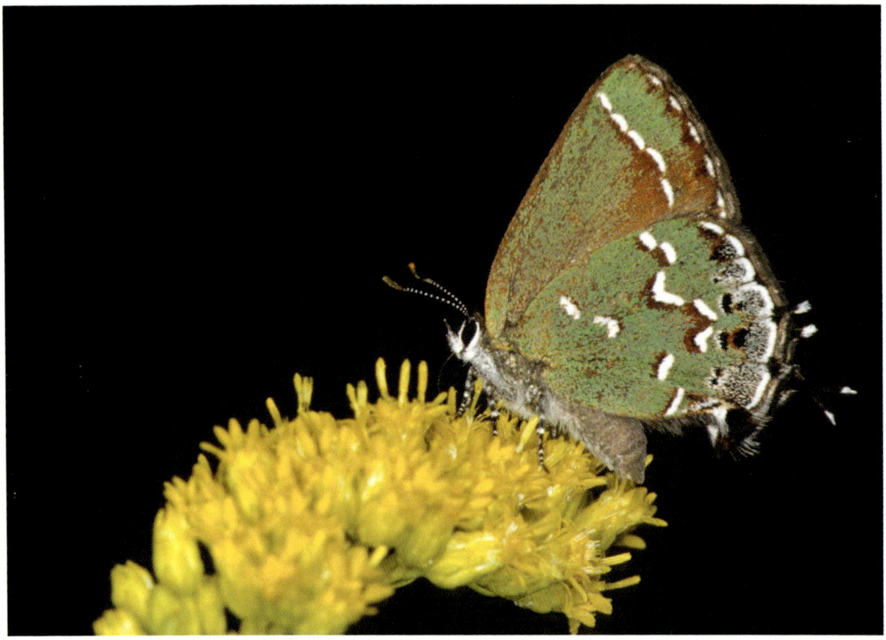

These images of the same butterfly show the advantage of using a longer focal length lens to select your background. Each was taken at f/22 at 1/60th of a second with balanced fill flash to bring out the color of the butterfly. The first image was taken against the green of the field, whereas the second was taken with a shaded juniper tree in the background, which produced dramatically different images.

Wide-angle to Normal Zoom Lenses

The wide-angle lens is the classic choice for landscapes with flowers and sweeping scenes. This lens works very well for photographing large fields of flowers or for placing flowers in the composition of a landscape where great depth of field is required to get everything in the image sharp. Most new telephotos that come with the camera are in the range of 18 to 70mm. You can purchase ultra-wide angle lenses in the 8mm range (this is one distinct disadvantage of the non-full frame cameras in that they multiply the focal distance by 1.4 to 1.6x, meaning your wide angle lenses have to be even shorter focal length to get the same effect), but they become quite pricey.

There are several keys to using a wide-angle lens, and one of them is to make sure the flowers are an integral part of the landscape and are emphasized or maybe even overemphasized and that they are sharp, sharp, sharp.

How do you obtain maximum sharpness getting both the foreground and background in focus? You obtain maximum sharpness by understanding the concept of hyper-focal distance or by using the depth of field marks on the lens. Unfortunately, most lens manufacturers no longer put depth of field marks on the front of their lenses, and that is unfortunate because it provided a quick and easy method of ensuring everything in the photograph was sharp and in focus. Because most new lenses do not incorporate this feature, I will not discuss it further. If you have an older manual focus, fixed focal length lens, consult your user's manual or ask a photo technician how to read the scale.

Telephoto Lenses

Medium telephoto zooms in the range of 80 to 200mm are wonderful wildflower lenses that typically go down to about one quarter life size if they have any macro capabilities. This can be expanded by adding close-up diopters. In general, extension tubes become limiting with these longer lenses because of vibration issues. Think of this lens as your workhorse for most medium to large flower portraits because it has lots of working distance and a fairly narrow angle of view that allows you to pick and choose your background. I have even used longer telephotos, up to 500mm, for some wildflowers that were particularly large and not approachable because of distance or some other hazard.

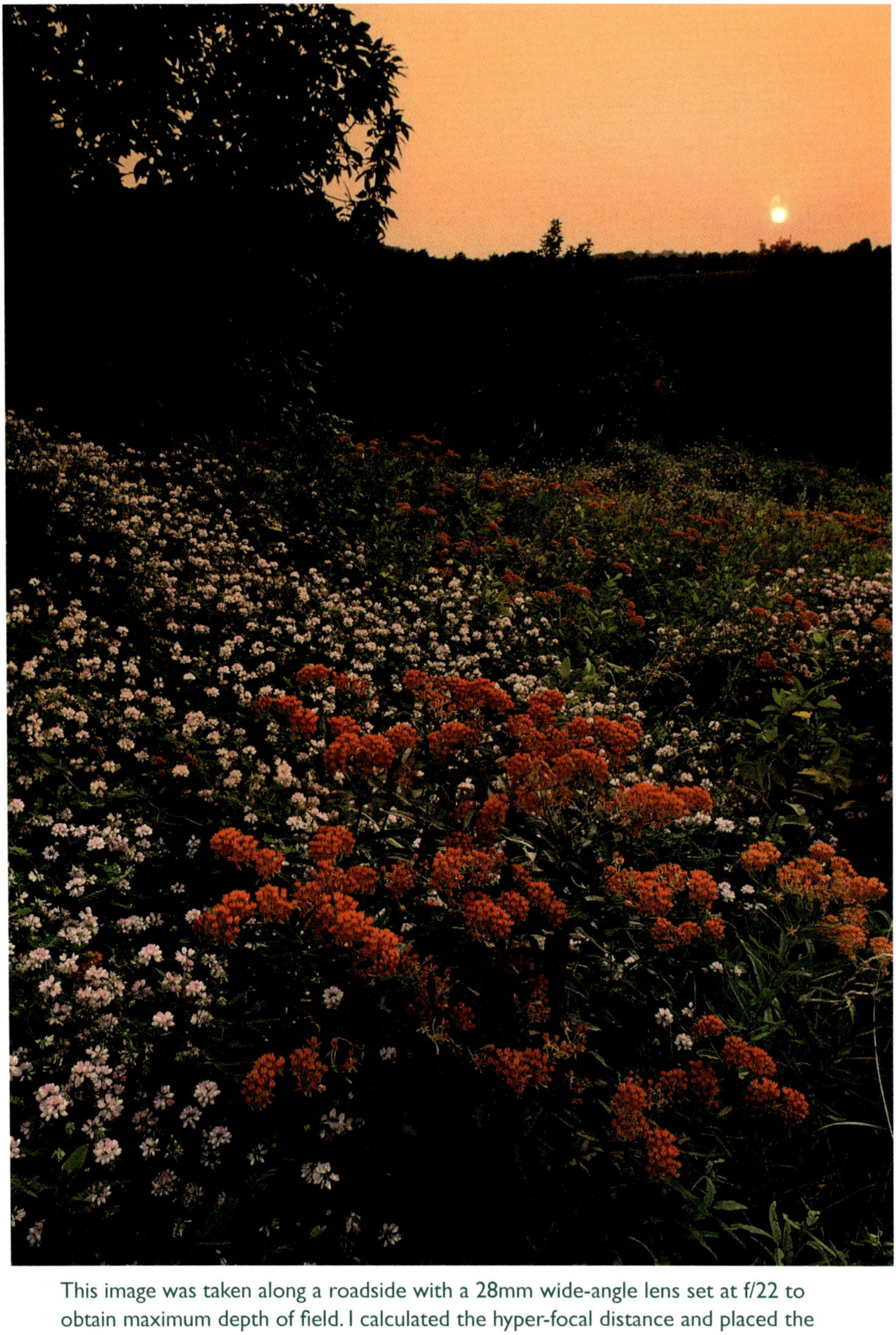

This image was taken along a roadside with a 28mm wide-angle lens set at f/22 to obtain maximum depth of field. I calculated the hyper-focal distance and placed the tripod and camera at that distance to make sure everything from the flowers to the distant sky was in focus. I wanted to balance the bright orange butterfly milkweed flowers with the hazy orange setting sun in mid-August. I used a +3 split neutral density filter to balance the available light of the sky with the darker flowers.

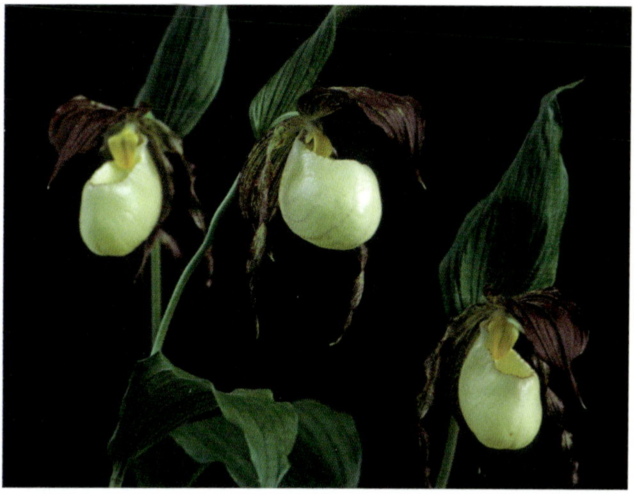

I used a 500mm lens to select out the background (in this case shade of some shrubs) and compress the amount of space so I could shoot at f/5.6 and get all of the flowers in focus.

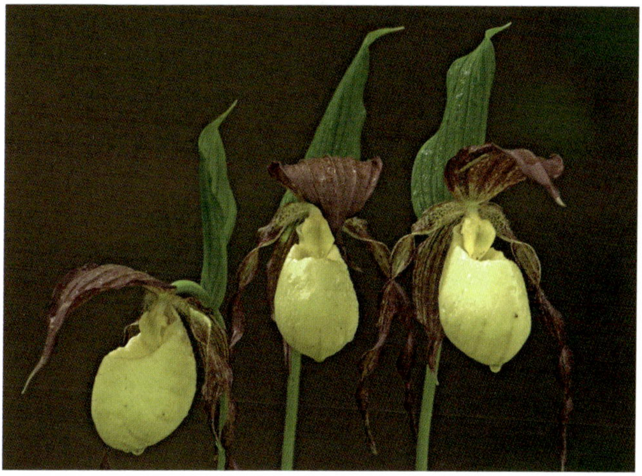

This is the same group of Kentucky lady's slipper orchids a year later. Notice the light conditions have changed dramatically. I still used a 500mm lens to select out the background and shot it at f/5.6.

Perspective Control Lenses

The final lens worthy of consideration is a perspective control or tilt-shift lens. These are standard equipment on large format, 4 x 5, or view-camera lenses. However, they are a highly specialized and expensive pieces of equipment for a DSLR system. These lenses were originally designed primarily for architectural work but are one of the nice luxury items for serious wildflower photographers. The biggest advantage of using a tilt lens is that you can photograph in windy conditions because you can obtain greater depth of field while maintaining a larger lens opening (smaller f stop number), and thus increase your shutter speed, often substantially.

These lenses work by creating a more parallel film plane to the subject and you tilt or adjust the front element of the lens upward

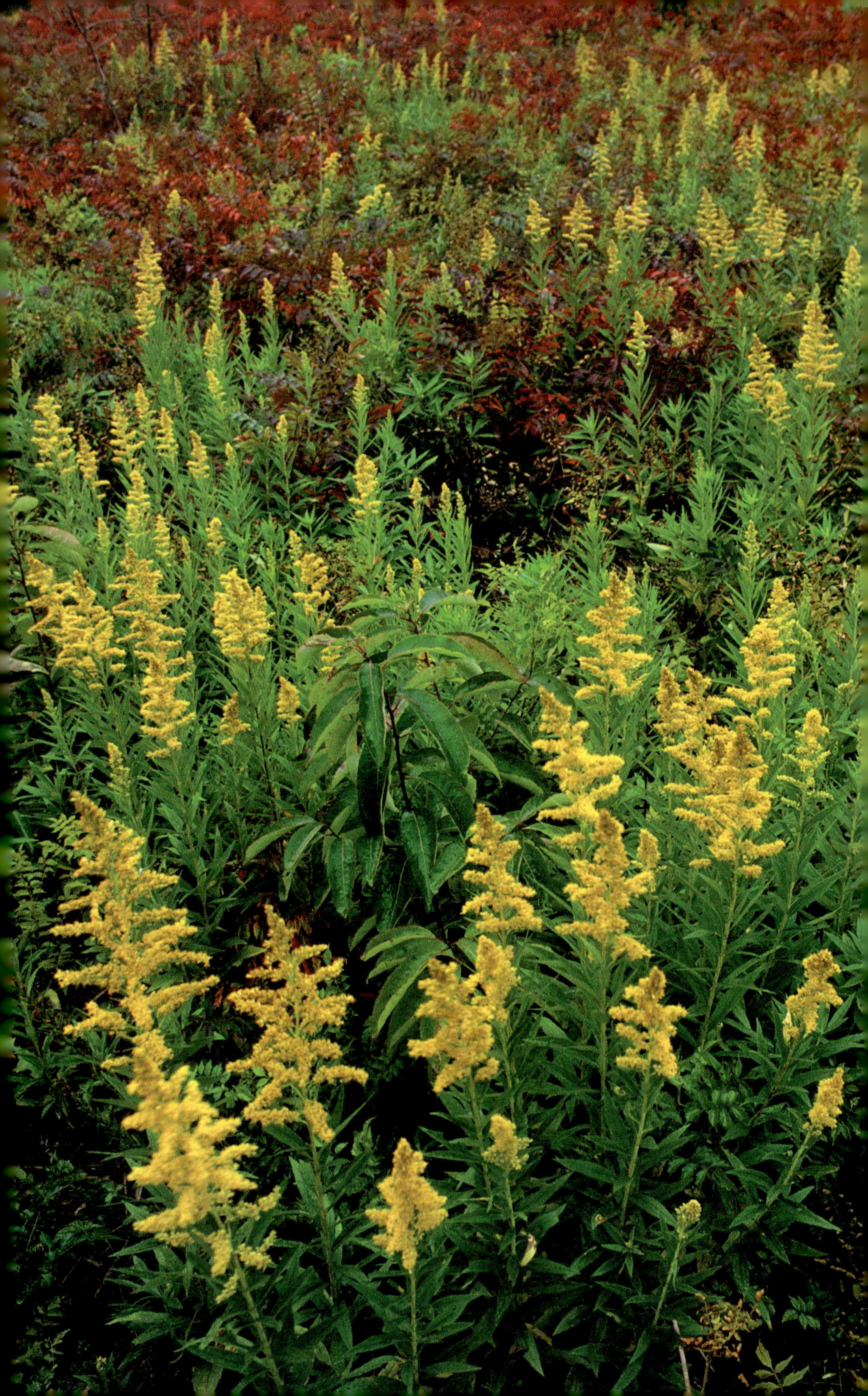

or downward, to align all the subjects you wish to keep in focus. Most of these lenses only work in the manual mode of your camera and must be operated manually with respect to controlling the aperture. Depending on the situation, you will need to step the aperture down to f/5.6 or more depending on the degree of tilting to get everything in focus. Use the depth of field preview button to see how wide open you can shoot and still keep everything in focus.

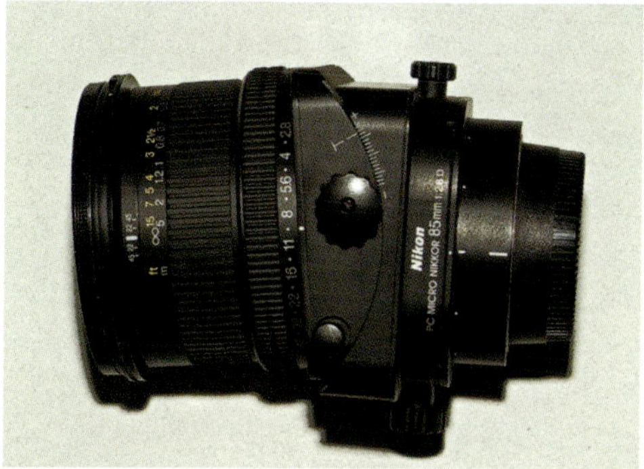

Tilt-shift lens

Close-up Lenses (filters) and Extension Tubes

The lens determines how big little things are on film because image size is based on a maximum magnification rate and a minimum focusing distance. There are two options for expanding the capability of any lens to make something little appear big on the sensor. The first option would be to increase magnification. The most common method of increasing the magnification of any lens is a close-up filter. Supplementary lenses or **close-up diopters** are filters attached to the front of the lens that increase the magnification by +1, +2, or +3.

Ah, but not all close-up diopters are created equal, and you should heed your inner voice telling you: quality versus cost. Don't be fooled by the camera store salesperson who sold you the set of single-

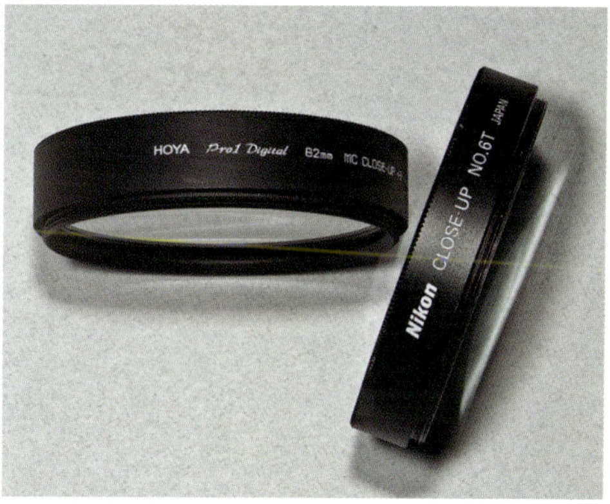

Close-up diopter

Opposite:
I used the 85mm tilt-shift lens because it was late in the evening with low light and a good stiff breeze was blowing the plants all over the place. I was able to move back away from the flowers and tilt the lens and took the image at f/5.6 at 1/250th of a second.

element diopters in a set of three. These are a cheap imitation for the good ones, which are two elements, achromatic (fancy words for high-quality) pieces of glass that have been coated to reduce flare and increase contrast.

The easiest of these diopters to find are made by Nikon or Canon but they can be used with any lens from any manufacturer. Nikon's terminology for these close-up diopters is 3T, 4T, 5T, and 6T. The 3 and 5T increase magnification by about 1.5x and the 4 and 6T increase by about 3x. The only difference is filter size as the 3 and 4 are made for 52mm filter size and the 5 and 6 are made for 62mm filter size. Canon makes the 250D and 500D in 2x and 4x for filter sizes 52, 58, 72 and 77mm. Others also make close-up filters and the Nikon and Canon versions are getting awfully hard to find.

My recommendation is when you find them available through eBay or whomever; don't think twice about purchasing one. One of the absolute best features about using diopters is that they do not cost you any loss of light as in the case of using extension tubes or a tele-converter.

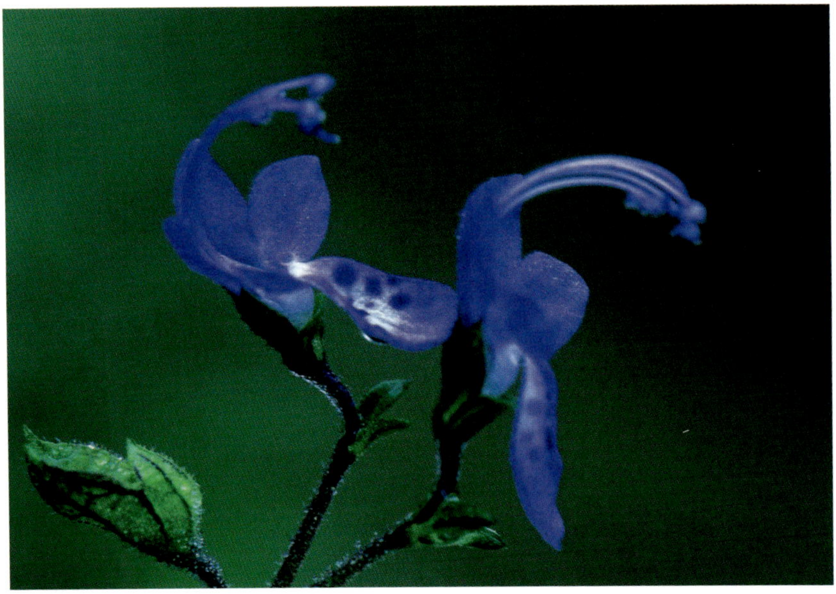

I used a close-up diopter to take this image of sandstone bluecurls because I needed the extra magnification to make the flowers bigger on the sensor because each individual flower is about one-half the size of a pencil eraser. To obtain maximum depth of field to get as much of the flower in focus (f/22) as possible, I used the diopter because it did not cost me light and I was able to shoot at a faster shutter speed (1/60).

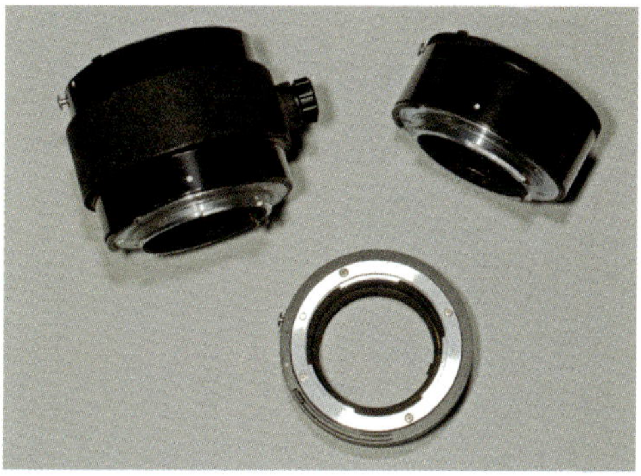

Extension tubes

The other option for making little things big on film is to make the lens focus closer. A true macro lens usually achieves 1x magnification with a short minimum focusing distance, i.e., if you look at a macro lens, the front end (barrel) of the lens simply moves out farther to create a shorter minimum focusing distance. Consequently, you can make any lens focus closer by putting some distance between the front of the lens and the film plane in the back of the camera. The easiest method of accomplishing this task is to put a hollow tube with no glass (called an extension tube) between the lens and the camera body. The closer you want the lens to focus, the more distance you need to put between the body and the front of the lens. The really great thing about using an extension tube made by your camera manufacturer is that the TTL (through the lens) metering is still going to work.

Another option is to use a tele-converter that increases the magnification (usually by 1.4, 2, or 3 times) and slightly increases the distance between the front of the lens and the film plane. If you select this option, which I typically do not, you lose about half a stop of light for a 1.4x, 2 stops for a 2x and 3 stops for a 3x. I would not purchase an inexpensive, off-brand tele-convertor because you really sacrifice the quality of the image. Purchase one that is matched to the particular camera and lens you are using.

Miscellaneous Equipment

There are a few other minor pieces of equipment that I consider a necessity for creative wildflower photography. The first is some form of translucent material that can shade the background or the flower from harsh sun and create sunny overcast conditions and to help with reducing the amount of wind swirling about a flower. Any of the following is an option for creating that type of environment: a photo umbrella (translucent), a collapsible translucent light disk, or a photo diffusion tent. I carry a collapsible light disk because they are less cumbersome and lighter to carry than either of the other options.

One essential item to carry is at least one extra battery. Most DSLR cameras do not function without battery power and if the battery loses power you cannot turn the camera on. These batteries are not cheap, but they are re-chargeable, and I always carry at least one extra, and sometimes two, depending on how close I am to someplace that a battery could be charged.

The other piece of equipment is some type of reflector to bounce light onto the flower. This doesn't have to be elaborate or expensive; it can be a small collapsible light disk. I carry a small mirror but you can even use aluminum foil.

The last piece of equipment that is really nifty is called the Whimberley Plamp. This is a plastic clamp attached to a bendable plastic stem with another clamp to attach the entire outfit to a tripod. The Plamp acts like a third hand holding flowers steady or even for holding a light diffusion device or card over the lens to prevent flare. These little devices cost about $40 but are worth the added cost.

Stuff You Might Want to Leave at Home

If you read some of the methods for wildflower photography, you will find different photographers recommending other types of equipment including focusing rails, bellows, lens stackers or reversers or using movie lenses for high magnification. In general, I do not use any of these for a variety of reasons. Ninety-nine percent of your wildflower photography can be accomplished without lugging all that extra expensive equipment around. Now, if you carry it in your car and don't get off the road much, you might be able to justify using this stuff.

Always remember technique over technology. There are multiple books in the market today that discuss the use of those pieces of equipment, and if you are inclined to using them, I would recommend you read those informative sources.

Summary of Essential Field Equipment

Let's review what we learned about the equipment required for making high-quality wildflower photographs. First and foremost is that equipment is not a substitute for good technique and that there is always a trade-off between quality and cost with photographic equipment. Second, the most important piece of equipment you will need is a good tripod and ball-head. Third, think like a minimalist and disregard everything you don't need like bellows, reversing rings, focusing rails, enlarging lenses, etc., and concentrate instead on the equipment you really need and will use.

Use a good single-reflex type camera with at least a 6-megapixel quality sensor with as many professional features like mirror lock-up, depth of field preview button, spot meter, etc. as possible. Use a cable release or the mirror lock up to reduce vibration or camera shake. Wide-angle and normal zoom lenses are best for scenic and habitat shots, not much else. Short to medium telephoto or zoom lenses are superb for portraiture when you want to isolate a single flower against an unobstructed backdrop. Specialized macro lenses, particularly in the medium telephoto range, are perhaps the best and most versatile wildflower lenses, but they are expensive and not absolutely necessary. If you need to make anything else bigger or to increase your magnification, carry some high-quality close-up diopters or an extension tube.

Other equipment might be a dedicated flash, some reflectors, extra camera batteries, and lots of imagination and creativity from your own mind. You could also keep a lightweight rain gear if you lay on the ground to prevent from getting wet.

Saving and Storing Files

File Formats

I stated that the thoughts expressed here represent my viewpoint, and if you asked 100 different photographers, you would get 100 different viewpoints on how to do something in the field, ways to post-process images, which software to use, and of course which file format to use to save the images in the camera. There is no right or wrong answer here, and I save mine as both RAW and JPEG. Why? JPEG stands for Joint Photographic Experts Group, which is the name of the committee that created this standard file format. Under this system, the image is compressed (hence a much smaller size file), but more importantly, it is a "lossy" compression, which means that visual information or quality is lost in the compression process. This is contrasted to lossless compression in which the exact information is reconstructed from the compressed data.

The JPEG file was designed to exploit the known limitations of the human eye. When you save your images in the JPEG format you are allowing the camera to make decisions for you and then storing the images in a compressed format, which can create difficulties in post-processing software. The advantages of using JPEG format would include, but are not limited to; the camera processes these more quickly, and you can therefore save time with in-camera processing (not such a big deal for wildflowers that do not move); they take up considerably less space on the memory card; and you can shoot faster because the camera buffers are emptied more quickly.

On the downside, data are lost each and every time you save a JPEG file; this is an 8-bit format (not 16-bit) which results in a loss of quality because continuous color tones are lost; and finally, and perhaps most important, is that all the information like contrast, white balance, color, saturation, etc. are built into the file, which makes post-processing more difficult and certainly causes a loss of quality.

Because of the last issue, you must absolutely accurately expose JPEG files. There is no room for error, and you should look at the histogram on your camera to ensure that no clipping occurs at either end of the spectrum.

RAW is nothing more than unprocessed data collected from the camera sensor. There is no single RAW camera format and RAW simply means that file contains minimally processed data from the sensor and they have not yet been processed. Think of RAW as a negative that you must convert to TIFF or JPEG to manipulate or print it (just as you would do to a photographic print using the old-fashioned method). The various camera manufacturers have their own file extensions for denoting RAW files and include .nef for Nikon, .crw or .cr2 for Canon, .orf for Olympus, .mrw for Minolta, and so on. Most camera manufacturers create proprietary software to post-process RAW files, or you can use Adobe Photoshop, Lightroom, or other software, which can usually accommodate most RAW files with the appropriate software.

The advantages of using RAW are that you can manipulate your images more in post-processing (setting things like actual color temperature versus daylight, incandescent, fluorescent, etc.; color saturation, brightness, and sharpness), and you do not lose any information or quality in the image. You can fine-tune your images, color correct them, sharpen them, and generally get the desired result you are looking for. Another advantage is that you can get 12- to 16-bit brightness files (compared to 8-bit for JPEG), which allow for capturing more fine details and it can handle major color or brightness differentials.

Another advantage is you can set the color space (either RGB or CMYK). The biggest disadvantage is time and storage space. If you shoot RAW, you are making the decisions, not the camera, and consequently you, by default, anticipate you will manipulate the image in the computer. Another disadvantage is that it takes longer to write the files to the card, and you cannot shoot many frames quickly, although this is usually not an issue for shooting wildflowers. Furthermore, RAW files are typically two to six times larger than JPEG files, which means you have to invest in good computing equipment with large amounts of file storage space.

Media Cards

Most digital SLR cameras today store the images on a digital media card, most commonly called a compact flash (CF) or secure disk (SD) formats. You should check the camera manual to see which type of card your camera requires. There seems to be a movement within the industry to standardize media card usage to the secure disk format, but, at the present time both are still in use, and the technology and storage capacity of the cards continues to improve.

Memory cards come in a variety of capabilities for storing images, and the price for more memory keeps plummeting. There are many manufacturers of these cards including Sony, Canon, Transcend, Verbatim, and Delkin, but the most popular brands are Lexar, Kingston, and SanDisk. What card should you purchase? It depends on how much money you want to spend, how many images you want to store on the card before downloading, how big the RAW or JPEG files are, and how fast you want those images downloaded. Since you are not dealing with shooting action or fast-moving action, you may not want to purchase the professional model cards like the Lexar 133X or SanDisk Extreme III, but instead go a cheaper route because you do not need the fast speed to clear the images from the camera.

For most people, a 2 GB card will be more than adequate as you can get about 110 RAW and high-quality JPEG images stored without downloading if you are shooting a 10-megapixel camera. If you are shooting JPEG alone you can get up to 400 images depending on how big the JPEG files are. But, remember, the more images you store, the more that could potentially be lost if something happens to the card. I personally use Lexar 2 GB Professional 300X UDMA compact flash cards. Of course, if you want fast downloads onto the computer, you have to purchase a card reader capable of fast downloads.

In the Field

Coping with the Ever-Present Enemy: The Wind

The final section deals with some specific issues that always seem to frustrate people in the field and some successful techniques I use to capture images. The first and probably the biggest issue any photographer faces when photographing wildflowers is the wind. Consider it enemy number one. There are multiple solutions to coping with wind, but the best advice I can give you is to develop a bit of patience.

It has been said that patience is a virtue and no one would ever consider not having patience when photographing an animal, but for a flower? The old adages about good things come to those who wait is definitely true in this case. Once you have set up your camera on the tripod, gotten the composition you want, and a breeze kicks in, don't tear everything down; just sit it out and wait and watch. It is actually pretty amazing what you can observe while simply waiting and watching in the outdoors. I once heard a bobcat scream, had a wild turkey come within six inches of me while I sat still, had a hooded warbler not more than six feet away bugging, and, most amazingly, have had butterflies land on camera gear and me.

Rarely will the breeze continue for hours on end, and if you have already set up, all you need to do is check for focus, and click away when the breeze dies down.

The second strategy is pretty much common sense: don't go out when the forecast calls for 10 to15 mile-per-hour breezes throughout the day. Stay at home or at the motel, relax, read a book, do some book research, and just chill out or better yet, check out potential sites for the next day. That said, there is the possibility of getting photos on this type of day depending on the terrain and your level of patience, because in some cove or protected area there will be times when the wind isn't howling, even on blustery days.

The third strategy is to photograph early in the morning and late in the evening. Although this will work for some species, it will not work for others that might only open during the day. This also happens to be when the light conditions are best.

Another strategy might be to increase the ISO rating in the camera and shoot at a faster shutter speed. I find this difficult to do because if the wind is strong enough to move the flower, then it is strong enough that you cannot create an effective composition to know exactly where the flower might be when you click the shutter. Now, you can increase the ISO dramatically to 800 or more, but be aware that the quality of the image will decrease dramatically because the noise will increase. This works on some occasions, and I will increase my ISO to 200 or at most 400 with the newer cameras that reduce noise more effectively.

The fifth strategy is something that I often do and that is to find some naturally occurring stem stakes, for example small twigs and branches, that I can prop the flower stalk or plant stem against. Of course, you can also use the commercially available Plamp that was mentioned in the equipment section. I have a tendency to minimize equipment in the field and have lost at least two or three Plamps; so I usually look around for sticks that have a "Y" branch that can be used and then find another small twig to place opposite the "Y" branch. Place them against the stem, and the support will decrease the amount of movement substantially. I do not carry wire, pipe cleaners, or other material into the field to attach stem stakes to flowers, because they have the potential to harm the plant and I am always losing these kinds of things in the field.

The biggest problem with using sticks is that they sometimes can get into the photo if you don't pay careful attention to their placement, and of course sometimes they break or are not sturdy enough. Other than these two drawbacks, this is a very effective technique to deal with movement.

Often in addition to using twigs or branches, I will need to create a wind barrier using a jacket or more often a large diffuser that I carry to bounce light. The diffuser I use is a translucent white, which creates soft lighting; I also use it to shade the background sometimes to make the subject stick out, so to speak.

Some photographers make their own wind barrier carrying plastic tarp material and stakes, but again I find this cumbersome and time consuming, and I believe it is just as effective to find whatever you can locate on site that nature has provided in the forms of branches, etc. to prop the diffusers up. If you have an inclination to do so, you can purchase a diffusion tent.

Flash is also an option for stopping movement but one that I rarely, if ever, use because it adds weight to the pack and I do not like the unnatural-looking light it produces although some photographers place diffusers and even colored fabric over the flash unit to alter the light. This is way too difficult for me to use and creates too much of a problem calculating exposure, so I prefer not to use a flash except as a source of fill light.

The last method of coping with wind is to use a tilt-shift lens which was discussed in some detail in the equipment section. Unless you plan on investing heavily in equipment, this is probably not justifiable for most amateurs.

Here are a couple of final tips when using your camera to photograph wildflowers. First, take the camera off autofocus because you, not the camera, need to be in control, as to the critical focusing point. Many cameras may not pick that same point to focus on and others may go in and out of focus trying to figure out what focus point is optimum.

Second, if you are using a vibration reduction lens, turn it off when it is on your tripod because if you do not, your images will be fuzzy (been there done that – experience is a good teacher).

Finally, check for critical focus in the camera on the LCD monitor. There is nothing more frustrating that getting images downloaded only to find they are not crisp.

Paralleling the Subject

Getting sufficient depth of field is always a problem when working with small flowers and wildflowers in general. As you increase magnification, you have the practical perception of decreased depth of field. Camera position becomes critical for obtaining adequate depth of field. You can optimize the amount of depth by ensuring that the camera axes are parallel to the flower you are shooting.

In addition, when focusing, you can follow the rules for hyperfocal distance discussed previously or just focus about one-third the way into the image. This will give you maximum depth of field.

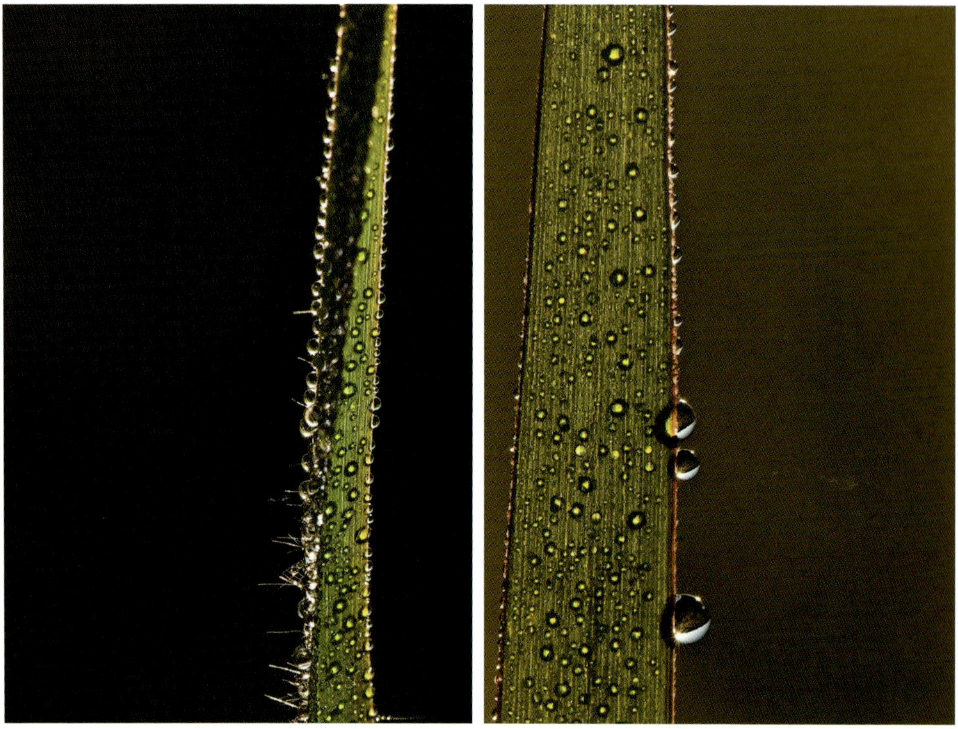

Note the difference between the two photos. The one on the left (a blade of little bluestem grass), was taken and the grass bends outside the region where the subject is parallel to the camera lens. This renders the top portion of the leaf out of focus. The image on the right (a blade of big bluestem grass), was taken where the entire blade of grass was parallel to the camera lens and the entire subject is in focus. Both images were taken at maximum depth of field (f/32) and both were three times life size.

Controlling the Background

Probably the one most irritating thing I see with wildflower photos is a distracting or cluttered background, and it seems in many cases it is the rule, not the exception, particularly with inexperienced photographers. Why is it so distracting? Cluttered backgrounds takes away from the center of interest of the photograph. One of the best and easiest methods to remove clutter from the background is to use a longer telephoto or macro lens that allows you to have a narrower field of view. One of the keys to using longer lenses to isolate flowers is that the background should be a good distance away because the closer the background is to the flower, the more distracting it becomes.

Once you have selected the background, use the depth of field preview button to see what aperture you can use that still keeps the

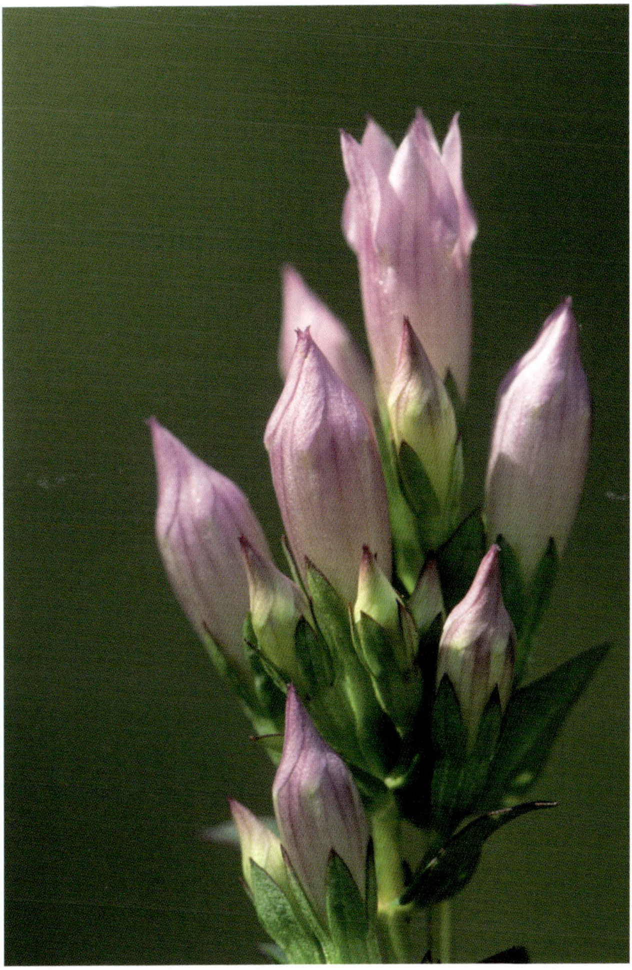

There is no mistaking the center of interest or subject of this image because the flower is the dominant element and it has a clear, uncluttered background without any distractions.

entire flower in sharp focus while having an out-of-focus background. With larger flowers, I often find this is about f/8 using a 300mm lens. Another way I create a better background is to use sticks and twigs to lie against a stem to gently move the flower to a more desirable location and place them so they will not show up in the image when the depth of field preview button is pushed. Once I have taken the image, I remove the stick and the plant comes back into its normal position, so no harm, and no foul.

If you are shooting habitat photos sometimes you can have some clutter. I have been known to selectively remove small twigs and other debris surrounding the flower, always being careful not to harm the habitat of the flower. I do not carry scissors or a knife or anything else to clip or remove vegetation surrounding the flower as some folks do. Besides being unethical, it is illegal to do so in parks, nature preserves, and other protected areas. Not that I am totally against it – just more junk to carry and deal with.

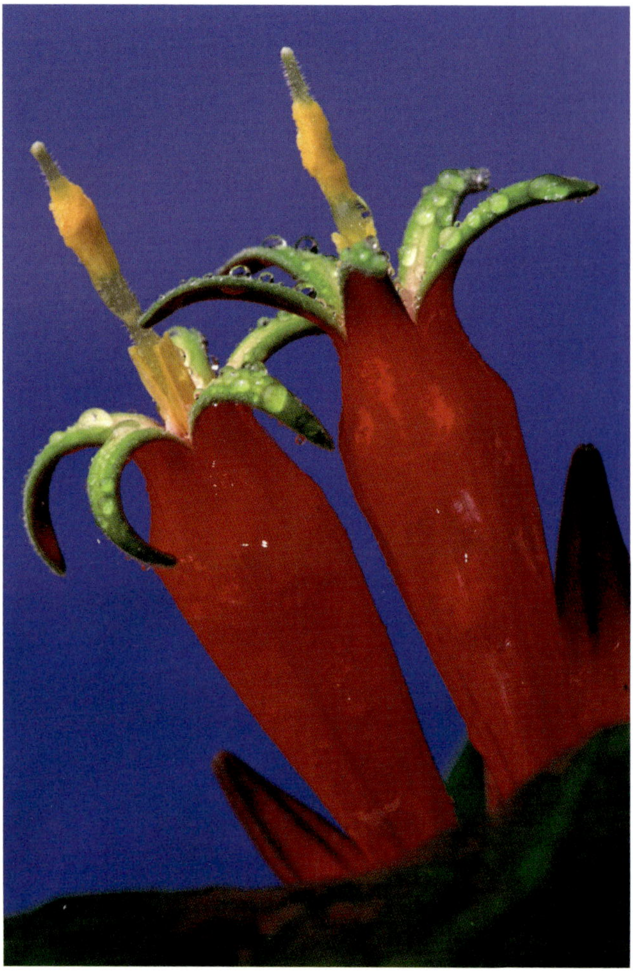

One way to minimize background is to think about color. For example, in a previous example I indicated how pure red and green clash for attention. In this example, I selected another color, blue (from the sky) for the background. Using a longer focal length lens and a polarizing filter, I took a lower angle and shot this against the blue sky because it has the primary colors in the flower, which work well against the blue background.

Capturing Flora and Fauna with Flowers

Have you ever been a Boy Scout and heard their saying "Be Prepared." That should be your motto in the field. Situations and circumstances come up all the time where preparation, a good knowledge of how your equipment functions, and maybe some luck all come together for a once-in-a-lifetime photographic opportunity.

Here is an example of how knowing your equipment and being prepared can pay off. I was taking pre-sunrise images at a state nature preserve for the book, *Kentucky's Last Great Places*. It was mid-June and there was nice heavy dew on the ground. I got to the location I had scouted and set up my camera with a wide-angle lens to capture the coneflowers against the pre-dawn sky. Things turned out and I got the image I wanted (the photo – opposite – was also

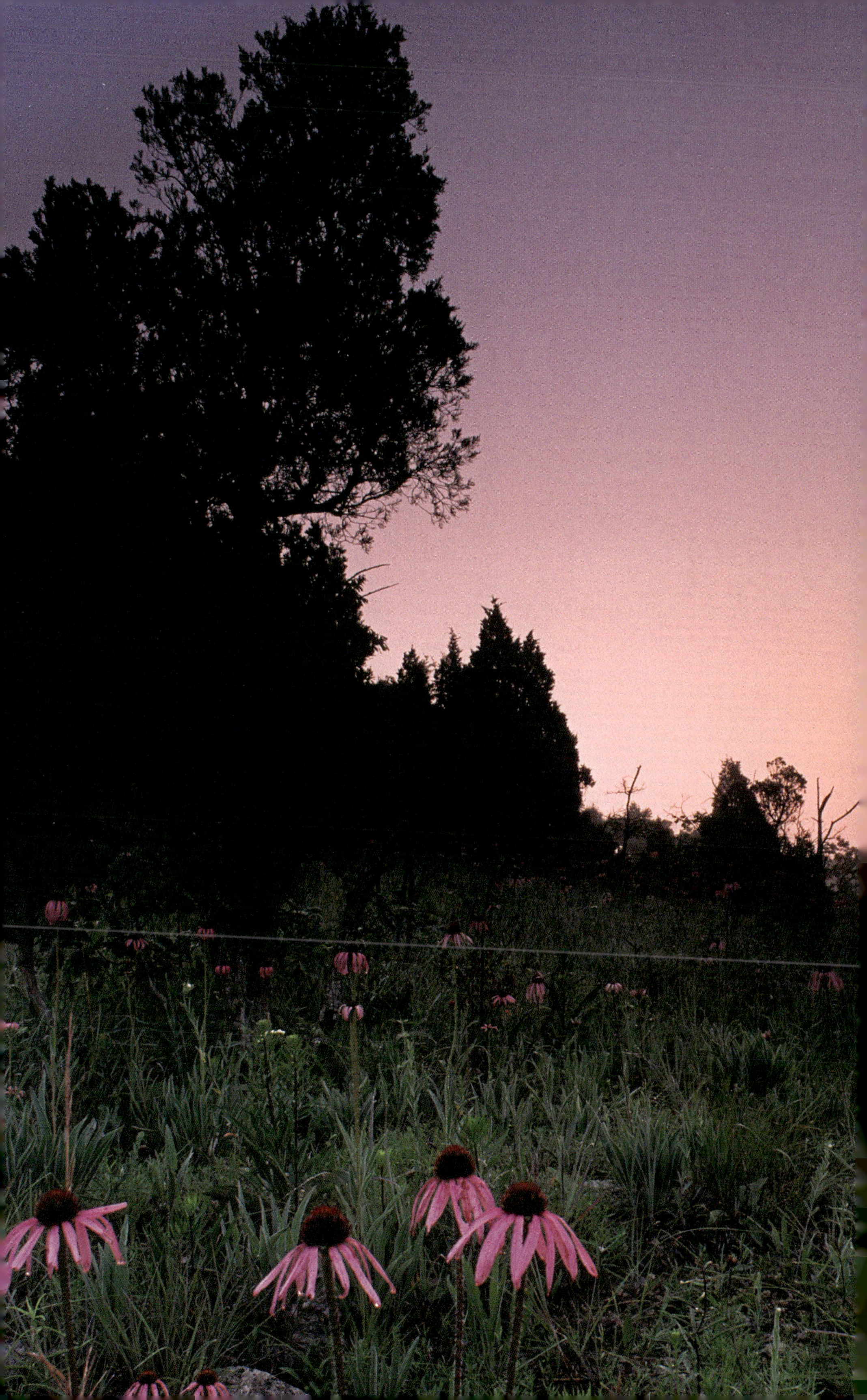

turned into a poster). As I was happy with the result, I began to look more closely about to see what other photographic opportunities existed. I stepped down and almost squished a smallish Cope's gray tree frog with my foot. It was on the ground, still as the cool morning air, which was beginning to get breezy because the sun was coming up and heating the atmosphere. Evidently this little guy did not appreciate almost getting squished and the next thing I know, he is climbing up a pale purple coneflower plant. I quickly took off the wide-angle lens and put on a 105mm macro lens (the only longer lens in my bag) and moved the tripod in place to get the frog on the flower. I managed to get two shots in before the frog reached the top of the flower. Once on top, he sat there for a few minutes and I took tons of images of the frog on top of the flower but the really good images are of the frog climbing up the stem, which made the cover of a nationalmagazine. Good luck or good preparation?

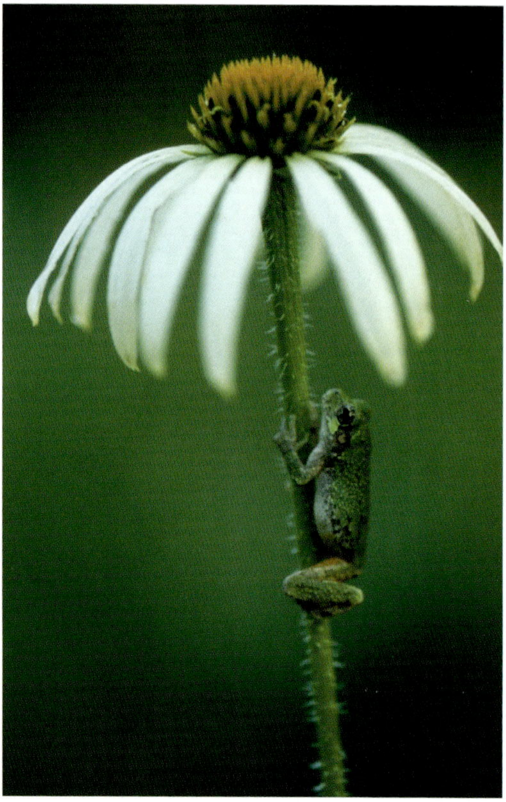

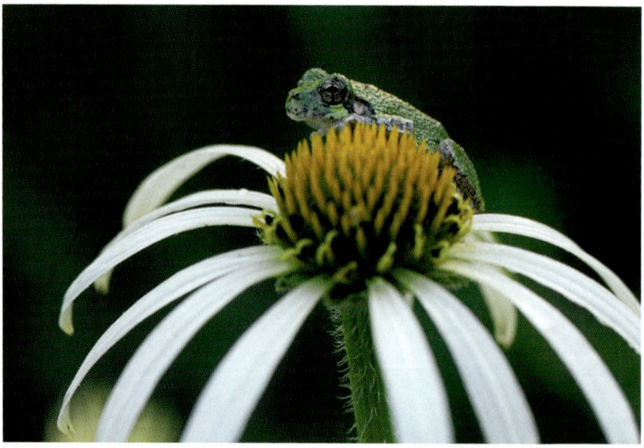

One of my favorite activities in the summer is

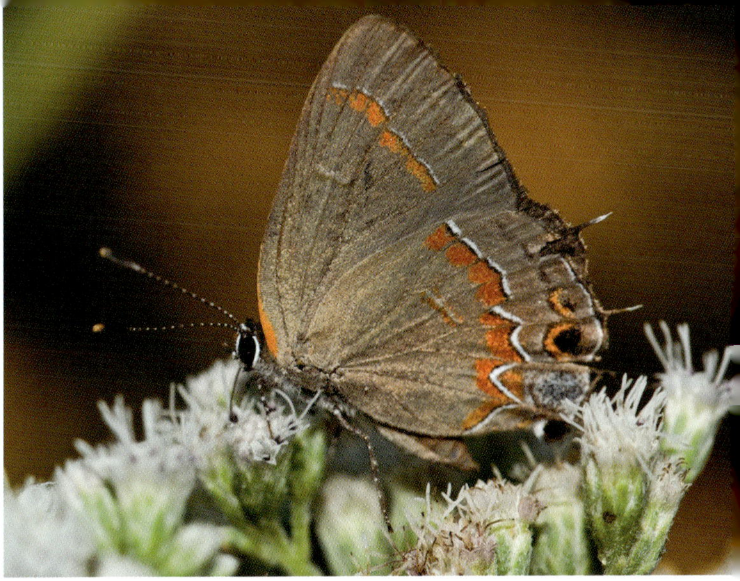

to photograph butterflies and insects on wildflowers. I use two basic techniques that I will describe below: one for small butterflies and tiny insects and another for larger butterflies on big flowers. The first thing to realize is that not all subjects will cooperate with you. Some critters are just plain skittish and I have found it is a waste of time and effort to pursue them. Others are just downright easy to work with. In addition, some butterflies are not that photogenic in that they have been flying around and have tattered or broken wings or scales missing and do not look that great. Finally, some of the flowers they visit might not be in great shape. So the key to being successful with respect to finding your subject is to get a cooperative butterfly that is fresh on a nice looking flower.

The next challenge is to use the right equipment for the right situation. This is a situation that calls for flash, which brings out the beautiful color on the scales of the butterfly. Use the largest flash made for your particular camera. In addition, this is where a longer focal length macro lens is worth its weight in gold, so to speak. I use a 200mm macro, which gives me enough working distance (the distance between the front of the camera lens and the subject) such that I can approach the subject carefully and not spook them off the flower. This is critical because if you shade the butterfly with your body, it will fly off and this extra working distance helps keep you away from the subject. This works particularly well for smaller butterflies like the hairstreaks. I do not use a tripod (although I will use a monopod on some occasions) and I make sure I put my autowinder on camera to high.

For larger butterflies on large flowers, I use a longer length telephoto (300mm or longer) and a short extension tube, which allows me to focus closer. This set up obviously requires the use of a tripod.

I still use a dedicated flash and in this case also a cable release to get my hands off the camera.

Here is the technique I use for capturing these critters on flowers. I set the ISO rating to 200 (good compromise between speed and quality), set the auto-winder to high, and set the aperture to f/16. I then shoot in aperture priority mode. I locate a subject that looks willing by watching the animal as it moves around a flower. If it is one that doesn't move from one flower on the cluster to another much, then I usually think it is a good candidate for photography. I then pre-focus the lens and look through the viewfinder moving slowly until the butterfly comes into focus, at which point I hold my finger on the shutter release and let the camera do the work. Using this technique I will generally get one really good, crisp and sharp image with others that vary because of movement of the butterfly.

For larger butterflies I watch and observe which flowers the butterflies seem to be gravitating to and then set up my tripod with camera and lens on that flower. I then pre-focus and in this case I set the aperture to f/8, set my camera to aperture priority and then, when butterflies land on the flower, begin to photograph them nectaring. I should mention that the best time to do this type of photography is from about 11 in the morning until 4 in the afternoon when the butterflies are more active. This is another reason that flash is important to use because it helps to control the contrast and shadows in this situation.

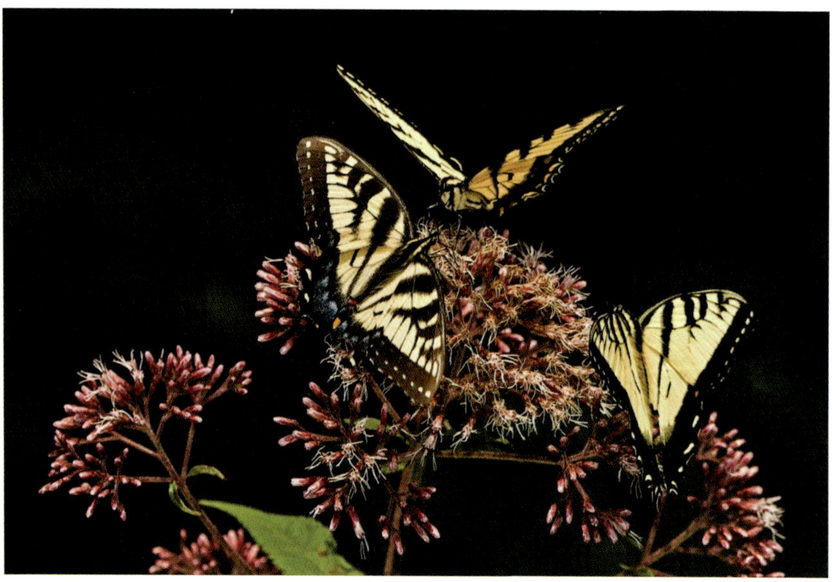

Putting It All Together

An old Chinese saying states that the "Journey of a thousand miles begins with a single step." I hope that you have begun a journey of learning how to photograph wildflowers and that you have taken the first steps by getting to this point in the book. I trust that you have gleaned some information about what type of equipment is best to use, how to use the equipment in the field, how you can use color to make more visually appealing images, and how visual design is the backdrop for creating more artistic photographs.

In the next series of images I want you to notice that these are all the same species of flower (Hepatica), but that each image conveys a different meaning depending on the various aspects of visual design that were emphasized in the image. This will hopefully bring all the concepts and principles I discussed earlier into focus and provide the final bit of clarity needed for you to go out and enjoy photographing wildflowers.

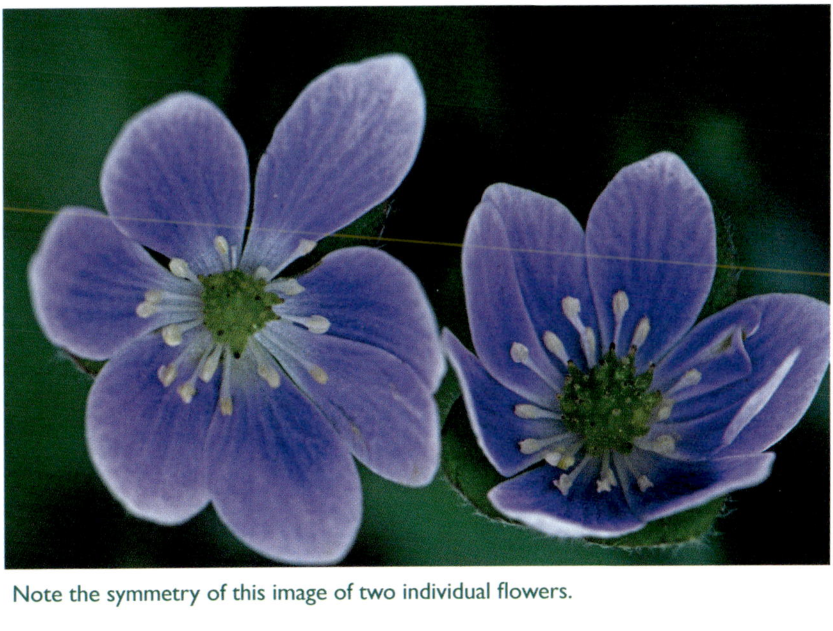

Note the symmetry of this image of two individual flowers.

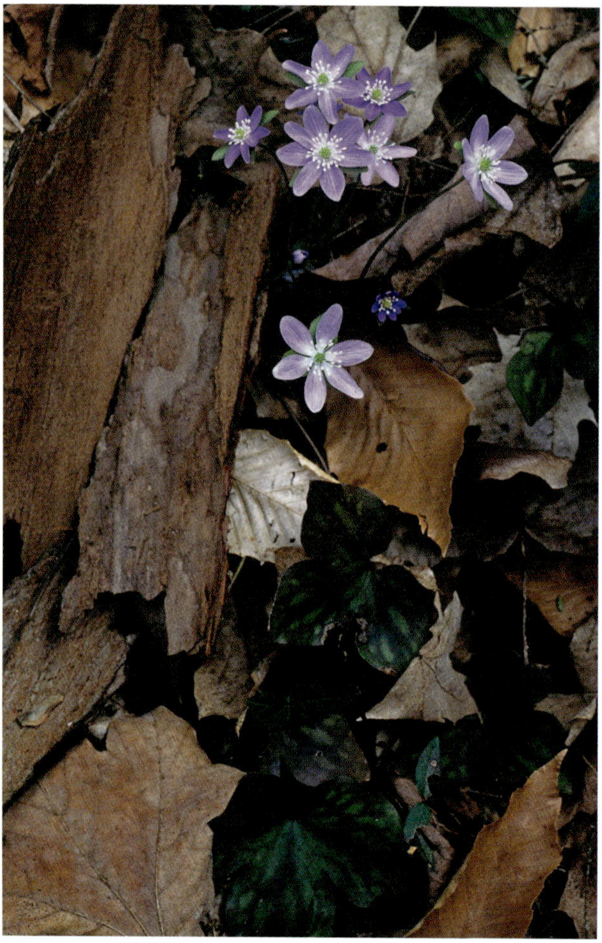

Note the leading lines and placement of the subject and then look at the image below, which is stronger because it was cropped more closely emphasizing the subject, the flowers. Notice the different orientation of the image from vertical to horizontal.

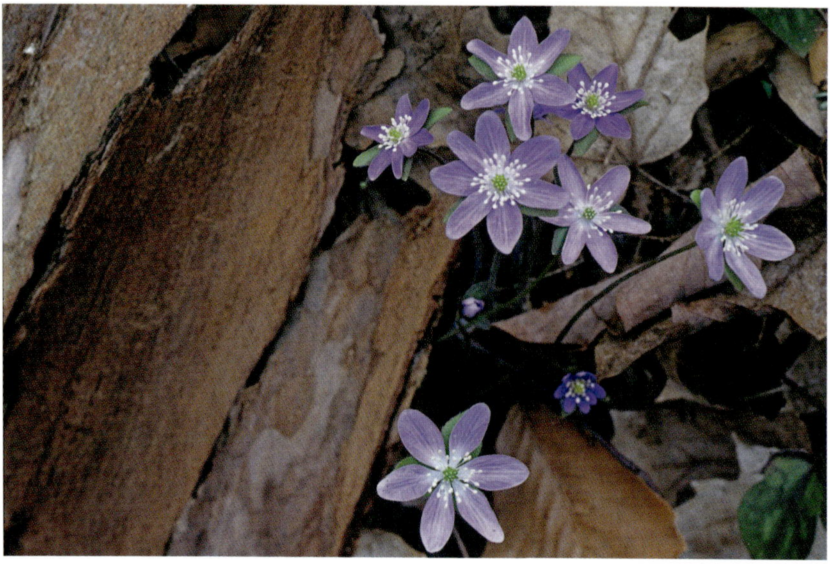

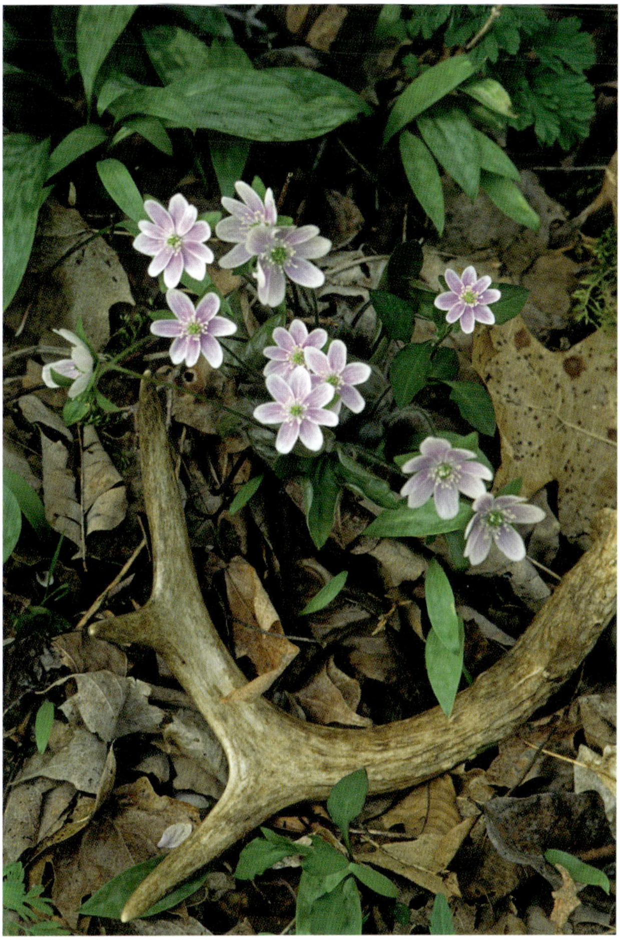

The deer antler serves as a frame around the primary subject. This was taken in February and is an example of being in the field as much as possible because rodents and other mammals usually gobble up shed antlers very quickly in the eastern woodlands and this one had already been chewed on the underside.

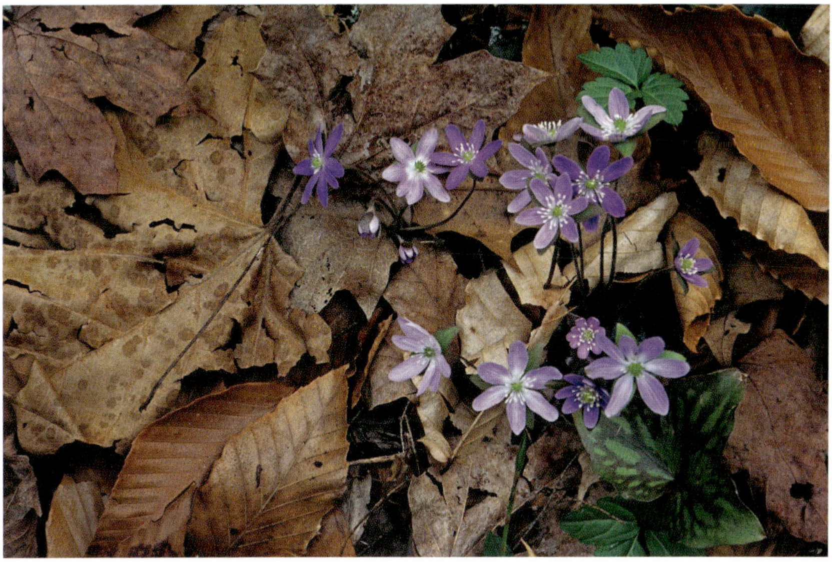

Notice the difference that color makes in an image, and how the lower image was taken on a sunny day late in the afternoon with the light diffused, giving it a warm appearance compared to the cool image above it and the one with the bright blue flowers.

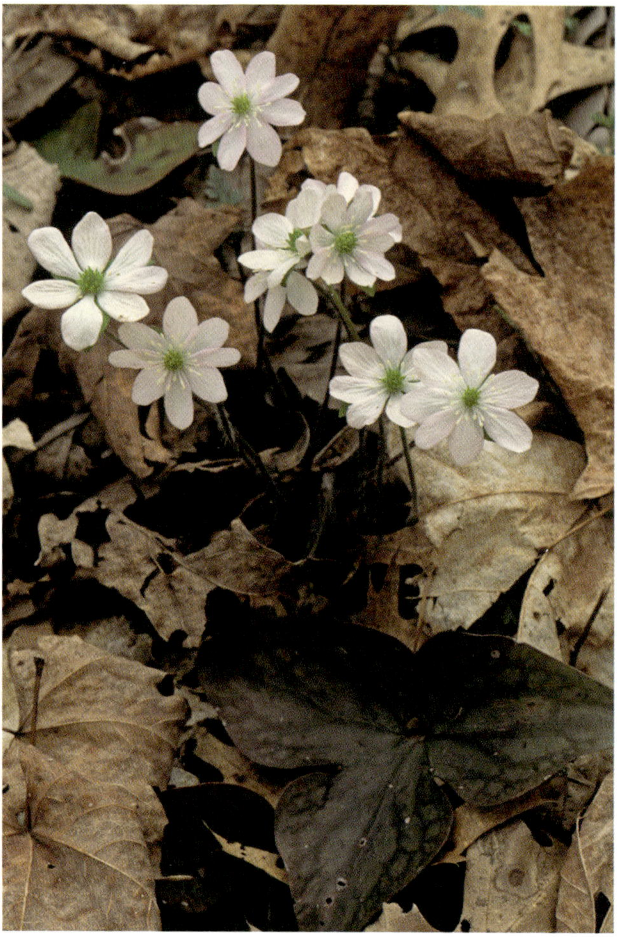

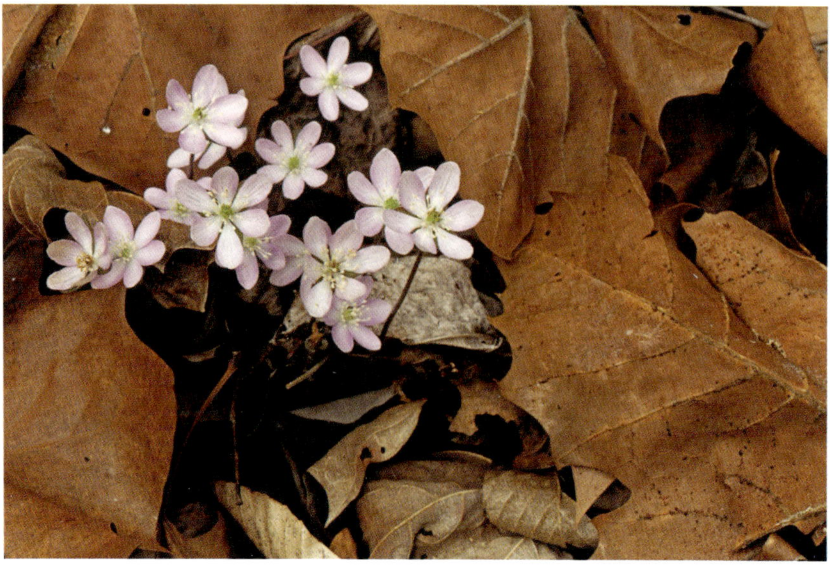

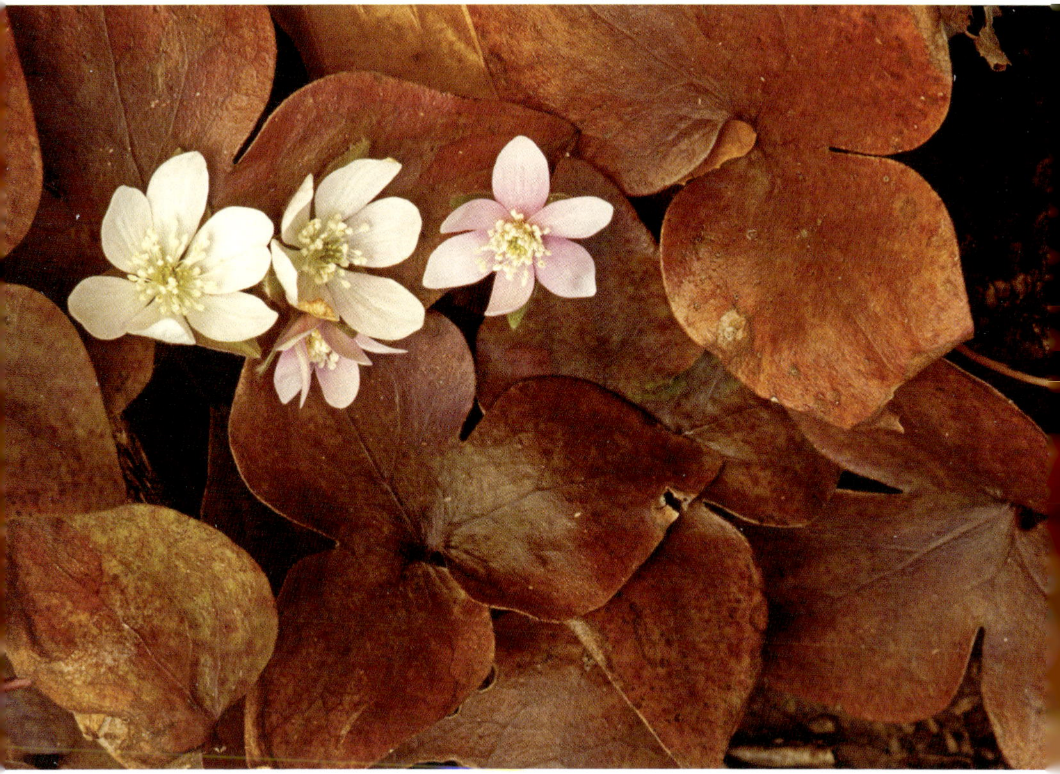

Note the interesting pattern of the leaves and the use of the rule of thirds.

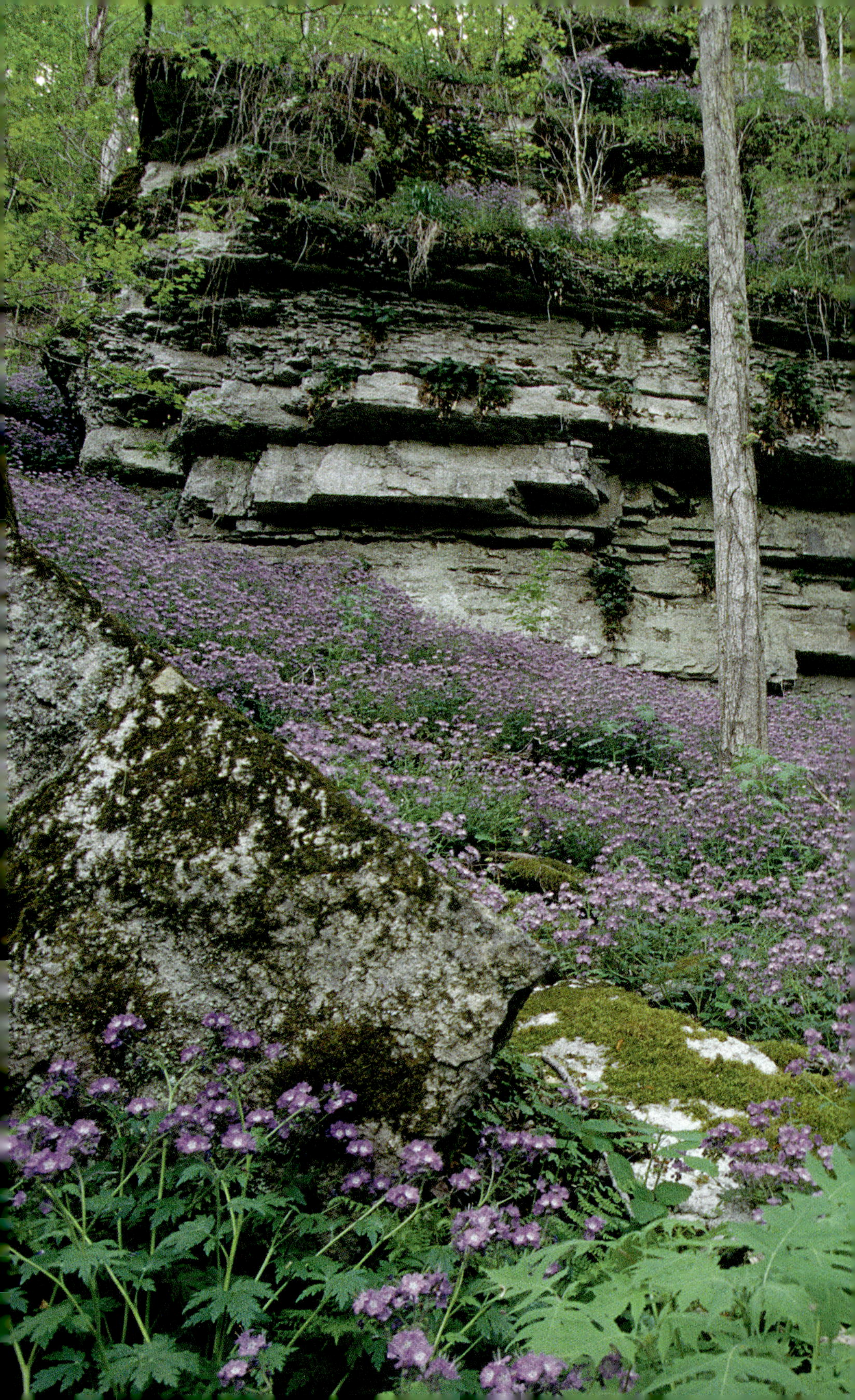

Locating Wildflowers

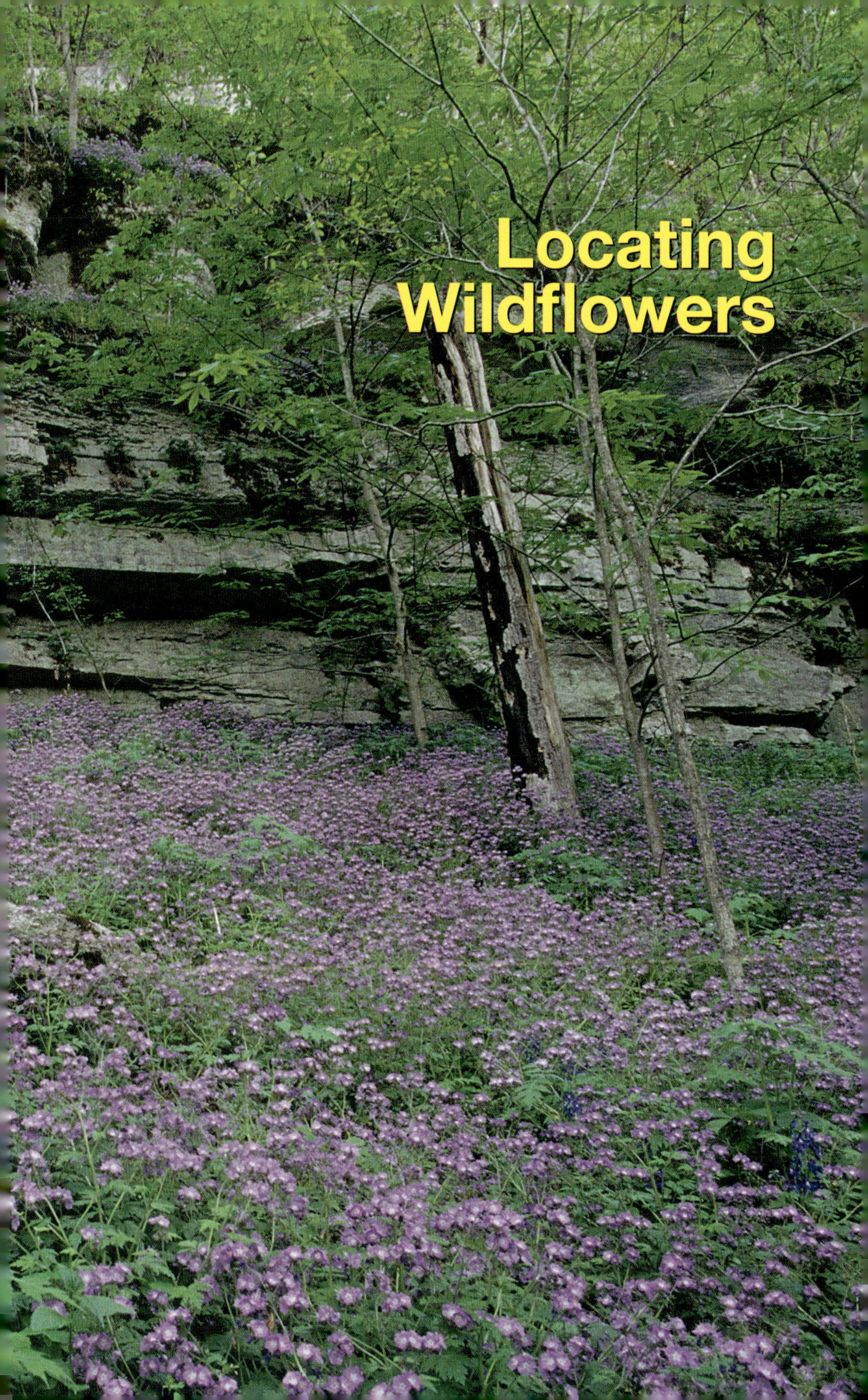

Finding Good Wildflower Locations in Kentucky

Now that you have the technical information on creating exceptional wildflower photos, where do you go to practice your craft? One of the best photo locations in all the United States for wildflowers is Kentucky. The reason? We are neither north or south, east or west, and we have a moderate climate with abundant rainfall and a variety of habitats ranging from the high elevation Appalachian Mountains on Big Black Mountain at 4,145 feet above sea level to gulf coastal plain swamps in Fulton County at 257 feet above sea level. In between we have Midwestern prairies and cedar glades. I have been fortunate to have traveled this state for over 20 years in my position as a Wildlife Specialist with the Kentucky Cooperative Extension Service and have walked hundreds of miles of trails and driven thousands of miles of back roads all across this state. While many will argue, and rightly so, that the Great Smoky Mountains are the best for wildflowers, particularly in the spring, we can argue that Kentucky has almost everything you can find in Great Smoky Mountain National Park except for the elevation gradient that allows for photographing early and mid- to late-season spring flowers. This simply means that the spring flower season progresses more slowly in Kentucky and you have to travel some to hit the best spots. But the upside is that you get the opportunity to photograph spring in one of the finest locations in North America.

Wildflower Phenology (sequence of blooms)

The wildflower blooming season in Kentucky can begin as early as February as harbinger of spring, purple cress and various draba species and mustards show their blooms. The season typically ends with a few straggling asters and goldenrods flowering in late October and early November. This gives the photographer ample time to spend outdoors finding and photographing wildflowers. The best advice when planning travel is to contact the naturalist at one of the state parks or a botanist familiar with the state to find out the status of the wildflower season and to determine what is exactly in flower.

That said, in general you can always count on the middle of April being a peak time for many spring species but if you want the lady's slipper orchids you will need to wait until the first week in May.

The Best Places to Find Wildflowers

I have listed those locations on the following pages that I consider to be truly outstanding where a large number of species can be found, are on public land or have public access, and are easily accessible for those in moderate physical condition. I have only listed one strenuous hike, that at Bad Branch in southeastern Kentucky, and if you take your time you can still do it but it will be taxing. I am sure there will be disagreements among many who look at this list and have their own favorite trails to find/photograph wildflowers. I am always looking for new places to go and welcome suggestions from other photographers, hikers, naturalists, and whoever would like to make additions to this list. For each specific trail I do not mention every single flower species found as it would require many, many pages of text. Rest assured that if a trail is mentioned, it is good and you are likely to find many more species (usually some of the most commonly found) to photograph.

If you are interested in finding a particular species and want to know when it flowers (in general), I would recommend you purchase the book, *The Wildflowers and Ferns of Kentucky* by Barnes and Francis, or two other books written by friends and colleagues, *The Wildflowers of Mammoth Cave* by Randy Seymour or *The Wildflowers of Land Between the Lakes* by Ed Chester. Using these references will help you plan your trip to make the most of the photographic opportunities in the least amount of time. The trails are listed by general region of the state: Eastern, Central and Western.

Eastern Kentucky

Big Black Mountain

The highest point in Kentucky rising 4,145 feet above sea level is one of the real gems for wildflowers in the entire state. A number of rare, threatened and endangered plants occur here and nowhere else in the state. This is an excellent place in the spring to see the rare species painted trillium, rosy twisted stalk, eastern waterleaf, and spotted mandarin. In mid-July, excellent finds include Turk's cap lily and Appalachian bunchflower. Late-summer rare species include Steele's Joe-Pye-weed, filmy angelica, Roan Mountain goldenrod, and Curtis' goldenrod. All these species are easily accessible from the main road that leads to the FAA radar tower. A number of years ago, the Commonwealth of Kentucky purchased the timber and coal rights on the mountain at elevations above 3,500 feet, but the land remains in private ownership. The paved road and right-of-way, is a public road and you can access the flowers from the road. My recommendation for both finding and photographing the various species on the mountain is to participate with an approved group such as the Pine Mountain Settlement School, which hosts the Black Mountain Wildflower Weekend annually during the first week in May. You may obtain contact information from the school's Web site. In the spring in addition to the numerous rare species you are likely to encounter are areas where the ground is white with large-flowered trillium with a smattering of southern red trillium, foamflower and other typical southern Appalachian species. There is a substantial number of wood anemone; pale mandarin; blue, white and yellow violets; wild strawberry; yellow trout lilies; jack-in-the-pulpit; wild geranium; blue cohosh; and many others. At the fire tower, look for Canada blackberry and red-berried elder. You will also notice the ground is carpeted with both color forms of wood betony near the tower.

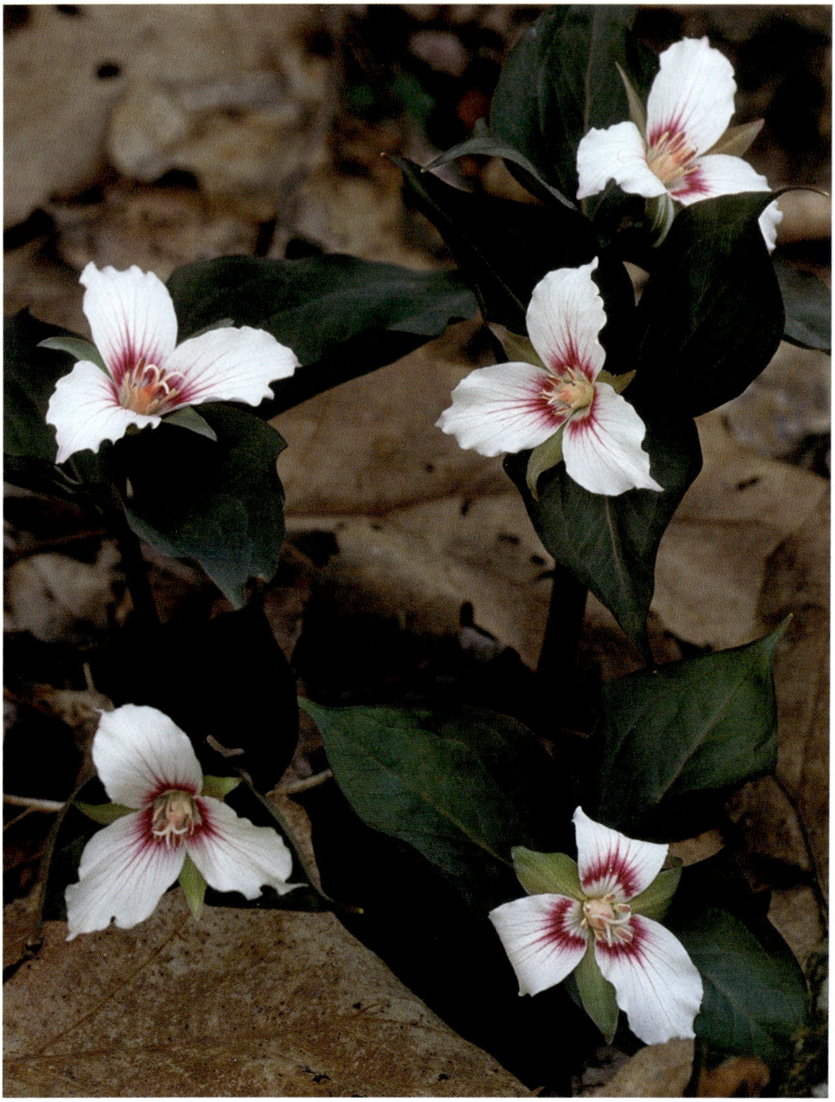

Painted trillium can be found in large groups on Big Black Mountain.

To Get There

Take U.S. 119 to Cumberland and exit on Kentucky 160 towards Benham and Lynch. Proceed through both of these communities up the mountain approximately 9.6 miles to the summit road just before the Virginia state line sign. Turn right and park in the gravel alongside the road and walk the paved road to the FAA radar tower. The best lodging option is the Benham Schoolhouse Inn run by the Kentucky Department of Parks. You will find comfortable accommodations here with 30 guest rooms. This facility was built by Wisconsin Steel, which became International Harvester as a school for children that lived in the coal camp and was used as a school until 1992. While in this area, if you have not visited the Kentucky Coal Mining Museum and Portal 31 mine, I highly recommend taking some time to learn more about how coal mining has shaped, and continues to shape, this part of the world.

Access Ratings

Driving Trails	**EASY**
Hiking Trails	**EASY**

Bad Branch State Nature Preserve

Mention Bad Branch Nature Preserve in Letcher County and most people automatically think of the 60 foot waterfall at the end of a mile-long, somewhat strenuous hike. This 2,600 acre nature preserve on the south slope of Pine Mountain was originally identified as significant by the famous botanist and ecologist E. Lucy Braun in the 1950's and 1960's. The original preserve was 435 acres and was purchased in 1985 for excellent scenic and ecological values. It is designated a state wild and scenic river and as you hike, you will hear the sounds of rushing water over boulders and notice high cliffs on either side which creates a Northern environment where more than 30 state listed rare plants and animals have been found. The trail follows an old logging road from the 1940's when the forest was harvested, although some of the hemlock stands in the lower portion are considered old growth and were not touched by loggers. The wildflower display in this preserve, particularly above the falls, is outstanding and the preserve has one of the largest concentrations of rare plants found in the entire state. The flowers along the beginning section of the trail, up to the waterfall, are nothing to celebrate except that you will find large numbers of one rare species, southern heartleaf and the uncommon round-leaf violet scattered all along the trail. You will find other typical Appalachian flowers like Quaker ladies and sweet white violets along the trail as well. As you approach the split in the trail with the right trail heading to the waterfall (an excellent side trip to photograph), the best flower displays begin on the trail that goes left above the falls. Here you will find several lovely patches of showy orchis, wild geranium, foamflower, meehenia, bishop's cap and other typical spring Appalachian flowers that carpet the ground. Once you get to the flattened portion of the trail around 2,500 feet and you begin to turn right onto the loop trail to the High Rocks area, keep a watchful eye for painted trillium in the spring and showy gentian in the fall. The trail near High Rocks isn't too exciting except right below the rocky outcrops (with lots of mountain laurel and Catawba rhododendron) is a large display of pink lady's slipper orchids.

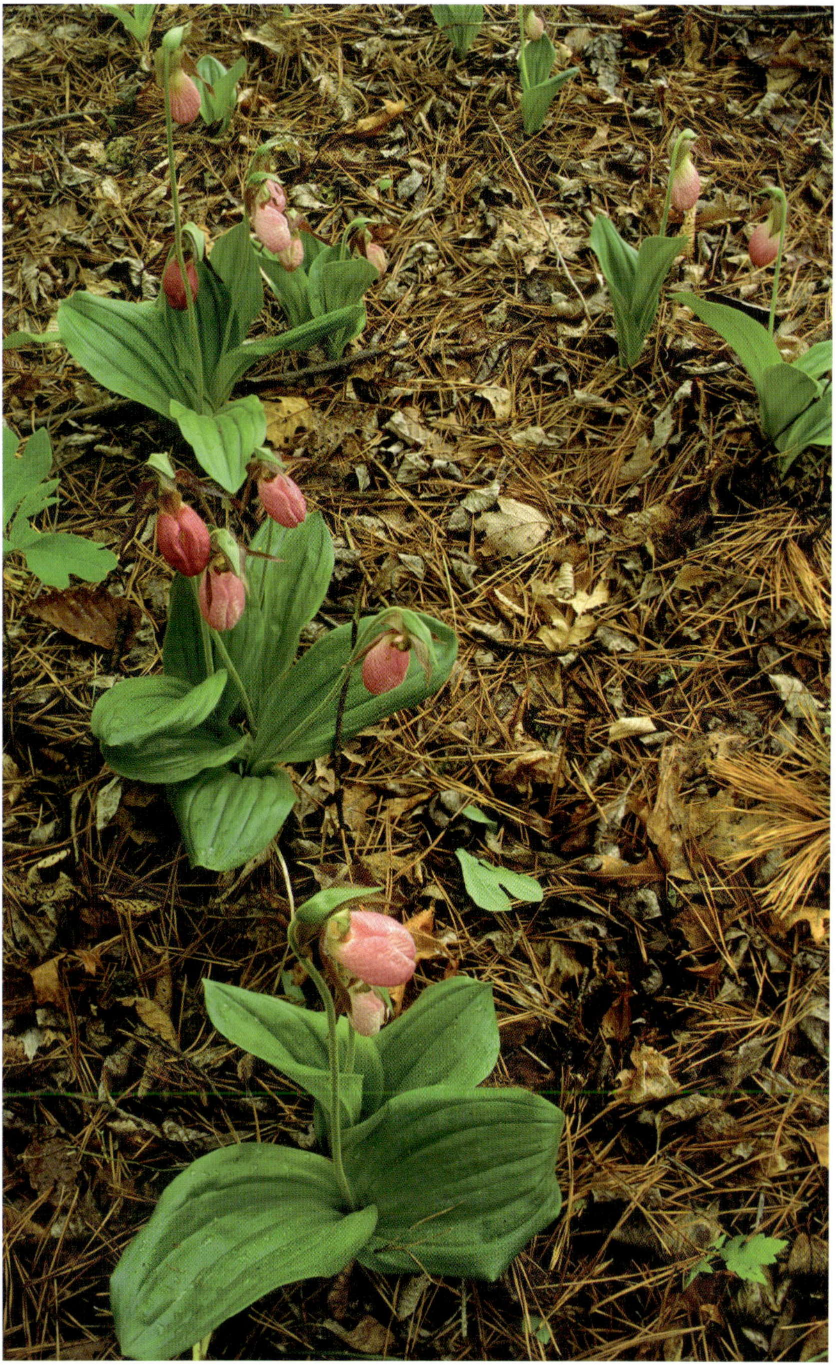

There is a large population of pink lady's slipper orchids near the crest of the trail at High Rock.

To Get There

From Whitesburg in Letcher County take Kentucky 15 to where it intersects with US 119 (look for the McDonald's restaurant on the corner) and travel over Pine Mountain approximately eight miles to Kentucky 932. On the way up at mile 5 to 6, look for several pull offs as these provide excellent opportunities for sunrise or sunset shots with layers of hills (Cumberland Plateau). Once you reach Kentucky 932 turn left, traveling east for two miles and then look for the parking lot on your left. The best lodging options in this part of the world are in Whitesburg, a short drive over the mountain on US 119. There are two options for lodging which include the Super8 and the Parkway Inn. Both are acceptable and comfortable.

Access Ratings

Hiking Trails

to waterfall	**MODERATE**
entire trail	**STRENUOUS**

Pine Mountain Settlement School and James Bickford State Nature Preserve

This is a real treasure for wildflower enthusiasts and photographers. Pine Mountain Settlement School was established in 1913 as an educational institution for children in the remote mountainous terrain of Eastern Kentucky. It also served as a social center for surrounding communities. While originally designated as a school, today it has a focus of providing environmental education and arts, crafts, and Appalachian culture to young and old alike. The school is a National Historical Landmark. I highly recommend you attend one of the two wildflower weekends: the Pine Mountain Wildflower Weekend on the third weekend in April and the Black Mountain Wildflower Weekend the first weekend in May. The staff at the school have been offering these weekends for more than 30 years and you will not be disappointed as the food is excellent, the lodging facilities comfortable, and the fellowship outstanding. Furthermore, this is perhaps the best way to get to Black Mountain and have access to all those rare woodland flowers on the top of the mountain. The other great thing about this location is that by contacting the school prior to your stay, you can get lodging and meals for a very reasonable cost and it reduces any travel time for getting wildflower images.

The campus at the school encompasses more than 625 acres mostly on the North side of Pine Mountain. Much of the area surrounding the campus has been designated a state nature preserve (348 acres) and you must follow all rules and regulations regarding use of the two trails at the school. The easiest trail is the Split-Rock Trail, one mile in length that begins just outside the Laurel House and proceeds at a very gentle rise into a beautiful setting with rocks and boulders and wildflowers covering the ground. Look for wood poppies, dwarf larkspur, spotted and pale mandarin, large-flowered and southern red trillium, large-flowered bellwort, wild geranium, showy orchis, bloodroot, and speckled wood lily. The best location for dwarf crested iris in a beautiful setting is just behind the Laurel House across the little stream. Furthermore, if you are interested in photographing three-birds orchids in August, there are some patches close to the Laurel House in the back of the gravel parking lot and some nice populations along the Dogwood Trail, which is the other trail at the school. The Dogwood Trail, one mile in length, begins behind the chapel. This is a much more challenging trail as it climbs in elevation before coming back down to the campus. You will find the same species as on the Split-Rock Trail. Depending on the time of year you may wish to contact the naturalist and botanist at the school for access to photographing such rare things as the summer coral root orchid, golden saxifrage, small yellow lady's slipper orchids, and a few other rare species on which location information is not available to the general public. Make sure you ask for a wildflower list while visiting as more than 130 spring wildflowers can be photographed on this campus and the surrounding environment. To make arrangements to visit and photograph and for meals/lodging, contact the settlement school at 606-558-3571, or 606-558-3542 between 7 am and 3:30 pm or go to its Web site at www.ppinemountainsettlementschool.com.

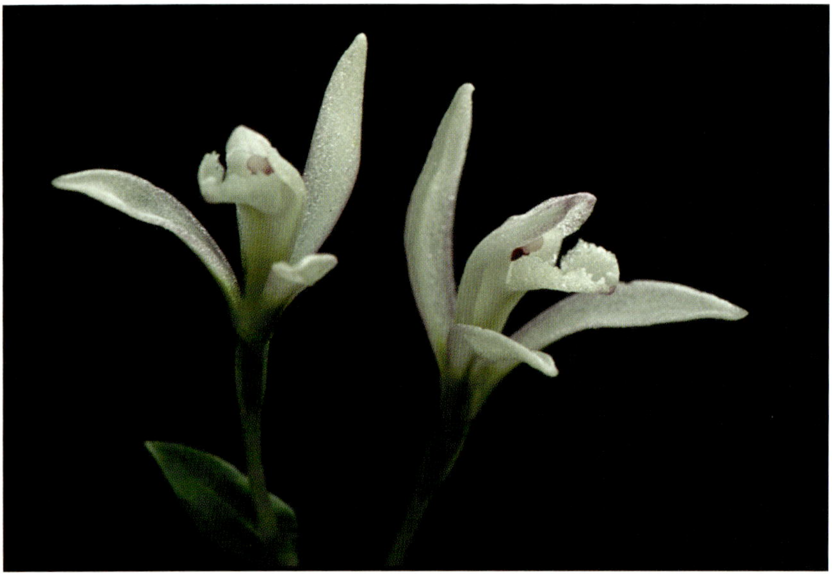

Three-birds orchid is easily found in early August near the lodge and about a third of the way up on the summit or Dogwood Trail.

To Get There

If you are coming from the northwest or north along the I-75 corridor, you can take exit 29 (Corbin U.S. 25 East) to Pineville. Take a left at the second stoplight (Kentucky 66/221) and follow this road for 1.5 miles (going east). At this junction, turn right onto 221 and go 24 miles to the intersection of U.S. 421 (Watch for coal trucks on these roads) and veer to the left (this intersection is on a curve) to stay on 421/221. In 0.9 miles, take a hard right to continue onto 221. Follow this for another 10 miles until you reach the junction of Kentucky 221 and 510 and veer to the right on 510 and take an immediate right into the Settlement School parking lot. If you are coming from the south, east, or Northeast, visit the school's Web site for specific directions. I would highly recommend you ask for lodging at the school as the closest motels are 45 minutes to an hour away in Benham, Whitesburg, or Harlan.

Access Ratings

Hiking Trails	**EASY to MODERATE**

Kingdom Come State Park

This would not normally be one of the "best" places for wildflower photography but there are some good things along the Raven Rock Trail that are worthy of photographing. This 1,200 acre state park hosts four nice overlooks for morning or evening photographs of Black Mountain or the Cumberland Plateau and is the epicenter of black bear sightings in Kentucky. One of the big features of the park is Raven Rock, which juts up 290 feet and occurs at a 45 degree slope. Stop at the Halcomb Overlook and park in the gravel lot. The Possum Trail descends towards Raven Rock and as you proceed approximately 0.25 miles down the trail, look on the left (east) side for the large whorled pogonia orchid (usually flowers the last week of April) and you will also notice a wet, seepy area to the left where a large patch of Canada lilies grow that flower in mid-July. Approximately 100 yards down the trail you will notice a spur to the right that will take you on top of the rock outcropping. There is a bench located at the junction and a beautiful pink lady's slipper orchid just beside the bench. Follow the outcropping to the east until you reach the power-line cut and look for the rare rock harlequin flower. This also occurs atop Raven Rock and the main trail takes you to the top of the trail. You can also easily access this particular flower at Pine Mountain State Park on the rocks at the original trail behind the lodge. Of other note at this state park is the large number of pink lady's slipper orchids along the trail and the pink Catawba rhododendron that flowers near the rocks in early to mid-May. The rock outcroppings at both state parks provide interesting areas to look for unusual mosses and lichens. As you get close to Raven Rock, look on your right hand side and you will see many nice populations of galax and Indian cucumber root. There are also several pink lady's slipper orchids after you cross the powerline and descend down the Raven Rock Trail (not the power line trail) about 100 feet into the woods.

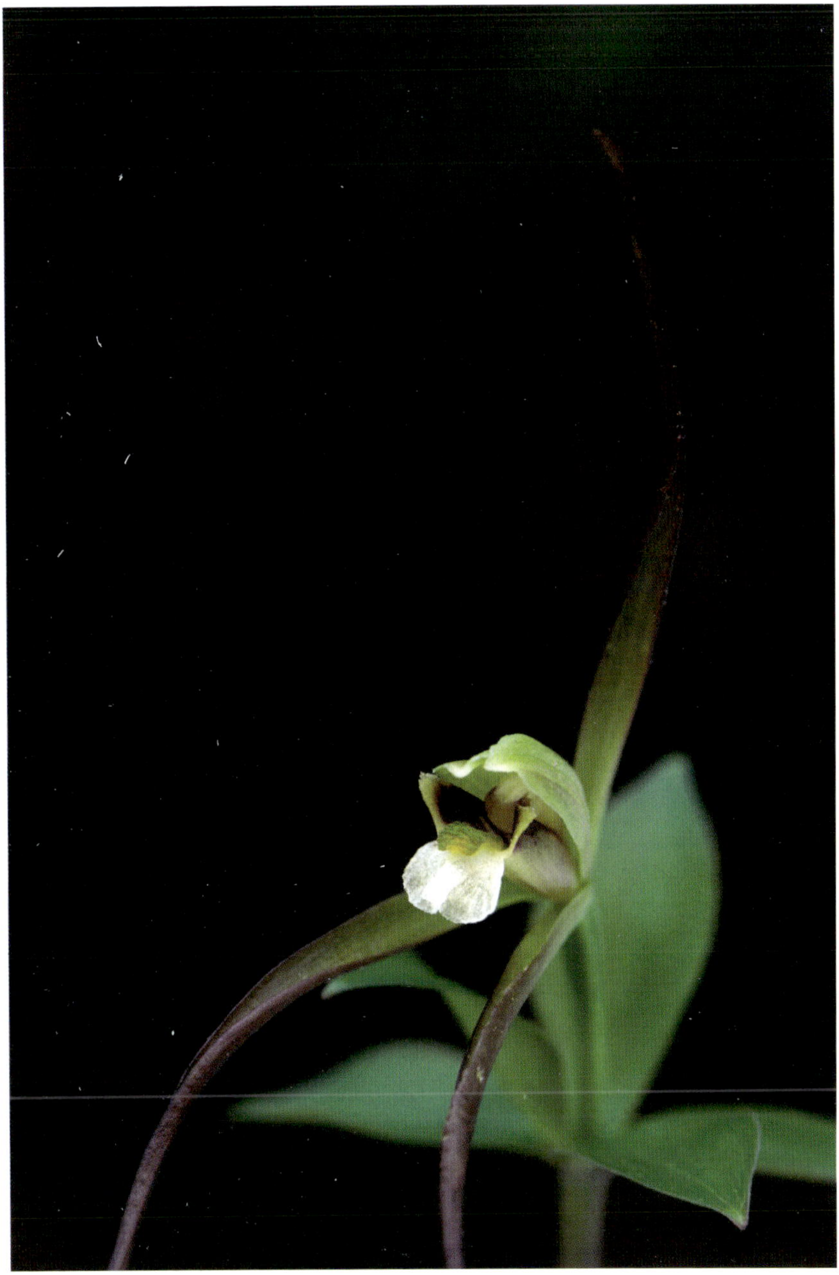

The large whorled pogonia orchid occurs just off the trail going toward Raven Rock.

To Get There

From the junction of U.S. 119 and Kentucky 160 in Cumberland, travel north one mile to the park entrance and proceed up on the main road to the top of the park. There is one exceptional overlook of Black Mountain on the way to the top. At the junction of the Little Sheppard Trail, take a left turn (west) and stop at the Halcomb Overlook. Lodging is available at the Benham Schoolhouse Inn or in Whitesburg or Harlan.

Access Ratings

Hiking Trails	**EASY**

Natural Bridge State Resort Park

Natural Bridge State Resort Park gets its name from the sandstone arch that spans 78 feet in length and 65 feet in height. This park has been a tourist destination since the late 1800s through access by the Lexington and Eastern Railroad. It became a state park in 1925 and was one of the four original state parks in Kentucky. The park encompasses more than 2,300 acres and has more than 20 miles of hiking trails. While the natural sandstone arch is the centerpiece attraction, along with Sky Bridge in the adjacent Red River Gorge, there are more than 100 natural arches in this region alone and more than half a million people a year visit the Red River Gorge and Natural Bridge State Resort Park. The scenic and landscape photographic opportunities in this region are unparalleled almost anywhere in Kentucky. I highly recommend you check out the book, *Red River Gorge: The Eloquent Landscape* written by my friend and colleague John Snell, before making travel plans because you can easily spend a week in this general vicinity and still not have captured the essence of the place. Not only will you encounter more than 200 species of spring-blooming wildflowers, but you can also photograph natural arches and bridges, towering cliffs, some waterfalls (seasonal like the small Creation Falls on the Rock Bridge Trail or the enormous Torrent Falls on private land just west of the park on Kentucky 11), and scenic streams like Swift Camp Creek and the middle fork of the Red River. The Kentucky Native Plant Society has always held its annual Wildflower Weekend at Natural Bridge State Resort Park, and it generally is held in mid-April to coincide with the peak flowering season in the spring. Natural Bridge and its environs including the Red River Gorge offer some of the best locations in Kentucky for photographing spring wildflowers and rivals or exceed the Great Smoky Mountains because during the week you will hardly encounter anyone on the trails early in the morning or late in the afternoon during the best times for photographing. While all the trails have some excellent photographic opportunities, and Hood's Branch offers solitude, I recommend the following trails, which have the best abundance and diversity of flowers that can be accessed in the shortest period of time to optimize your photographic endeavors. These trails are the Original Trail, Rock Garden, and Whittleton Branch (part of the Sheltowee Trace of the U.S. Forest Service trail system in the Daniel Boone National Forest).

Natural Bridge State Resort Park

Original Trail

At the base of the lower parking lot by the concession center near Hoedown Island, you will begin climbing along a paved trail that will ultimately take you to the natural arch. This trail was built in the 1830s by the railroad, and it is the shortest and easiest route to the natural bridge. A few yards from the starting point on the right, look for a nice patch of blunt-leaf waterleaf that will be flowering in late May. As you move up the trail about midway to the split where you can go to the nature center or the lodge, look on the left for a very nice patch of cancer root. Once you get up on the main level trail, turn to the right and follow the elevated path to the stairs on the left. Just before the stairs, look over the railing, and you will find some of the deepest blue hepatica I have ever seen in my life. As you turn to the left and climb the steep set of rock steps, look on your right for some spring coral root orchids. Once you have reached the top of the steps, you have the option of going left or right, and you will want to turn to the right and begin looking for columbine on the cliffs, meadow rue under the wet cliffline, and lots of interesting ferns like walking, bulbet, and cliff brake on the limestone outcroppings. You will also find some nice patches of wild ginger and purple phacelia. As you reach the end of the cliffline, you will turn back to the left and begin the ascent to the natural bridge. You will notice many large, white-flowered trilliums, southern red trillium, and other species along the trail. Once you reach the first of four shelters, look for the round-leaf violet along the trail. This is the best place to see this in Kentucky other than at Bad Branch State Nature Preserve. On the steep portion of this trail you will find partridge berry. In the middle of the summer, look for spikenard on the left half way up the trail. Opposite this area, on the right, is a really nice patch of showy orchis. As you continue to climb, look for halberd-leaf violet and along the base of some cliffs, look for cliff rue, and as you get close to the bridge, look for a wide variety of spleenwort ferns. Once reach the top of the bridge you can wander around the trails and find bird's foot violet and pink lady's slipper orchids.

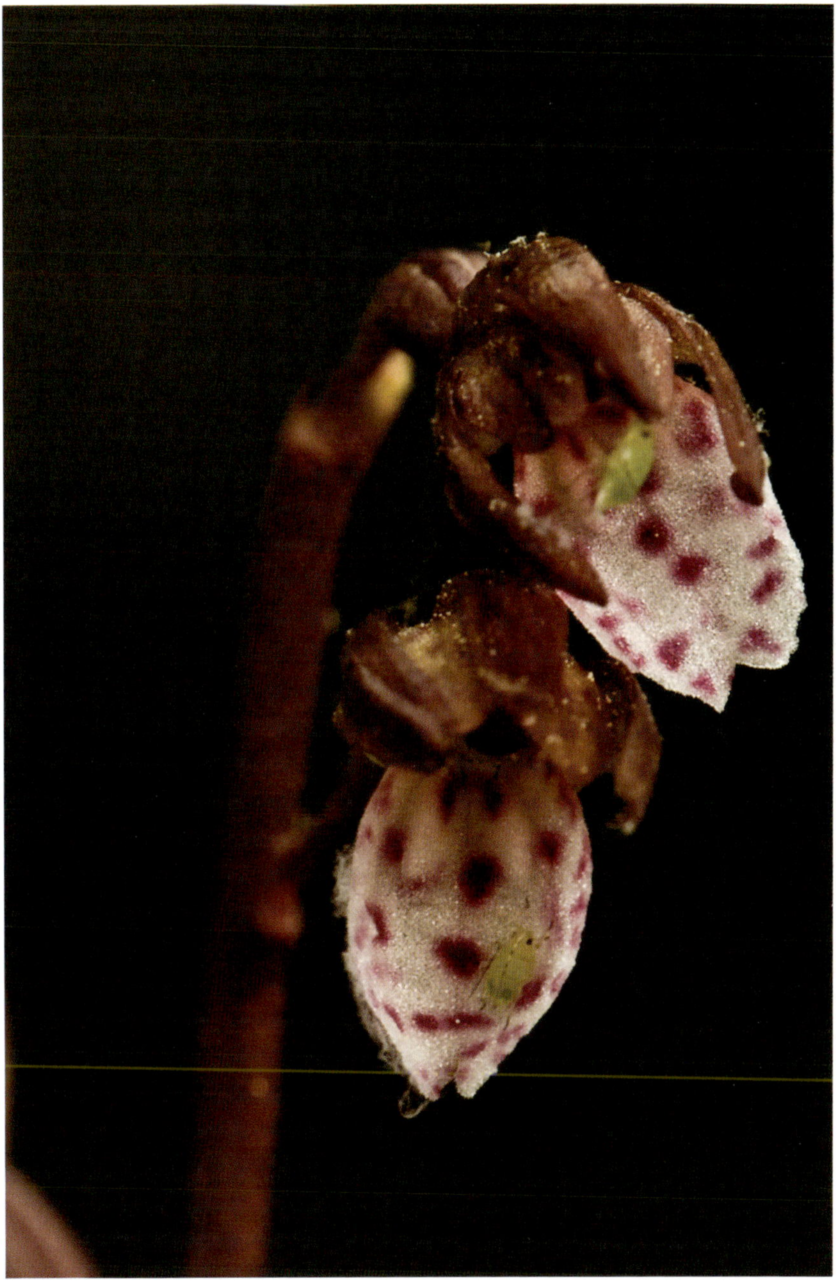

As you head up the stone stairs, just after the stream, look for spring coral root orchids around step number 14 – 20 on the right hand side over the wooden rail fence or look on the upslope of the parking lot by the nature center.

To Get There

Take I-64 east from Lexington or west from Ashland to the Mountain Parkway, and head southeast towards the Slade exit (number 33). Exit to the right to Natural Bridge State Resort Park. Follow Kentucky 11 for two miles and the park will be on your right. Obviously lodging is available at the park but you must reserve your room well in advance, sometimes a year or more, since the lodge and cabins are usually booked during the wildflower season. There are a great variety of other lodging options available including Natural Bridge Cabins. A quick web search will delineate hundreds of lodging options outside the park but be sure to book well in advance. Planning is essential since this is such a popular area. On a side note, a meal at Miguel's is a worthy endeavor if nothing more than to savor the local climbing culture and a taste of some pretty good pizza.

Access Ratings

Hiking Trails	**EASY to DIFFICULT**

Natural Bridge State Resort Park

Rock Garden Trail

This used to be my favorite trail in the park and Red River Gorge. Unfortunately, several years ago an exotic pest plant arrived, annual chickweed, and began carpeting the ground, crowding out native flowers. The allure of this trail was the incredible diversity of flowers, but, more importantly from a photographic standpoint, was the profusion of flowers growing on top of giant rocks and boulders that had tumbled down from the scenic cliff on this north-facing, mature forest stand. There are still ample opportunities for portraits and habitat shots, but the great landscape shots with a foreground of trilliums with cliffs in the background is no longer possible as you are most likely to see a mat of the unphotogenic chickweed. This trail begins as it hooks up with the Original Trail behind Hemlock Lodge. After the first short, steep, incline you will reach the cliffline and you will turn to the right and go down into a small depression (filled with tons of trilliums) and onto the trail that follows a ridgeline directly above the lodge. Once you turn left from this mostly south-facing slope onto the north-facing slope, the wildflower action really picks up and you will begin to notice the cliffline with trilliums in large patches. Continue along the trail for another quarter-mile and you enter a "natural" garden complete with large boulders covered with purple phacelia, foamflower, stonecrop, violets, jack-in-the-pulpit, and trilliums galore. If you poke around, you are likely to find showy orchis, star chickweed, stonecrop, alumroots, mandarin, bellwort, and dwarf crested iris. As you proceed out of the garden and turn to the left, you will enter a completely different habitat with nothing much to photograph until you get under the sky lift near the top and begin to find bird's foot violet.

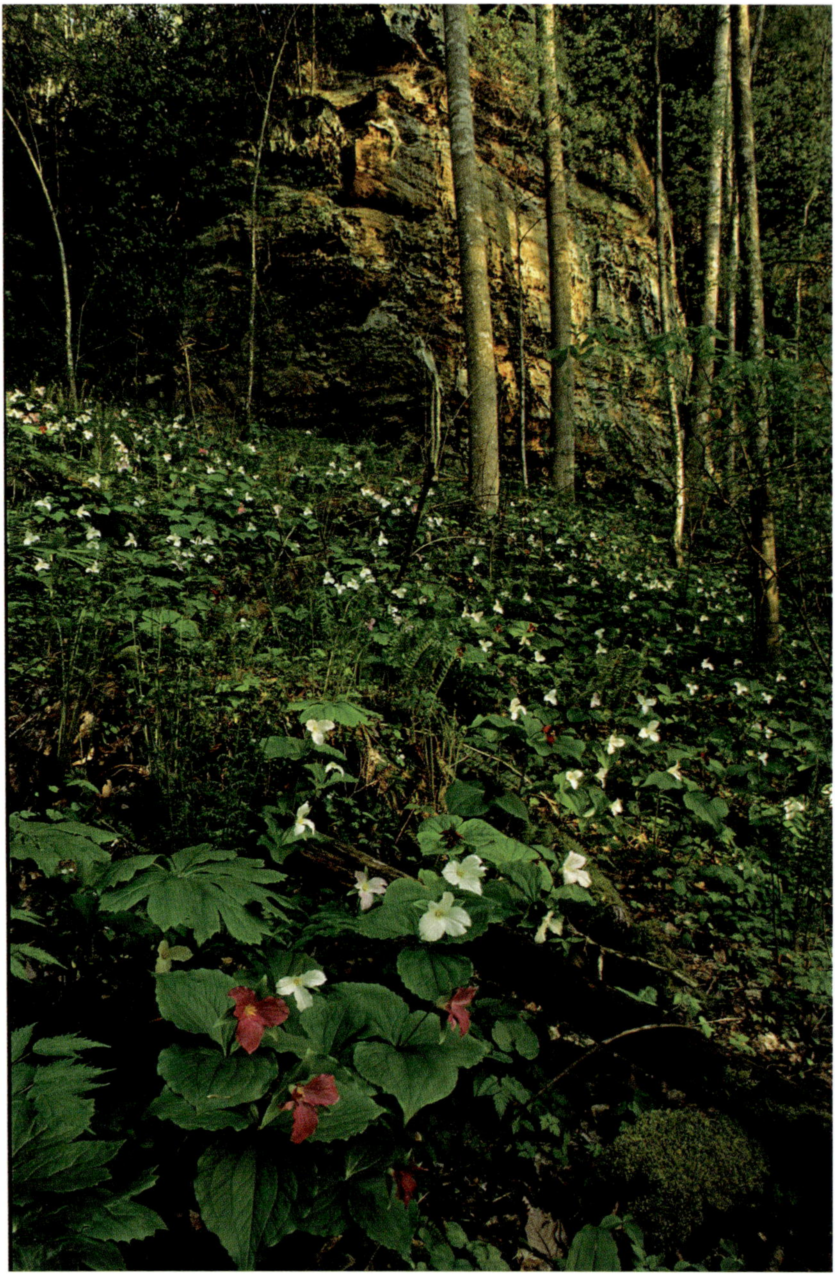

This scene, along the Rock Garden Trail, is a common occurrence all throughout Natural Bridge and the Red River Gorge area.

To Get There

Take I-64 east from Lexington or west from Ashland to the Mountain Parkway, and head southeast towards the Slade exit (number 33). Exit to the right to Natural Bridge State Resort Park. Follow Kentucky 11 for two miles and the park will be on your right.

Access Ratings

Hiking Trails	**MODERATE**

Natural Bridge State Resort Park

Whittleton Branch

This is undoubtedly the easiest walk in the entire Red River Gorge area and one of the absolute best for wildflowers. The walk is mostly level but does gain some elevation after the first mile from Whittleton Arch to the end of the trail at Kentucky 15. To access this trail, you will need to park at the entrance of the middle fork campground and walk the paved road until it ends and the walking trail begins. There is not much in the way of photographic opportunities until you reach the end of the pavement. Right before you begin the walking trail, if you veer off into the woods on the left you will find wood betony in abundance. You will also see Carolina vetch, blue phlox, wild geranium and numerous other species like false rue anemone and violets. Coming out of the woods going toward the trail, you will notice a large amount of horsetail in a wet area, and just beyond the wet area not too far from the trail, look for some nice showy orchis by the sign on the left. The trail for the most part follows the stream and there are several exceptional scenic vistas where you can take photos with a foreground of large white trillium and the stream. As you begin the hike, you will notice a great variety of species including golden ragwort, blue phlox, wild geranium, and violets of all colors and sorts. The first significant landmark to look for is about 100 feet down the trail. Look on your left for a downed tree and what appears to be a make-shift trail going up a somewhat steep embankment. If you look about 50 feet up the slope, you will see perhaps the most photographed yellow lady's slipper orchids in Kentucky. When the tree toppled over a number of years ago, it wiped out a good many of the orchids, but there are still more than a dozen at this location. As you continue on the trail, the next significant stop is where the stream makes a fairly sharp turn to the left. Where the trail narrows, you will find on the slope many bishop's caps; pale mandarin; southern red, Sulcate and large-flowered trilliums in abundance; and bellwort. When the trail makes the left turn, you will see a small flat area between the trail and the stream. This little patch is worth a day's photography as you will find trilliums, numerous showy orchis, and wild geranium in profusion, almost too thick to comprehend. Be careful where you step as the ground is literally carpeted with wildflowers at this location. Continuing up the trail you will cross several bridges. Look for the dwarf crested iris by these bridges and in the summer look for the rattlesnake plantain orchids, which occur here in abundance. Other species you are likely to encounter as you continue up the trail will be meadow parsnip, foamflower, star chickweed, sweet cicely, baneberry, white Clintonia, bluets, jack-in-the-pulpit, and several other species. There are a few more yellow lady's slippers close to the trail as you approach the arch and a few pinks up near the top of the trail. Most people make the trip to the arch – not a very photogenic arch but quite large – and return back to the campground for an easy two-mile loop.

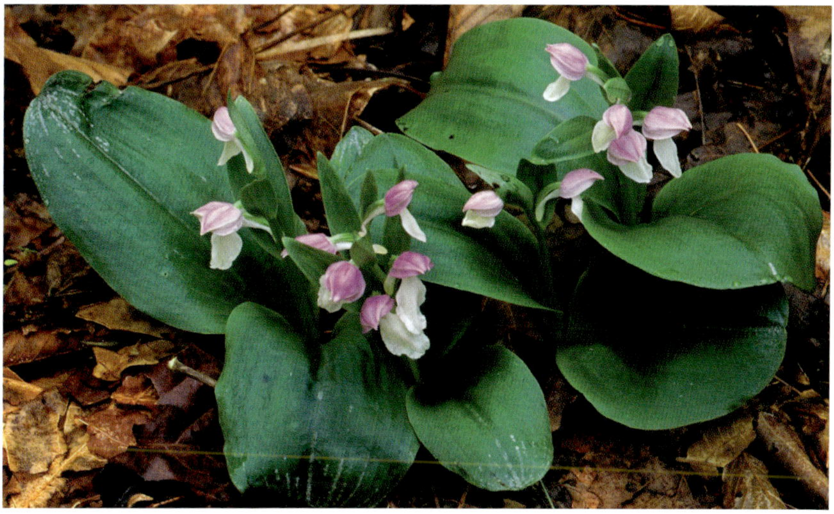

Showy orchis are abundant on the Whittleton Branch trail at the base of the sign and in the flats to the left between the trail and the stream.

To Get There

Take I-64 east from Lexington or west from Ashland to the Mountain Parkway, and head southeast towards the Slade exit (number 33). Exit to the right to Natural Bridge State Resort Park. Follow Kentucky 11 for two miles and the park will be on your right. Continue another quarter-mile for Whittleton and look for the campground on your left.

Access Ratings

Hiking Trails	
to Natural Arch	**EASY**
to Kentucky 15	**MODERATE**

Red River Gorge

Of all the areas covered in this book, the Red River Gorge, which lies immediately across the Mountain Parkway from Natural Bridge, is perhaps the most well known because of the number of natural arches and its scenic beauty. The upper Red River is both a state and national wild and scenic river. The gorge itself is known as a great camping, hiking, and rock climbing paradise. The gorge is part of the Daniel Boone National Forest and 29,000 acres encompass the Red River Gorge Geological Area so designated in 1974. In 1976, the National Park Service designated the area a National Natural Landmark. In 2003, 37,000 acres were placed on the National Register of Historic Landmarks. The 12,646 acre Clifty Wilderness Area overlaps the gorge area on the east and the National Highway Administration made 46 miles of road a national scenic byway in 2002. Obviously, this is a great area for outdoor and nature photography. If you are camping outside a campground, you will need a permit that costs a minimal fee. It is available from a variety of local vendors. Because this area receives so many visitors, locking your vehicle and keeping valuables out of view is absolutely essential. The photographic opportunities, in addition to wildflowers, include natural arches, cliffs, scenic vistas and an outstanding river. Wildflowers can be found in proliferation on all the trails but the most accessible occur along two roads, Forest Service Roads 23 and 9. A visit to the Gladie welcome center located on Kentucky 715 (scenic loop several miles past the intersection with Kentucky 77) is worth the effort and you can pick up some pointers on flower locations and maps.

The Forest Roads 23 and 9 Driving Trail is a 7.3-mile road that has an impressive array of wildflowers and you can expect to find large patches of Virginia bluebells along the river or Indian Creek; in many places, they literally carpet the ground. You can also find several large patches of large-flowered white trillium, in some places covering a hillside on Forest Service Road 9 after you cross the creek. Like all areas in the gorge, there are unlimited opportunities for photographing flowers and moss-covered rocks, streams, and clifflines. The view from the Kentucky Highway 77 Bridge looking north is wonderful and photogenic. The first part of this road, turning left off Kentucky 77 immediately after crossing the bridge, is gravel, and then toward the end it becomes pavement and then, when turning right after 2.5 miles, is gravel once again. These roads are not well traveled during the week, but on weekends there can be significant vehicular travel, which does not bode well for flower photography. The list of flowers seen along these roads is impressive, and for those who have limited mobility this is a great place to photograph many of Kentucky ephemeral spring wildflowers. The flowers really get abundant after you make a right-hand curve and the slopes face north. Look for blue phlox, golden ragwort, white wood vetch, wild geranium in profusion, alumroot, may apple in profusion, large-flowered white trillium, wild ginger, foamflower, large bellwort, Jacob's ladder, smooth yellow violet, rue anemone, bloodroot, wood poppy, blue cohosh, Solomon's and false Solomon's seal, and lavender waterleaf, and boulders covered in stonecrop, star chickweed, cut-leaf toothwort, yellow trout lilies, dwarf crested iris, jack-in-the-pulpit, and long-spurred and Canada violets. After this 2.4 mile trek, you can turn right onto Forest Service Road 9 and pick up southern red and erect trillium in abundance, several large patches of bishop's cap, and patches of bluebells along the creek that, in some cases, cover more than an acre. There is also one small patch of twinleaf about half a mile down the road on the right immediately adjacent to two very large moss-covered boulders. Later in the season you can find valerian, synandra, white bergamot, Carolina phlox and fire pink on some of the drier sites. Look for the yellow lady's slipper orchids at mile 0.1 on the right hand side of the road. There is no time during the year when these roads do not have spectacular flowers and in early summer you can find purple coneflower, black-eyed Susans, orange-flower, Indian physic, and sun drops. Late in the season you can find Joe-Pye-weed, ironweed, yellow wing stem, cardinal flower and great blue lobelia. There are a couple of side road trips to take while in the gorge, and the first is to take the loop road (Kentucky 715) near Sky Bridge. Look for vernal iris along this road. If you want to walk the Rock Bridge Trail, you can pick up trailing arbutus and much round-leaf violet and dog-tooth violet along the lower section of the trail. In early fall, you can photograph the federally endangered white-haired goldenrod at the Nada Tunnel but do not get out and walk around the cliffs where the plants are growing as this is a violation of federal law. There are plenty of plants that can be photographed without getting up along the cliffline.

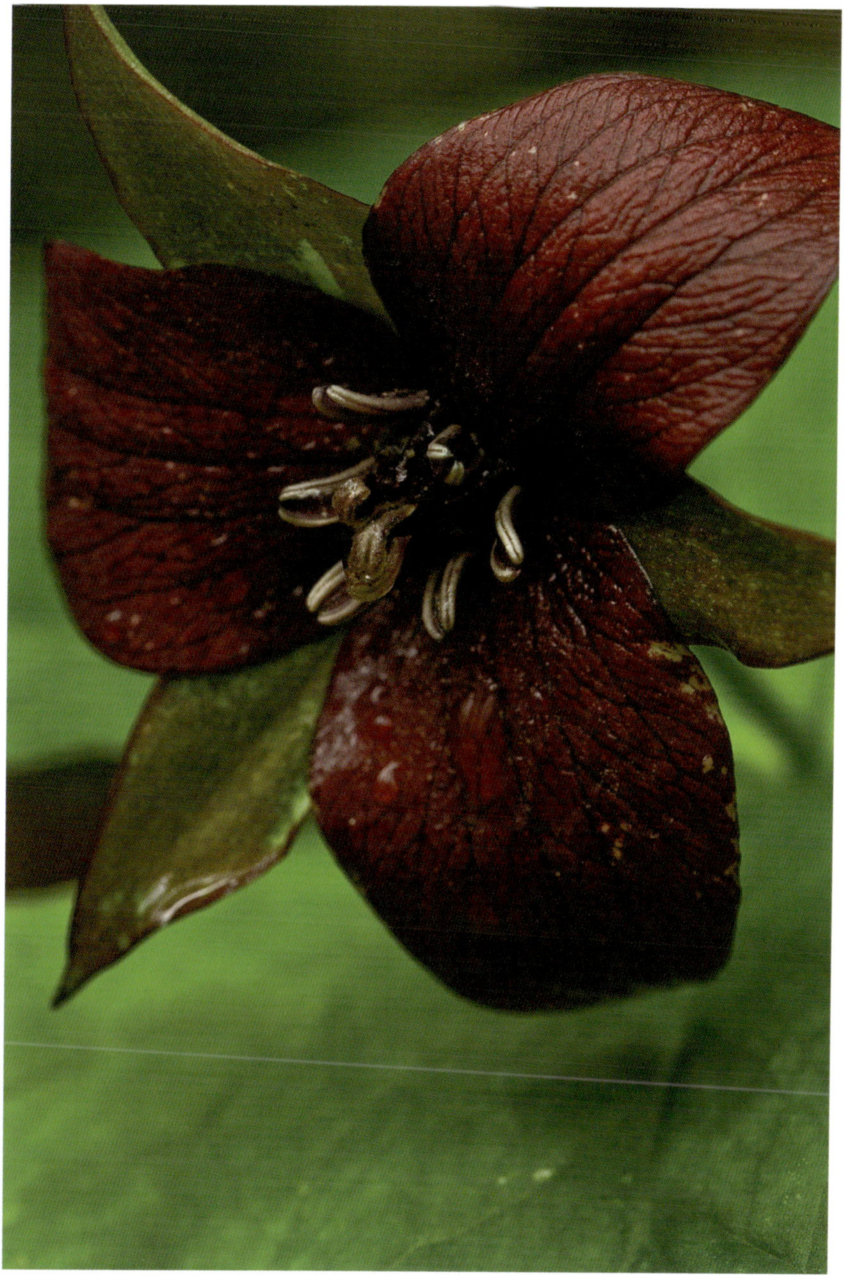

Red and southern red trilliums occur along these roads in abundance.

To Get There

Take the Mountain Parkway to the Slade exit (number 33) and turn to the east (left). That road will dead end in a tenth of a mile. Turn left (going back north) on Kentucky 15 for two miles until you reach Kentucky 77 and the community of Nada. Turn right and follow this road until it dead ends in about six miles. At two miles, you will go through the Nada Tunnel and be in the Red River Gorge. When you cross the metal bridge and come to the stop sign, turn left. This gravel road is the beginning of Forest Road 23. For lodging options see the section on Natural Bridge.

Access Ratings

Driving Trails	**EASY**

Laurel Gorge *(Elliott County)*

Laurel Creek is owned by the U.S. Corps of Engineers as a backwater of the Grayson Lake Project. The stream has its headwaters many miles west in Rowan County but empties into the Little Sandy River near the town of Sandy Hook. This largely unknown wildflower location is one of the finest in the entire eastern Kentucky region because the two mile trail is essentially flat, there are three waterfalls located adjacent to the trail, and the diversity and abundance of flowers are nothing short of spectacular. The trail begins at the Cultural and Heritage Center. Immediately outside the building is a wildflower garden that provides opportunities to photograph species like the showy orchis, trilliums, and other typical woodland species found farther down the trail. The first quarter mile of the trail is accessible to those with special needs. There is nothing spectacular about the flowers until you reach a large population of pink lady's slipper orchids growing under the cliffline on your right-hand side. Once you get past the more accessible portion, you can take an old abandoned trail that will take you down to Laurel Creek where there is a profusion of trout lilies, trilliums, and all sorts of other goodies. As you travel down the trail and get to the first stream crossing, you can follow a smallish, informal trail up to the cliffline on the right and see Dog Falls, a very ephemeral waterfall that can be spectacular if it has rained in the last day. There is a nice population of columbine up near the cliffs. If you continue on the main trail you will begin to see a profusion of large-flowered white trillium and both southern red and red trilliums mixed in with wood anemone, foamflower, violets, wild geranium, meehenia, star chickweed, dwarf crested iris, ginger, and other species. Continue along the trail and as you round the bend and the trail is close to the creek, look for large populations of bloodroot on your right. Farther down the trail you can find violet wood sorrel and once you approach the second major creek, you can go off trail up either fork, and there are seasonal or ephemeral waterfalls at the cliffline which is about a quarter-mile walk off trail. As you get back on the trail, look for cancer root on the left in this section along with valerian later in the spring.

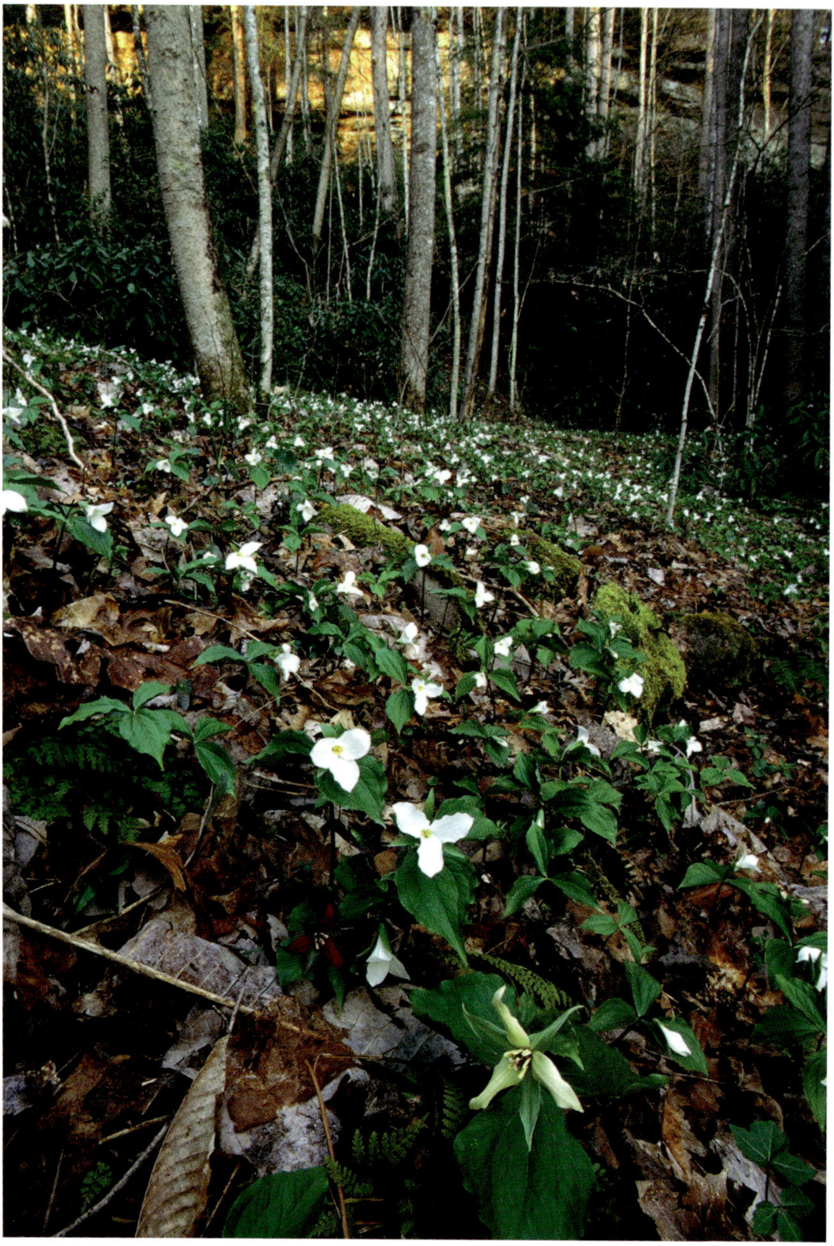

You can find large-flowered, southern red and Sulcate trillium in abundance in the Laurel Creek Gorge area. In mid-summer, the large-leaf rhododendrons can be spectacular along the trail as well.

To Get There

From I-64 take the Grayson exit (exit 172) and travel south through Grayson on Kentucky 7, past the lake and past the intersection with Kentucky 32 approximately 20 miles. You will be approximately three miles north of Sandy Hook. Slow down because you can easily miss the sign that directs you to old Kentucky 7 on your left. Take old Kentucky 7 approximately one-half mile, and look for the gated entrance to the cultural center on your right. Follow the road to the parking lot under the new Kentucky 7 highway bridge. The lodging options here include the Laurel Gorge Inn which is located just a mile south of the cultural heritage center. The next closest lodging would be at exit 172 on I-64 at Grayson.

Access Ratings

Hiking Trails	**EASY**

Carter Caves State Resort Park

This park is most well known for bat caves, which harbor thousands of federally endangered Indiana bats. There are more than 20 caves in this park but it can be a photographer's paradise with sheer limestone cliffs, bats in caves, a 30 foot tall cascade in one cavern, a picturesque lake, a handful of state listed rare plants including mountain lover, Walter's violet, Canada yew, and mountain maple, and more than 20 miles of hiking trails. While you can walk one of the many trails in the park, the absolutely best area to photograph wildflowers is along the main road. There are ample areas to pull off and park, and the left side of the road is a wonderful north-facing slope while on the right side is a small perennial stream with caves littered among the cliffline. You will notice the great populations of large-flowered trillium once you turn into the park. At mile 0.15 and 0.25, you will see large boulders on the right hand side of the road near the stream. Each of these large rocks is covered in columbine with some stonecrop and a handful of other species. If you continue up to mile 0.75, the road turns to the left and you will see a cave with cascades coming out from the base. You can park here and find wood betony, dwarf crested iris, jack-in-the-pulpit, bishop's cap, and a handful of other species. From this point to the gift shop, the flowers decline as the aspect changes and you do not have the rich mesic forest. However, right before the gift shop on the right you will see another cave. There is a wonderfully rich wildflower area here as well. The common plants you will find along the road include large populations of the large-flowered white trillium, blue cohosh, and wild ginger. You can also find typical rich forest species like blue phlox, large-flowered bellwort, pale mandarin, Solomon's and false Solomon's seal, star chickweed, rue anemone, bloodroot, stonecrop, wild geranium, and May apple. There is a small number of yellow lady's slipper orchids that occur at the Y in the road where you turn to go to the lodge or over to the maintenance or picnic areas. If you are interested in hiking, most of the same flowers can be found along the two-mile Horn Hollow trail. The park maintains a list of spring wildflowers and, as with most state parks, the naturalist can direct you to locations for specific species found on the list that are not found on the main road or on the Horn Hollow trail.

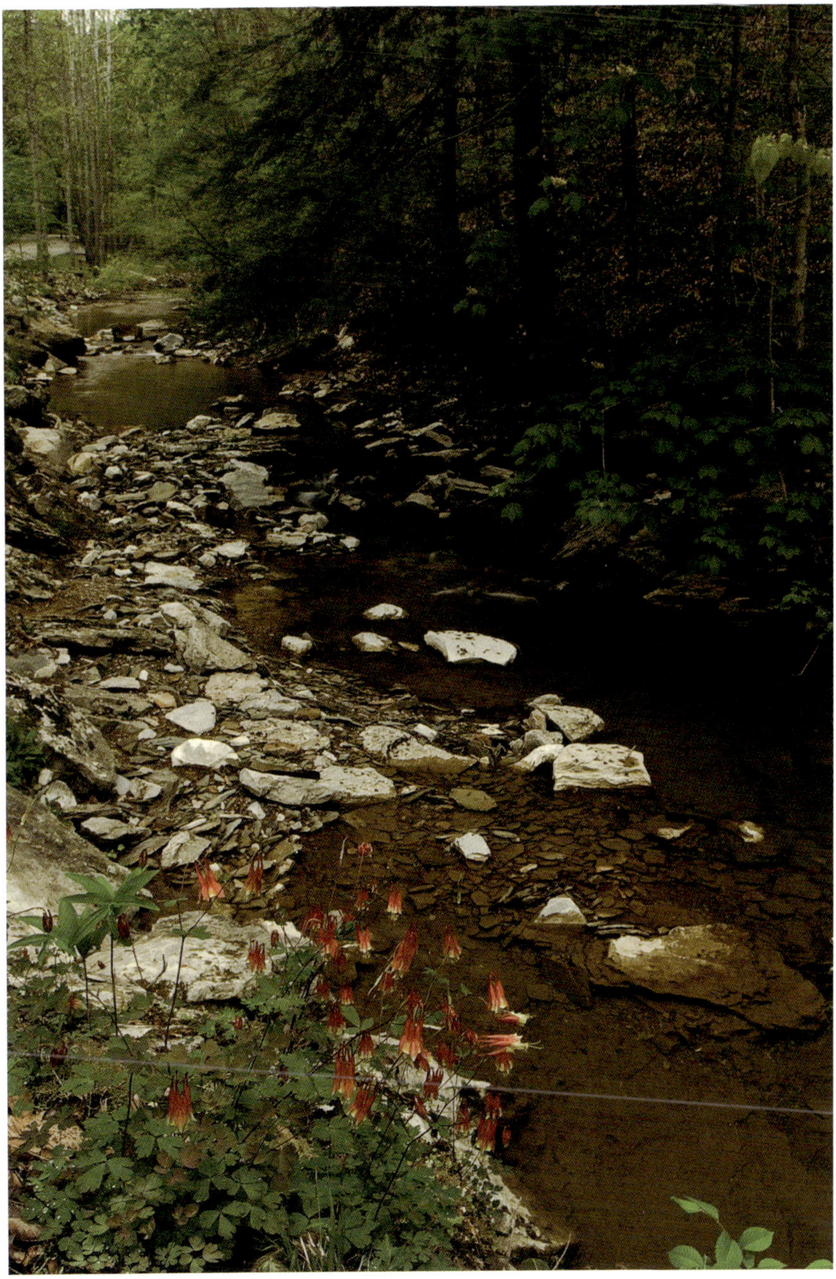

On the right hand side of the road at mile 0.15 and 0.25 are two large boulders covered with columbine.

To Get There

From I-64 take the Olive Hill exit (exit 161) traveling north on U.S. 60 and Kentucky 182. Go northeast approximately two miles until you reach the junction where Kentucky 182 and U.S. 60 split and turn left going north on Kentucky 182. Travel approximately three miles north and the park entrance will be on your left shortly after you cross Tygart's Creek. Lodging is available at the park and this is the best option. The next closest lodging would be at exit 172 on I-64 at Grayson.

Access Ratings

Driving Trails	**EASY**
Hiking Trails	**EASY**

Cumberland Falls State Resort Park

Cumberland Falls is most noted for the famous "moonbow" or rainbow that appears over the falls on nights with a full moon. The park offers more than just looking at the "Niagara of the South" which drops 68 feet into the Cumberland River. There are many photographic opportunities for other waterfalls including Dog Slaughter, Amos, and Eagle; massive clifflines and rock shelters, and of course wildflowers. The Park maintains a list of wildflowers and lists the trails that individual species can be located on. The best trail inside the park is Trail 12, The Wildflower Loop Trail. This is an easy 1.25-mile walk that begins by the swimming pool on the north side of Kentucky highway 90 and ends behind the dance pavilion. Much of this trail follows sandstone cliffs and rock houses, which means you should look for typical dry upland species like halberd violets, trailing arbutus, and little brown jug scattered all along it. One of the most spectacular aspects of this trail is walking along the cliffs and rock shelters and the multiple large populations of galax. The best flowers occur near the end of the trail which is behind the swimming pool. If you are only interested in rich mesic-type species, then you could only walk a quarter-mile down the trail starting at the back end by the pool. If you start at the beginning you will notice some Robin's plantain and several large patches of fire pink. Go down the trail a bit farther and you will descend into a small ravine. Look to the left, across the ditch, and you should find one or two showy orchis. You will then intersect with trail 1, the Sheltowee Trace; follow it for a short distance, and then veer off to the right. In this section, you will find much galax, and in the summer, there is at least one patch of rattlesnake orchid. Once you cross the paved road that leads to the sewage treatment center, the flowers get a bit better, and you can look for foamflower; two-leaf and slender toothwort; star chickweed; blunt-lobed hepatica; sweet white and long-spurred violets; dwarf crested iris; mayapple; Indian cucumber root; white baneberry; bellwort; Solomon's and false Solomon's seal; and rue anemone. There is also some wood vetch along this trail. The yellow lady's slipper orchids in the park are located along Kentucky 90 and since there is no parking along this road, you must walk down from the parking lot about 0.5 miles. As the road takes a sharp left, look for the orchids on the right side of the road. Other things to find here would be round leaf catchfly on the Eagle Falls trail and a great scenic view of Cumberland Falls. Dog Slaughter Falls is also quite scenic and there are a few pink lady's slippers on this trail. At the beginning of the trail, a few yards off the gravel road you can find one or two fairy wands. Later in the spring, the beardtongue and eared coreopsis along the gravel road, are absolutely outstanding. In addition, in the early summer, look for native wisteria, American water willow, and vetchling pea vine (on the state list of rare plants) at the base of the cliff near the falls in the sandy soils. Also look for smooth and pinxter flower azaleas in this area.

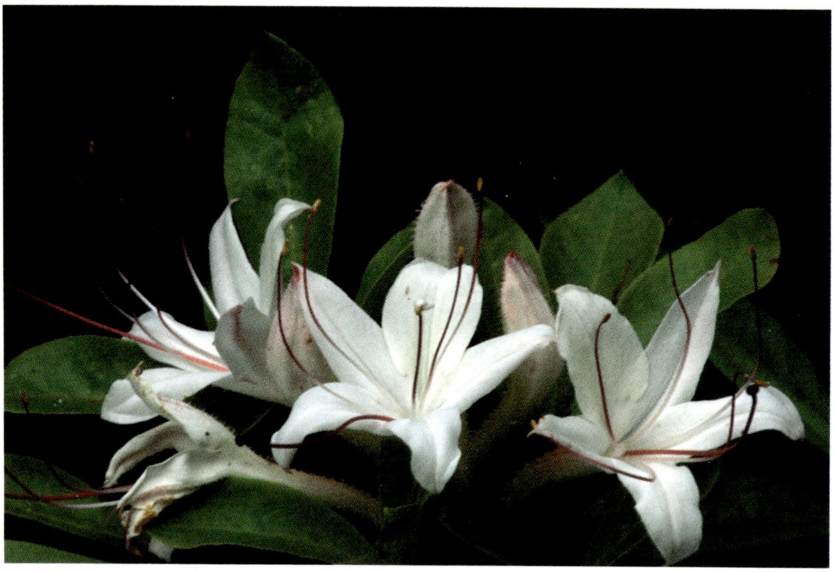

Smooth azaleas are common along many of the streams in the Cumberland Falls vicinity. Look for it to flower in May.

To Get There

From the north on I-75, take the second Corbin exit (exit 25) and travel approximately 7.5 miles turning right onto Kentucky Highway 90. From the south, take the second Williamsburg exit (exit 15) and travel north for 5.8 miles and turn left onto Kentucky Highway 90. Go west on Kentucky Highway 90 for 7.5 miles to the park. Turn left into the lodge area, and take the first left turn and an immediate left into the parking lot and park here as it is the closest point to the beginning of the trail. From US 27, take Kentucky 90 East for 13 miles and turn right into the DuPont Lodge parking area. The best place to stay is at the lodge because other lodging is limited and more than a 45 minute drive to Corbin.

Access Ratings

Hiking Trails	**EASY**

Big South Fork National River and Recreation Area

Lick Valley Trail

Lick Valley Trail, with Princess Falls and Lick Creek Falls (Forest Service trails 631 and 631A and B joining the Sheltowee Trace in the Big South Fork), is a 4.5-mile trail that may well be the most scenic hike in the entire state of Kentucky. From a wildflower photography standpoint, the rich mesic forests along the trail from the Yammacra Bridge to Princess Falls (about one mile) are the best. You can find yellow, toad shade, southern red and erect trillium; dwarf ginseng; dwarf crested iris; blue phlox; wild geranium, hepatica, yellow trout lily, pale mandarin, Solomon's and false Solomon's seal, Canada, long-spurred, smooth yellow, halberd-leaf and sweet white violets; foamflower; rue anemone; jack-in-the-pulpit; mayapple; stonecrop; and four patches of cancer root. When you get near Princess Falls, look for marsh blue violet near the stream. If you decide to continue to Lick Creek Falls, there are some nice patches of flowers for the next half mile and then you can begin to look for several nice patches of pink lady's slipper orchids. Along the side trail up to the falls is a nice patch of Clinton's white lily. At Lick Creek Falls, you can find lots of cliff meadow rue and if you decide to continue the rest of the trail, look for more pink lady's slipper orchids, round-leaf violets, and lots of cliff meadow rue. My suggestion for walking this trail is to begin in Stearns at the old Forest Service ranger station and walk the trail down. The first mile is pretty boring because it is flat and goes through several clearcuts; however, look for a huge patch of pinxter flower azalea on the right about a quarter-mile into the trail. On the road, you will find yellow star grass, sweet white violets, and lyre leaf sage. As you begin to descend after the first two sets of stairs and get over the cliffline, look for a very nice patch of pink lady's slipper orchids after you pass the massive cliff. You will then descend farther into the Lick Creek Valley and begin finding red trilliums and typical mesic forest wildflowers. On your way to this trail, look for several large patches of bird's foot violet along U.S. 27 on the east side of the road just north of Whitley City. The trail at Yahoo Falls, going on the lower trail, is also good for spring flowers (the upper portion is boring, so take the lower trail). In late July, if you take the upper trail, look for the rare lesser rattlesnake orchid growing in the moss on the side of the stepping-stones as you begin to descend prior to crossing the creek.

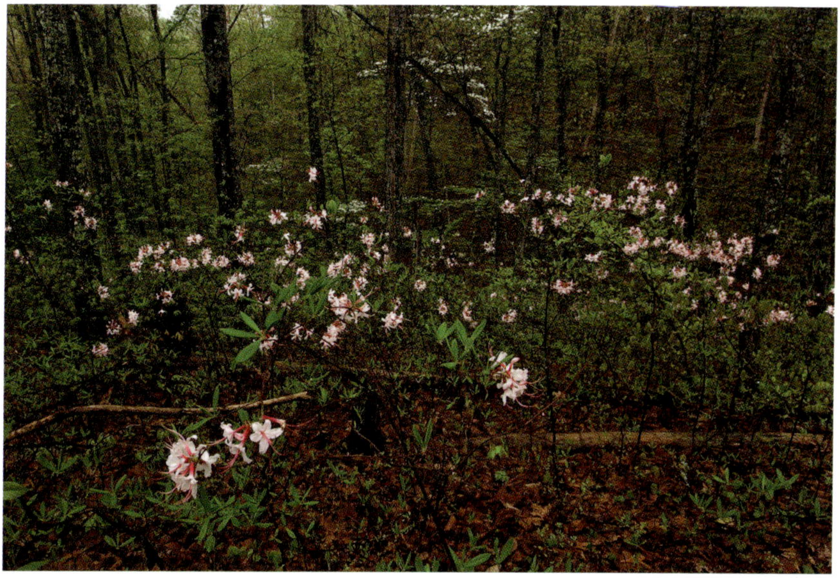

The pinxter flower azaleas occur in a large patch at the top of the Lick Creek Trail about one-half mile hike from the old Stearns ranger district office trailhead.

To Get There

From U.S. 27 take a right on Kentucky 92 into Stearns and continue past the fork in the road. Travel about three miles to the bottom of the hill and look for a sign that says Yammacra. Pull into the gravel parking lot and walk north. If you are walking the trail from the top down, follow Kentucky 1651 north (at the visitors' center) for approximately two miles and look for the road sign that says Stearns Ranger Station Road. Turn left and travel 0.1 miles to the trailhead. My recommendation for meals is to eat at either the Stearns restaurant in the old historic building or at the Coal Miner's Diner in the historic Barthel camp. Lodging is somewhat limited to the Best Western, Parkland Motel, Barthell Coal Mining Camp or the Big South Fork Motor Lodge.

Access Ratings

Hiking Trails	**MODERATE**

Big South Fork National River and Recreation Area

Bear Creek Gauging Station Trail 206

The first part of this trail heads out from the Bear Creek overlook parking area and heads south to Trail 206, which is nothing more than a gravel road taking you down to the river near the confluence of Bear Creek and the Big South Fork River. There is nothing to see or photograph along the first half-mile down to the river, but once at the river, turn to the right and follow this trail approximately two miles to Big Shoals on the west side of the river (you will hear the rushing water from the trail). Once you begin heading north on the trail, look for Cumberland spurge, on the state rare plant list, scattered along the first mile or so of the trail. You will also notice lots of dwarf ginseng and southern sessile trillium along with some southern red and large-flowered trillium. You will find that the best time for the trail is a little later in the spring when you will find three large patches of green-and-gold (the primary locations of this plant in Kentucky), star tickseed, and along the river at Big Shoals, the federally endangered Cumberland rosemary. If you cross the river, and you should be very careful here because of strong currents and the potential for deep water, you will find the entire shoals covered with blue false indigo and hairy phlox which put on quite a show. In addition you will also find Barbara's buttons and sweet fern as well as numerous other common prairie-type plants. In late summer, look for small headed blazing star on the shoals. The river is usually quite easy to cross in late July and August. In late spring to early summer (June) look for the very showy sweet mountain camellia at several locations along the trail. While in this area you should probably walk the short (0.7 mile) trail at Split Bow arch because you will find some pretty good flowers like red trillium and wild geranium in good abundance. The arch is also photogenic.

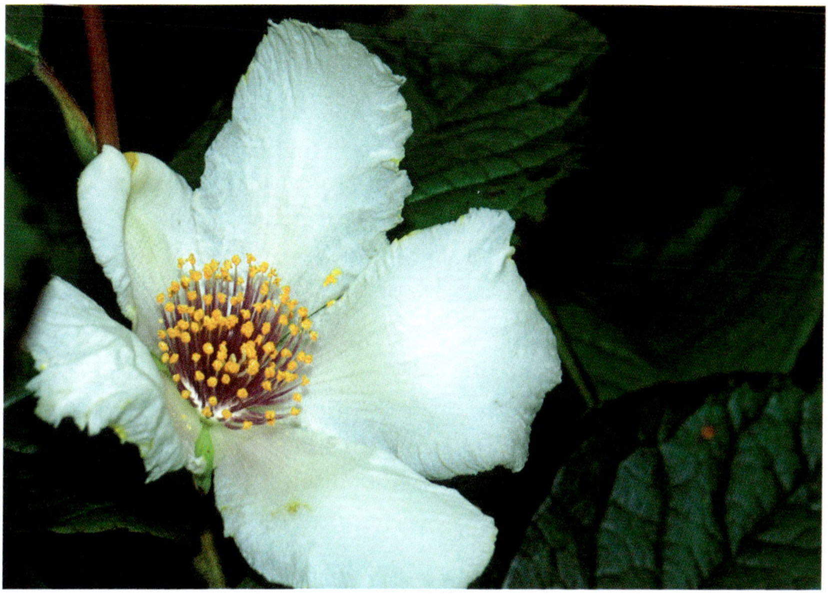

The sweet mountain camellia is a small tree with exceptional flowers that horticulturalists have been trying to breed for years. In June this trail is the best place in the state of Kentucky to find this showy species.

To Get There

Take US 27 to Stearns and turn onto KY 92. You can obtain a map and other information at the visitors center which is just a quarter mile from US 27 on KY 92. If going to the Bear Creek Overlook, take US 27 south of Stearns and turn onto KY 1470 going west until you reach the park border and keep going straight, following the brown signs to the overlook parking area. The road down to the hiking/horseback trail is to the south about one-quarter mile.

Access Ratings

Hiking Trails **MODERATE**

Bee Rock, Rockcastle River, Daniel Boone National Forest

This is one of my absolute favorite trails because it is not heavily traveled. There are excellent flowers along this trail as well as the very scenic Rockcastle River. Because the campground is not yet open for the season when the spring flowers are at their peak, you must park at the gate and walk through the campground. Look for blue phlox, wood vetch, and golden ragwort as you walk through this area. Once you enter the trail at the end of the campground, there isn't much exciting in the first 100 yards, but when the trail takes a bend to the left and it appears to split, just after a small ravine where there are many large boulders on the left, look on the left side for a small population of wood anemone. The next thing of interest will be a large patch of blue phlox at about a quarter of a mile down the trail. Once you get to marker 0.5, the excitement really begins with numerous large patches of wild geranium and Jacob's ladder, some as large as a quarter of an acre. Beginning in this section, you can find rocks literally covered with stonecrop; hepatica; halberd-leaf, Canada, sweet white, common blue, and long-spurred violets; yellow trout lilies; foamflower; red trillium; bishop's cap; rue anemone; star chickweed; large-flowered bellwort; pale mandarin; Allegheny spurge; and baneberry. One of the most significant flowers along this trail is a large population of dwarf ginseng and a handful of goldenseal. Later in the spring around mid-May, walk the first two miles of the trail and where it takes a sharp bend to the left, you will notice where a makeshift trail heads off to the right through some hemlock trees. This little trail will lead you to a cobble or gravel bar at the head of the narrows. On this gravel bar, you will find golden Alexanders and lots of blue false indigo and the view of the river and flowers is nothing short of spectacular. Later in the season in July, there is a nice population of tassel-rue. About this time, you can also look for the wild bean at various places in the rocky areas along the banks of the Rockcastle River. Other prairie- or open-type flowers that can be found here include things like goats rue, flowering spurge, pencil flower, and in the spring, lots of smooth azalea.

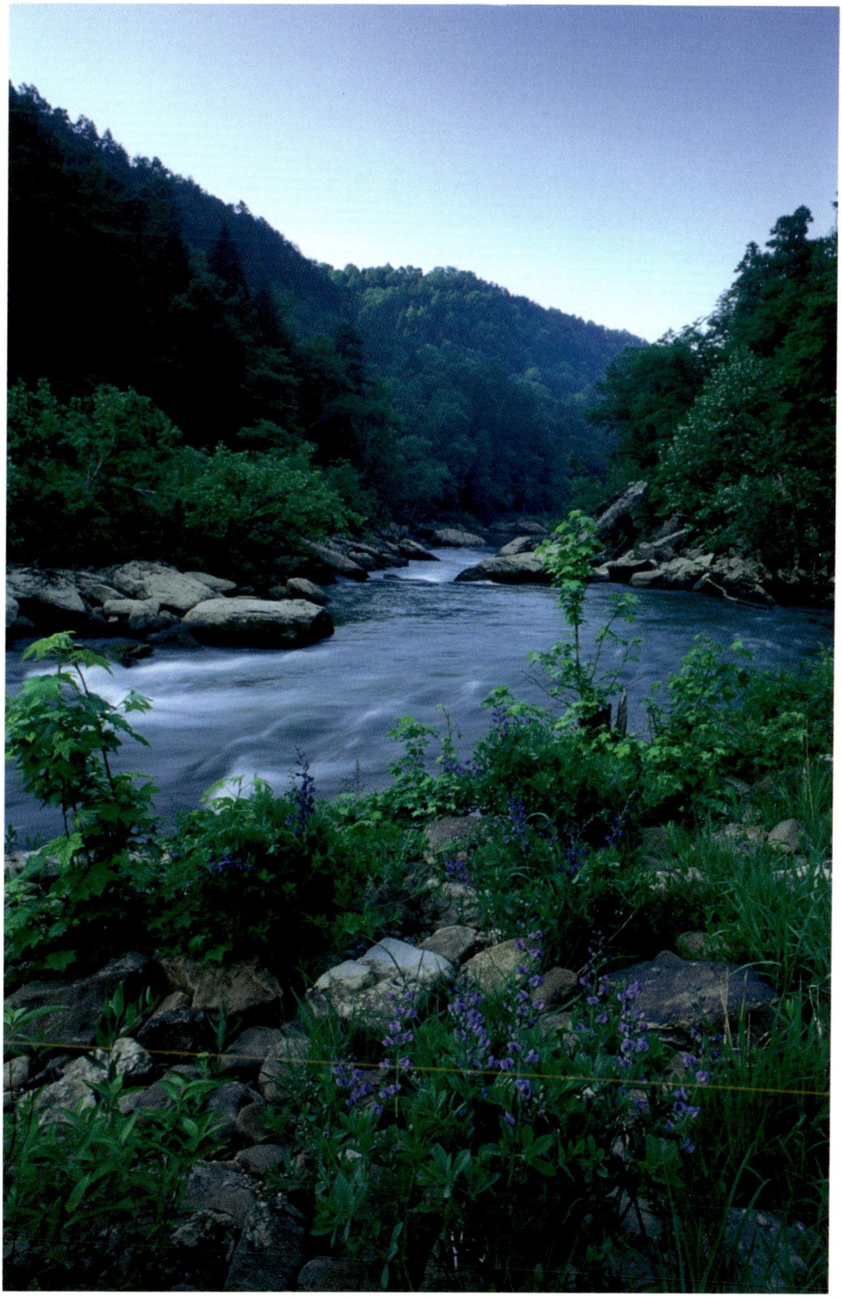

There is an outstanding gravel/cobble bar located two miles from the trailhead that has an outstanding display of blue false indigo in mid-May.

To Get There

From I-75 Take exit 38 (Kentucky 192) west for approximately 18 miles. Cross the Rockcastle River Bridge, and turn right into the campground. From Somerset, take Kentucky 192 East from the bypass 22 miles and turn right into the campground. Make sure you are on the Pulaski County side, not the Laurel County side (south or east). If you go in the spring, you will need to park at the gate by the walking bridge over the river that connects the two campgrounds. The closest place for food and lodging will be in either London or Somerset and either one will be at least a 30-minute drive to this site. A quick web search will reveal many places, although for lunch you can hit the little diner on Kentucky 1193 just south of the intersection of Kentucky 192 and Kentucky 1193 at Bald Rock.

Access Ratings

Hiking Trails	**EASY**

Anglin Falls

This 124-acre state nature preserve is named for the former president of Berea College, John B. Stephenson. The wildflowers in the gorge are spectacular along this one mile walk to the 75 foot waterfall that is seasonal and photogenic after a good, heavy rain. The first one-third section of the trail is mostly dominated by ground cedar and has few flowers, but look for several crane fly orchids (they flower in July) and some common woodland flowers like blue phlox and star chickweed. Once you cross Anglin Creek and begin ascending the hill, look on both sides of the trail for large groupings of southern red and red trillium, both the maroon and cream forms. There is tremendous potential for shots of diverse groups of wildflowers with clifflines or boulders in the backdrop and trilliums or other flowers in the foreground. There are also some excellent opportunities for photographing clusters of flowers in and among the rock boulders, especially near the top of the trail by the waterfall. As you proceed up the hill, look for several very nice large clusters of puttyroot orchid, and as you approach the waterfall, there is a significant population of American columbine. This is a very rich site, and you can expect large populations of harbinger of spring, sharp-lobed hepatica, blue woodland phlox and other common spring ephemerals. I found nice populations of rue anemone, small-flowered bellwort (near and along the rock boulders), large clusters of sedum on the boulders, bishop's cap, long-spurred, yellow woodland, and Canada violets, false and true Solomon's seal, wild ginger, dwarf larkspur, blue cohosh, baneberry (doll's eyes), Dutchman's breeches, squirrel corn, bloodroot, star chickweed, yellow trout lilies, foamflower, May apple, yellow mandarin, wild geranium, synandra, and sweet cicely. There is one patch of dwarf crested iris and a few wild leeks (ramps) and celandine poppy, but they are not abundant.

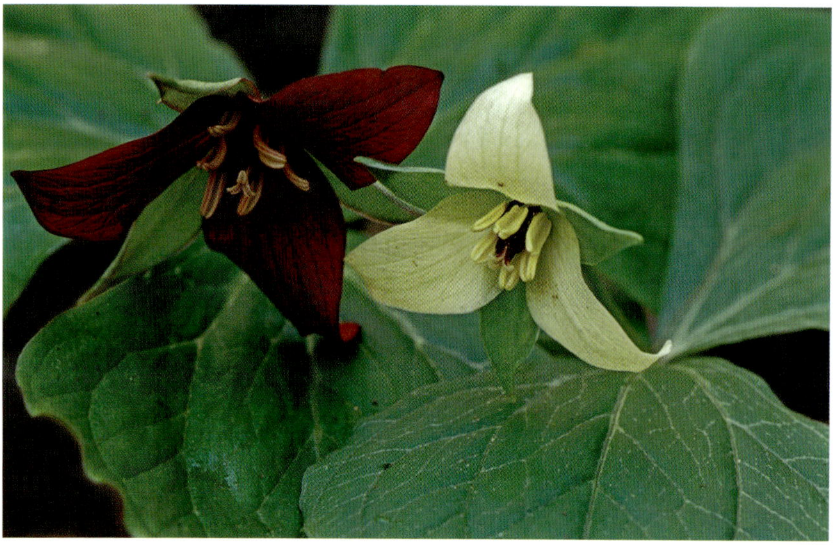

Both the maroon and cream color forms of southern red trillium can be found growing together.

To Get There

From the center of Berea (Boone Tavern and Hotel) travel five miles east on Kentucky 21 until the road dead ends. Turn right onto U.S. 421 South and drive 2.6 miles up Big Hill. Look for Burnt Ridge Road on your right after you reach the top of the hill. Turn right and drive 0.2 miles. Turn left onto Himanns Fork Road, and travel 3.4 miles. At this point, look for a red brick house on the right, and in 0.1 miles take a hard, sharp left onto Anglin Falls Road. Travel about 0.9 miles, and look for a sign that says Anglin Falls next to a mailbox (just before Anglin Creek). Turn left into the parking lot. The signage to this preserve is poor and I recommend you look at a county map or gazetteer map because there is an alternative route that is a bit easier to follow. I would recommend staying at the historic Boone Hotel and eat at the tavern. There is also a good Italian restaurant, Papalleno's and the coffee shop next to the tavern is a great place for breakfast or lunch. There are other lodging or meal options close to Interstate 75. While in town make sure to check the variety of artisan and craftsman shops in Old Town or at the Kentucky Artisan Center (I-75 exit 77).

Access Ratings

Hiking Trails	EASY

Central Kentucky

Raven Run Nature Sanctuary *(Fayette County)*

This 734-acre city nature preserve is known throughout Kentucky and much of the eastern United States for its outstanding display of blue-eyed Mary flowers that peak in mid-April. In a good year, more than 40 acres of the ground are literally carpeted blue and white. More than 600 species of plants have been observed in the park, and it has many outstanding populations of twinleaf, bloodroot, yellow and white trout lilies, false rue anemone and dwarf larkspur. The preserve is bounded by Raven Run Creek on the north and Chandler Creek on the south. There is a small overlook (with tons of red columbine surrounding the rocks that are dotted with fossil coral and nautilus) where a small section of palisades can be viewed. Raven Run has more than 10 miles of trails, but from a wildflower photography standpoint, the Main Trail (red) and the Flower Bowl Trail (yellow) are really the best, hands down.

After checking in at the nature center, the quickest way to the good flower patches is to take the Meadow Trail to point E on the red trail. At this point, take a right to points D and C and then the short hop to the overlook. If you want to photograph some excellent patches of sharp-lobed hepatica, fire pink, Dutchman's breeches, and twinleaf, take a sharp right at point C, and return up the trail about 0.2 miles where you will see large numbers of early saxifrage growing out of the moss in the rocks along the trail. As you return to point C, turn left and continue on the red trail (look for white, blue and pink colored hepatica, harbinger of spring, and yellow trout lilies in March) until you reach point D. At this point take the yellow trail into the flower bowl. You can spend the remainder of the day in this area alone as you will find not only the blue-eyed Mary flowers, but also false rue and rue anemone, dwarf larkspur, wood poppy, Jacob's ladder, wild ginger, common blue, yellow woodland, and cream violets, wild blue phlox, stonecrop, several early mustards and buttercups, and in selected locations some nodding or bent trillium. The best place to see these trilliums is to take the spur trail that goes down slope to Raven Run Creek; you will find both the white and maroon forms. In late spring, on the red trail from points F to G is an outstanding display of wild hyacinth. As you continue out of the flower bowl on the yellow trail back to where it connects with the red trail, look for some nice patches of Dutchman's breeches, squirrel corn, yellow corydalis, wood poppy and twinleaf until you reach the power-line opening. Just prior to and immediately after the power-line opening look for large populations of bloodroot and twinleaf. Continue on the red trail until you hit point K, and look for Allegheny spurge in this area. Once you reach Evan's Mill there is a nice convergence of two streams and a little cascade. Around this area and up to the power-line cut, look for sharp-lobed hepatica, and near the ridge, white trout lilies. As you continue on the red trail from this point you are mostly going to see bloodroot and fewer numbers of flowers that you have observed in the other areas of the park. At point N you can get back onto the Meadow Trail and return to the nature center.

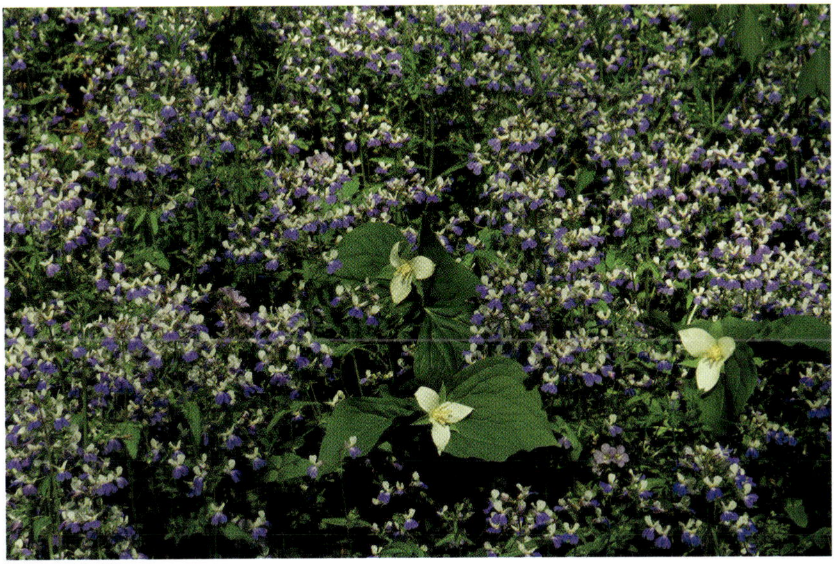

Raven Run is known for the spectacular display of blue-eyed Mary in mid-April. The entire flower bowl area of this nature preserve is carpeted with these flowers shown here with nodding trillium and Jacob's ladder.

CENTRAL

To Get There

Take Richmond Road south from Lexington until you reach U.S. 25 where you will see Jacobson Park on your left. Turn right at the light and proceed 3.5 miles to Jack's Creek Pike. Continue on Jack's Creek Pike for approximately 5.5 miles, and you will see the large fenced entrance on the left. Drive about 0.4 miles to the parking area on the right. Proceed to the nature center where you can obtain specific information about what is blooming and where. This is also an excellent location to bring a larger lens with you, as deer and turkey are quite abundant and used to people. The hours of operation are basically from 9 a.m. until 5 p.m. but there are extended hours during some seasons. Check the Lexington Fayette Urban County Government Web site for specific information and details. Lodging and meal opportunities are almost unlimited in the Lexington area but the closest facilities will be at Exit 104 on I-75.

Access Ratings

Hiking Trails	**EASY to MODERATE**

Tom Dorman State Nature Preserve *(Garrard County)*

Originally called the Palisades State Nature Preserve, this little gem is one of the best places to get a view of the 200- to 300-foot tall towering cliffs called the Kentucky River Palisades. These are the oldest exposed rocks in the state of Kentucky, and the rich limestone soils give rise to an exceptional spring flower display. While this preserve does not have the abundance of blue-eyed Mary that you find at Raven Run, it does have a similar flora, and it is more accessible with longer hours, which means more hours for photography than Raven Run. From the parking lot, take the Palisades trail to the left for the best flower displays. You will not find much of anything of interest for the first quarter-mile but once you cross the head of two drainages and loop toward the river down the slope the flowers begin to appear it seems almost out of nowhere. Look for all the typical bluegrass spring species like bloodroot, yellow corydalis, squirrel corn, Dutchman's breeches, sessile trillium, wood poppies, Jacob's ladder, false rue anemone, and rue anemone. The best flowers are on the slope down to the river and up the drainage, and once you cross the drainage into the flats, there is not much of anything interesting unless you are interested in seeing the old broken structures and Knight's Ferry Landing on the river. The trail on the other side going up holds nothing of great interest from a photographic standpoint.

CENTRAL

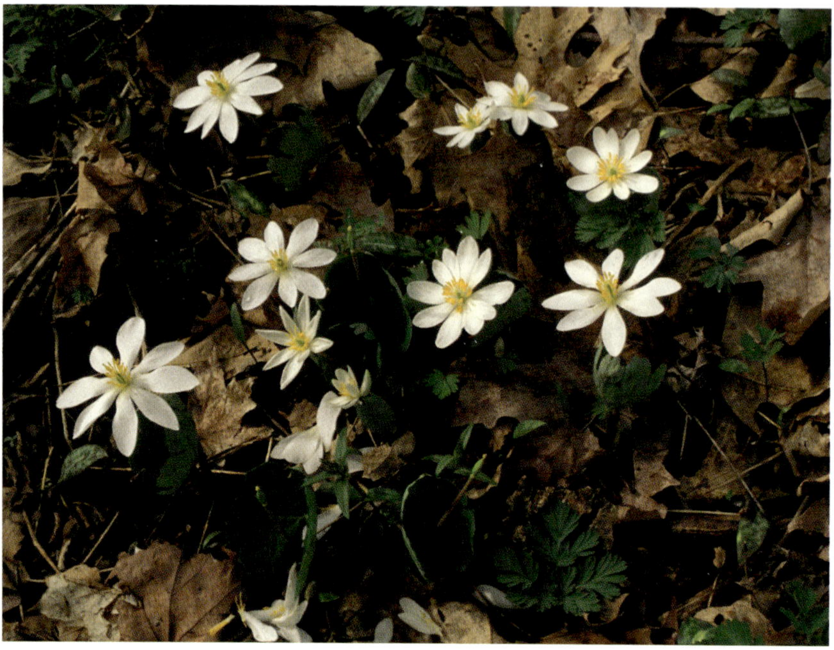

Bloodroot grows in profusion in the forests along the palisades of Central Kentucky.

To Get There

From Nicholasville take U.S. 27 South for nine miles until you cross the Kentucky River. Continue another 1.25 miles, and then turn right onto Kentucky 1845 traveling west. Continue for one mile and turn right on Jess Brim Road (look for Lambert's Chapel at the intersection). Continue down this road for 0.75 miles (stay straight), and park in the gravel lot. Lodging is available in Nicholasville at the Super 8 or Holiday Inn Express. To experience some local food check out the Oak Street Diner or JD Legends.

Access Ratings

Hiking Trails	**EASY**

University of Kentucky Arboretum and Matthews Garden

Wildflower photographers might not think of finding great flowers in the middle of Lexington, but they would be wrong. There are two wonderful locations on the University of Kentucky campus that provide numerous photographic possibilities for either spring woodland wildflowers (Matthews Garden) or Summer/Fall prairie flowers including some very rare species in the state. The Matthews Garden is located at the corner of Limestone Street and Washington Avenue behind an old house. The garden is bordered by a white fence, and the postage-stamp-size garden is located behind the fence. Don't let the size of the garden discourage you because there are more than a hundred species of native woodland wildflowers including trout lilies, bloodroot, trilliums, Jacob's ladder, twinleaf, Virginia bluebells, rue and false rue anemone, wild geranium, all the native azaleas, purple phacelia, shooting star, wood poppies, foamflower and lots more.

The other great location for shooting summer or prairie flowers is the Lexington Fayette Urban County Government-University of Kentucky arboretum or state botanical garden located on Alumni Drive across from Commonwealth Stadium. If you want to shoot spring flowers in a more natural setting, there is a remnant 40-acre woodlot where you can find sessile trillium and a handful of other spring flowers. However, the showcase of the arboretum is the "Walk across Kentucky," specifically the Pennyrile region prairie gardens. Here you will have access to more than 100 species of prairie flowers, including some that are very rare in Kentucky. Don't limit yourself just to flowers, because all along the walk you can find many woody species, some of them like September elm, Allegheny chinquapin, white walnut, and water locust, are on the official list of rare, threatened, and endangered species in Kentucky. The entire walk is about two miles long and paved. Additional photographic opportunities also exist in the more formal or horticultural gardens located behind the Dorotha Smith Oatts Visitors Center. In the Pennyrile prairie gardens, the rare species you can photograph include sweet Susan, purple prairie clover, cream wild indigo, blue false indigo var. minor, Price's aster, silphium sunflower, compass plant, and western silky aster. More common prairie species like New England aster, purple coneflower, various goldenrods, bee balm, and rattlesnake master are all accessible in these gardens. The arboretum is open from dawn to dusk daily every single day of the year.

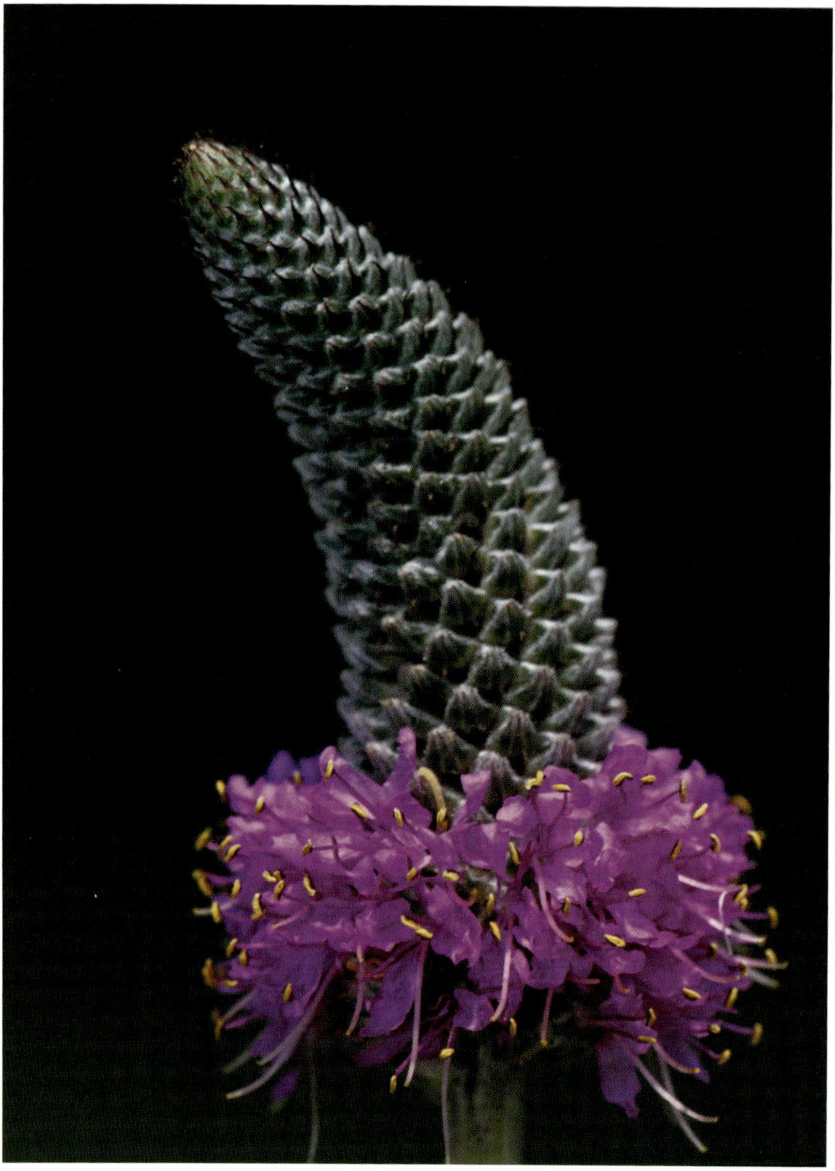

Purple prairie clover is just one of the rare wildflowers that can be found in the Pennyrile prairie gardens in the walk across Kentucky at the UK Arboretum.

To Get There

From I-64/75 take the Newtown Pike exit (exit 115), and turn towards town. Follow Newtown Pike (Kentucky 922) 3.3 miles to W. Main Street. At West Main Street, turn left at the light and go 0.6 miles to South Upper Street. Turn right. Continue straight (this street will turn into South Limestone Street or U.S. 27) for 0.8 miles to Washington Avenue. Matthews Garden will be on your left. Continue an additional 0.3 miles to Alumni Drive (you will see Commonwealth Stadium on your left) and turn left on Alumni at the light (the senior citizens center is located on the left corner). Go 0.7 miles, and the Arboretum entrance is on the right.

Access Ratings

Hiking Trails	**EASY**

Cherokee Park *(Louisville)*

Finding the spring wildflowers at Cherokee Park isn't all that difficult, and the display can be outstanding in the spring and again in late summer (August). Once you parked at the junction of Cochran Road and Scenic Loop, head across the road on the asphalt trail, and cross the wooden bridge over Beargrass Creek. Take an immediate left onto a dirt trail that parallels the creek. You will notice a large population of large-flowered bellwort. Continue down this trail for 50 yards or so and look for hepatica and twinleaf. On the rocks, you will find some columbine and stonecrop. Turn around and before you get to the asphalt trail, look to the left on the rise, and you will see the largest patch of rue anemone in the park. Then go back to the asphalt and begin a slow walk along this trail. You will notice on your left the woods, which are in the process of being restored; bush honeysuckle, garlic mustard, and other exotics are being removed, and the native species are coming back in droves. As you get about 40 yards down, you will notice some Virginia bluebells on both sides of the trail, and one white plant is on the right in a cluster of typical blue-flowered ones. Once you get to the spring, turn around and head back, up to the dirt footpath on the right (or continue on up the hill and cross the road to Wildflower Hill). As you walk through this section you will notice that there are some large patches of sessile trillium (the nodding or bent trillium occurs in four or five patches that are seen from the asphalt trail or this footpath) and blue cohosh. Also notice in places that the ground is literally carpeted with lavender waterleaf. Other species to look for include Dutchman's breeches, squirrel corn, harbinger of spring, rue anemone, false rue anemone, yellow trout lily, cut-leaf toothwort, May apple, twinleaf, bloodroot, bent trillium, Solomon's and false Solomon's seal, dwarf larkspur, stonecrop, early meadow rue, early spiderwort, wild ginger, celandine poppy, star chickweed, Jacob's ladder, Jack-in-the-pulpit, and ramps or wild leeks. In summer near the spring area growing in and around the ephemeral stream you can find arrowhead, peltandra, southern blue flag iris, Joe-Pye-weed, cardinal flower, great blue lobelia, and in patches along the path, look for wild golden glow, purple coneflowers, ironweed, and other summer blooming species. One last area to look for in this park; after returning to the main road take a right and follow the road for 20 yards or so to where Beargrass Creek crosses the Scenic Loop you will find a trail on your left. Take that a few yards, and you will notice a very large patch of wild hyacinth.

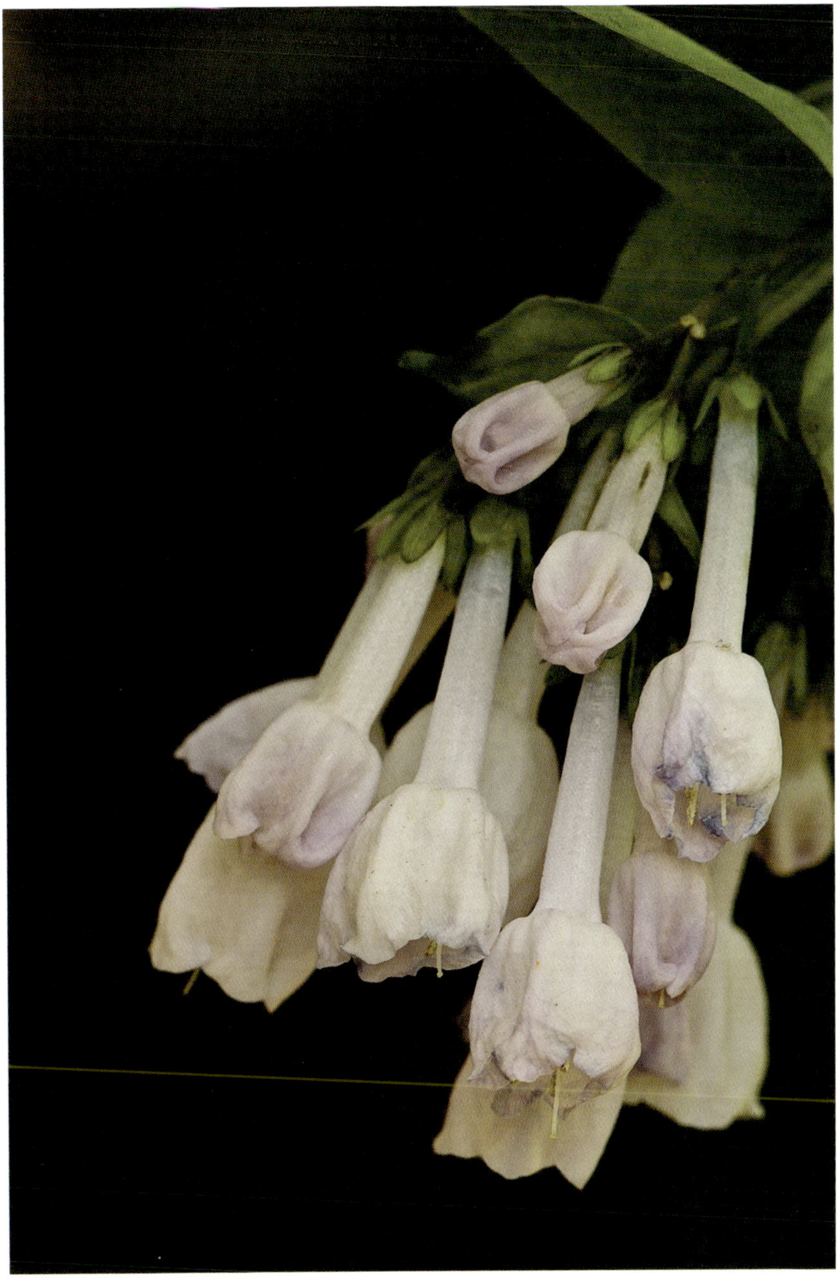

Light colored Virginia bluebells occur in one location along the paved trail.

CENTRAL

CENTRAL

To Get There

Take the Grinstead Drive exit from I-64 (exit 8), and turn to the south going under the freeway. When you come to the first light, which is Lexington Road, take a left and go about a quarter-mile up the hill to Cochran Road and turn right into the park. You can park at the bottom of the hill on the right where Cochran Road and Scenic Loop intersect.

Access Ratings

Hiking Trails	**EASY**

Tioga Falls

You would think the waterfall is the most significant feature of this trail, and you would be correct. But the lower trail falls hosts a wide variety of spring flowers, and the hills come alive in mid- to late-April. In early spring, I would recommend taking the high trail part of the loop to the falls because there is an incredible amount of bloodroot in many nice clusters of 10 to 20 flowers and some early meadow rue along the rocks. You will also see some yellow trout lilies on the upper trail. In late spring, the upper trail isn't very good, but the lower trail is good. The best flowers begin just past the overhead rail bridge with a decent patch of dwarf larkspur on the left. At this point you will begin to see several large patches of wild ginger and nodding trillium in groups of two to ten scattered about the trail all the way to the falls. The best patches of trillium occur just before you reach the falls. About halfway down the trail on the left, you will notice the remains of an old stone structure, and there is a nice patch of goldenseal on the left in this area. Other plants of note along the trail include a couple of patches of celandine or wood poppies, a large number of white baneberry (doll's eyes), Canada and yellow violets, Solomon's and false Solomon's seal, and rocks covered with stonecrop. Near the waterfall, on the south side (you have to cross the creek) are several nice patches of goldenseal. There is also quite a bit of bladder pod (tree or shrub) scattered along the trail.

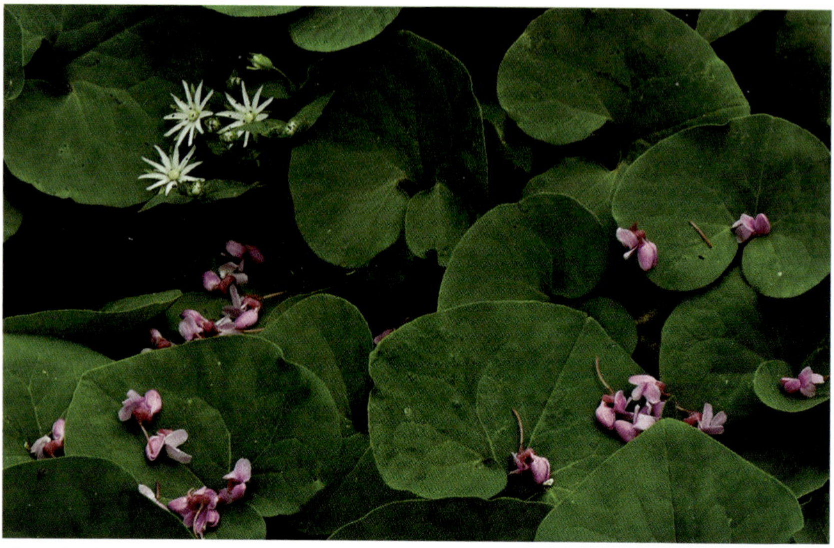

Star chickweed growing in wild ginger near the creek.

To Get There

From the Gene Snyder Freeway (I-265) in Louisville take the 31 West south exit (also called Fort Knox or Dixie Highway exit 1) and travel about eight miles to community of Westpoint. Once you have crossed the Salt River and into Hardin County look for a brown sign that says "Bridges to the Past" and turn left (you will also notice signs for the River of Life Church). Go one mile and park at the entrance of the hiking trails, or if you want to walk only the lower trail, turn right, and the road dead ends in a half mile with a turnaround. Park here and walk the trail from this point. From south I-65 take the Joe Prather Highway exit (exit 102) and turn to the west (left off the ramp). Continue to 31 West and turn right. Follow 31 West, north through Muldraugh. When you get to the bottom of Muldraugh Hill, begin to look for the brown sign that says "Bridges to the Past", and turn right. There are many places to stay close to this area in Louisville, Radcliff, Vine Grove, or Fort Knox.

Access Ratings

Hiking Trails	**EASY to MODERATE**

Boone County Cliffs

Boone County Cliffs Nature Preserve is a 74-acre area owned by the Nature Conservancy but is a dedicated nature preserve within the Kentucky Nature Preserves Commission system. The trail is about 2.4 miles long, but the first third is the only part that is worthy of wildflower photography. The preserve gets its name from the 20- to 40-foot tall glacial conglomerates (smallish rock outcrops or "cliffs"), and on the top of the first one on the trail is a population of bloodroot that is truly outstanding. If you stay on the trail a bit farther, you will come into a population of near old-growth beech trees that is photogenic. The best flower photography occurs from the parking lot to the top of the hill, and make sure you stay on the trail as the stream contains some rare creatures, which is one reason the preserve was created. You will find all the typical bluegrass spring species on this preserve including yellow corydalis, white trout lilies, rue anemone, wild ginger, baneberry, dwarf larkspur, squirrel corn, Dutchman's breeches, bloodroot, wood poppies, violets, waterleaf, bishop's cap, blue phlox, and, on the rocks early saxifrage and stonecrop. On the route up to the preserve along Middle Creek Road look for large patches of blue-eyed Mary. In late spring, you can take a quick two-mile diversion to Dinsmore Woods to photograph the federally endangered running buffalo clover which occurs at the beginning of the trail behind the buildings. Unfortunately, the wildflowers in both of these properties are declining because two invasive exotic plants, annual chickweed and garlic mustard, are crowding them out and it will only be a matter of time before these properties are no longer on the list of outstanding areas.

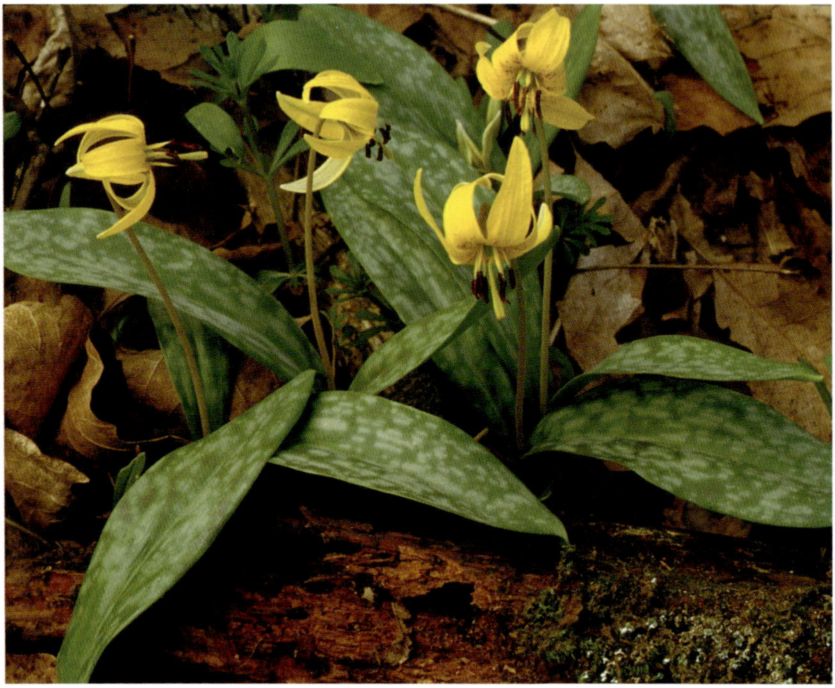

Yellow trout lilies occur in abundance and flower in March or early-April.

To Get There

From I-75 take the Burlington/Florence Kentucky Highway 18 exit (exit 181) and go west for 11 miles (through the town of Burlington) to Middle Creek Road on your left. Turn left, and go 1.9 miles to the parking area, which is on your left. The lodging and meal opportunities for northern Kentucky are almost unlimited and the closest food and lodging will be at Exit 181.

Access Ratings

Hiking Trails	**MODERATE**

Highland Cemetery

Who would think that in the middle of the Cincinnati/northern Kentucky suburbs of Fort Mitchell you would find a 150-acre woodland with four miles of hiking trails? Highland Cemetery, established in 1869, totals more than 250 acres. Highland Cemetery has the typical spring bluegrass wildflowers, and they occur in the middle of a city, which means that you will hear the sounds of traffic as you walk the trails in this urban wooded oasis. As you begin heading down the trail from the trailhead, you will notice some nice large patches of yellow trout lilies, and later in the spring look for the uncommon synandra in this upper portion of the trail. You will then stay on the yellow trail, and the most striking aspect at this point is that the ground is carpeted with Dutchman's breeches. There is the usual cut-leaf toothwort and sessile trillium in this section as well. The most abundant flower here, the white trout lily, is the next thing you will notice, and the first large patch occurs at the junction of trails 1 and 3 just before you cross the stream on the left. There are several other large patches in the back that are more than an acre in size. The best flowers occur on the trail that hugs the creek (the lower section). Look for blue phlox, squirrel corn, Jacob's ladder, wood poppies, and yellow, blue and white violets. When you get to trail 3, take the lower route, and you will see some nice patches of bloodroot; on the upper section of this trail, there is a large number of wild hyacinth, although I do not know how well they flower because the deer have nibbled them down pretty seriously. Continue down trail 3 and onto trail 4 where you will find a large patch of white trout lilies and several nice patches of bloodroot. There is no question that the best flower display occurs along trails 4 and 5. When you get to trail 5, look for a small amount of twinleaf and nodding trillium. This is the only place I found rue anemone on the property. Other good things on trail 5 include jack-in-the-pulpit, Solomon's and false Solomon's seal, blue cohosh, and plants typical on the remainder of the trails – squirrel corn, yellow corydalis, spring beauty, lavender waterleaf, mayapple, wild ginger, golden ragwort, and harbinger of spring. The waterfalls on trail 5 are nothing to write home about but the water drops a couple of feet over a small cascade which can be a nice retreat sitting on one of the numerous benches in that area.

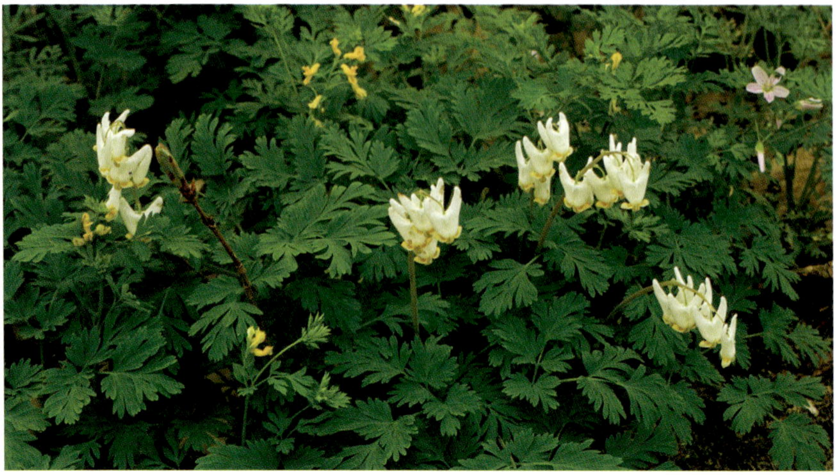

Dutchman's breeches, yellow corydalis and spring beauties abound at this location.

To Get There

Take I-75/71 to the Fort Mitchell Dixie Highway exit (exit 188). From the exit ramp coming from the south, turn right and you will see the cemetery right in front of you. Turn left into the property. Coming from the north, turn left (headed south), cross over the interstate, and take the first left into the cemetery. Once in the cemetery, stay on the main road, but take all right-hand roads and you will head down a slight hill (notice the woods on your left). You can park at the white sign (kiosk) on the left side of the road. This is the trailhead. Since this is private property, the cemetery does accept donations to defray expenses, and there are brochures highlighting the common spring flowers at this kiosk.

Access Ratings

Hiking Trails	**EASY**

Western Kentucky

WESTERN

Mammoth Cave

Writing about this International Bio-reserve Site is easy because my friend Randy Seymour has written a wonderful book, *The Wildflowers of Mammoth Cave National Park* and Appendix B, the flower-hunting guide, has which species of flowers can be found on which trails. As for photography, I chose only two locations in the park, both very good and easily accessible. One is a gravel road, Ugly Creek, on the north end of the park, and the other, Cedar Sink Trail, is on the southern end and is a short hiking trail to the most scenic place in the entire park. There are approximately 870 plant species found in the park, and at least 21 state rare species are found within the park. There is one species, uncommon in Kentucky, the striped gentian that can be found flowering in October along the back portion of the Sloan's Pond trail right of Kentucky Highway 70. For more detailed information other than the two areas I mention, just look through Randy's book for specifics.

Mammoth Cave

Cedar Sink

As you park in the lot and begin down the trail you probably are thinking, "This is one of the best wildflower trails"? Ah, first looks can be deceiving. This 0.8-mile trial is mostly level until you get to Cedar Sink, the largest sinkhole in Mammoth Cave; it is so large you do not even get the sense that you are in a sinkhole. As you begin down the gravel path, look for partridge berry, cinquefoil, wild strawberry, and some goldenseal in the first stretches. Then when you get to the first footbridge that crosses an ephemeral stream, you will find a great abundance of Jacob's ladder, rue anemone, spring beauties, and foamflower. As you travel farther down the trail and pass the dense cedar thicket on a rise begin to look for wild geranium, lyre leaf sage, wild comfrey, jack-in-the-pulpit, dwarf larkspur, cut-leaf toothwort and several nice populations of the uncommon toothwort or fork leaf toothwort and two-leafed and slender toothwort. Close to the cedar forest, you will notice one hillside that is literally covered with wild geranium, probably an acre of more. Once you reach the overlook at the sinkhole look for a few shooting stars to the right of the wooden structure. You will now begin descending into the sink, and once you reach the iron stairs you will notice the cliffs, moss-covered rocks, a stream coming out of the base of the cliff, and lots of early saxifrage. At this point, you will observe a very rich, mesic and quite scenic forest with white stonecrop on the rocks and typical limestone spring flowers including sessile and bent or nodding trillium, Dutchman's breeches, squirrel corn, celandine poppy, yellow trout lilies, early spiderwort, wild ginger and yellow corydalis. As you walk down the trail just before the other overlook looking back towards the previous overlook on the top of the cliff you will find a patch of more than 30 putty-root orchids. Other spring flowers in these rich woods include columbine and hairy alumroot on the cliffs and lavender and Canada waterleaf, Solomon's and false Solomon's seal, white baneberry, and golden ragwort.

If you get to this location in midsummer, look for Michigan lilies just before the parking lot on the north side of the road. In the summer, look for a fairly large population of early ladies' tresses orchid on the right side of the trail about halfway down. There are also a variety of interesting sunflowers, wingstem, black-eyed Susans, orange coneflowers, crane fly orchids, and agrimony along the trail

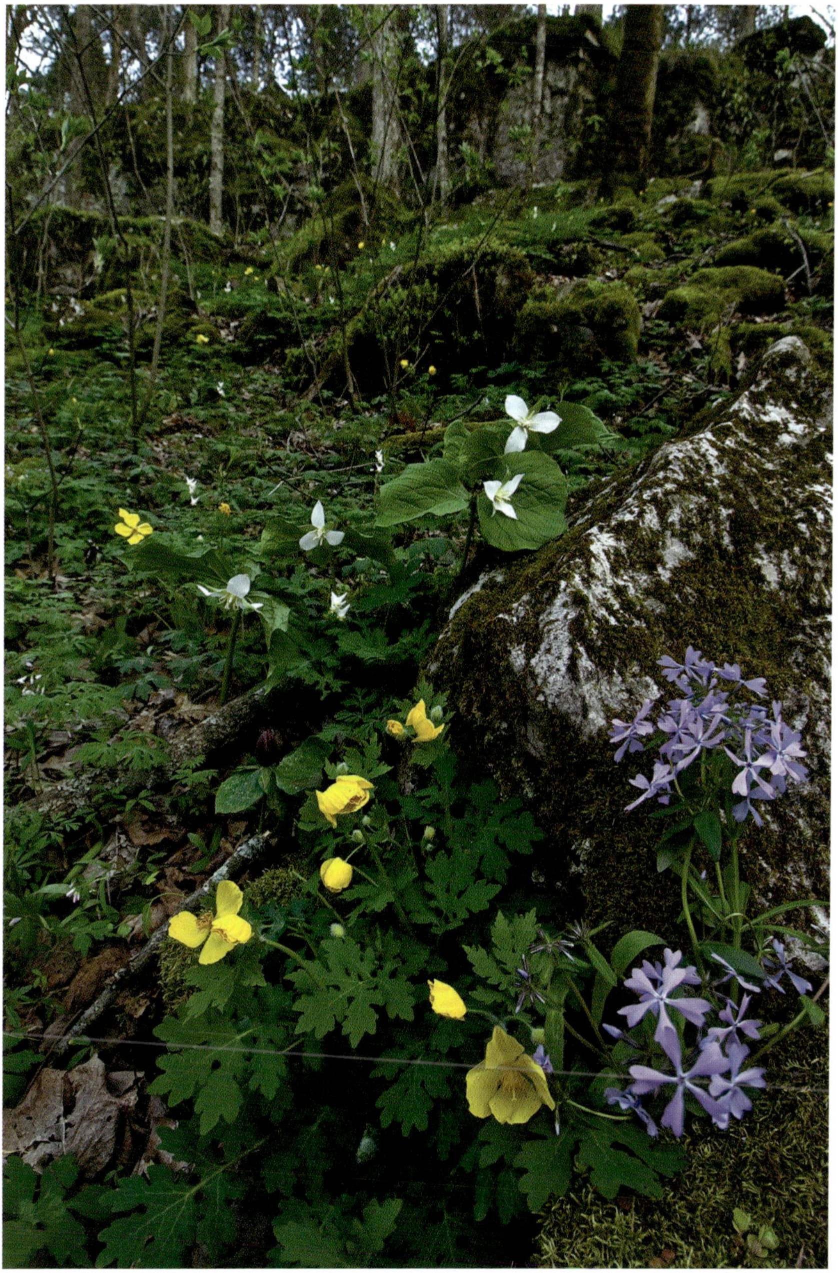

There is a great diversity of flowers including wood poppies, nodding and sessile trillium, blue phlox and Dutchman's breeches as you descend into Cedar Sink.

WESTERN

To Get There

From I-65 take the Park City exit (exit 81) west into the national park (Kentucky 255) for 2.3 miles and turn left onto Kentucky 70. Stay on Kentucky 70 past Sloan's Pond and turn left onto Davis Road (turns into Kentucky 422), and look for the park signs that indicate the community of Pig and Cedar Sinks. Go one mile and the parking area is on the left. One of the best places to stay while in this area is the hotel in the national park. They also have meal service available. Other options include many hotels and restaurants in Cave City, which is a close 15 minute drive.

Access Ratings

Hiking Trails	**EASY**

Mammoth Cave

Ugly Creek Road, Little Jordan Road or Dennison Ferry Road

As you enter this gravel road from the asphalt, you will not find anything interesting until the road makes a right-hand turn after a mile and begins to descend a steep slope. Look for early saxifrage on the rocks and as you descend on the road, you will find fire pink, cut-leaf toothwort, blue phlox, wild geranium, rue anemone, bloodroot, early meadow rue, star chickweed and foamflower. At mile 1.4, you will have reached the bottom of the hill, and you will notice the stream on your left. Pull off the road here, and walk around the bottoms near the stream and look for bent trillium, moss-covered rocks loaded with bishop's cap, stonecrop, and foamflower. Other species in the bottom include putty-root orchids, dwarf crested iris, sweet white and white violets, wild geranium, yellow trout lilies, wild ginger, bloodroot, hepatica, rue anemone, Jacob's ladder, blue cohosh, lavender waterleaf, lots of bergamot, and spiderwort. In midsummer at the first sharp turn downhill, look for the rare wood's false hellebore at the bottom of the hill on the left. As you climb the hill, you can turn around because the remainder of the road is high and dry unless you want to continue for a couple more miles and see Big Woods, which is a couple of hundred acres of old-growth forest.

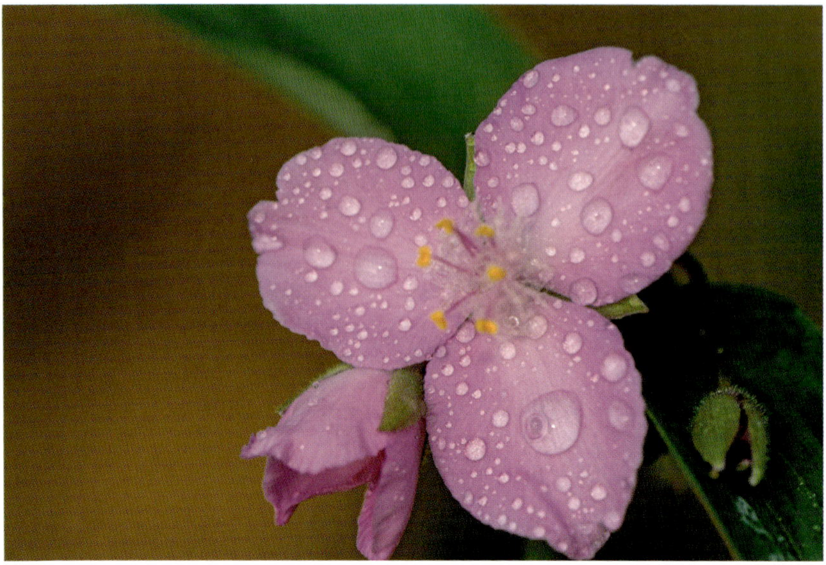

There is an abundance of spiderwort at this location.

WESTERN

To Get There

From Kentucky 70 inside the park, take the Deer Park Hollow Road. It will intersect with the Green River Ferry Road. Turn left and this will take you to the ferry across the river. After crossing the river on the ferry, continue for a couple of miles until you reach the first right-hand turn (gravel road), and this is Little Jordan Road. From the north you can reach this road by going west on Kentucky 88 from Munfordville (on I-65) at exit 68. Go through town (going east) until you reach Kentucky 88 and turn right. Follow this road for almost 13 miles until you reach Kentucky 728. Turn left after a half mile and then turn left again onto Kentucky 1827. Follow this for about 6.2 miles. Turn left onto Kentucky1352 and go one mile, and you will see the gravel road on your left.

Access Ratings

Driving Trails **EASY**

John James Audubon State Park

This is undoubtedly the best location in western Kentucky for spring wildflowers, which typically peak around the middle of April. As you drive in the entrance from U.S. 41, you will notice several nice patches of blue-eyed Mary; in good years, these patches can be outstanding. Once you arrive at the visitor's center, you will notice the beginning of the trail system that leads into the state nature preserve. There are more than 5.5 miles of trails that meander through this mostly "old" forest (approaching old growth in its characteristics) that is highly photogenic. As you begin entering, take the short King Benson trail, and you will find a very nice patch of recurved trillium just below the little hill. Continue along this trail until you reach the top of the rise. From there you have a variety of options and all the trails have similar flowers. One of the distinctive characteristics of this forest from a photography standpoint is the carpeting by a single species during different points in the spring flowering season. In early spring the ground is literally covered with squirrel corn and Dutchman's breeches followed by a carpet of wild ginger, and then later in the spring by lavender waterleaf. In addition, there are several nice patches of blue-eyed Mary. Look closely for the rare baby blue eyes. This diminutive flower can form carpets in some areas along the trails. The other significant find is near the highest point where several trails converge by a campfire stone structure. Here is a nice patch of bloodroot and green violets. Other typical spring flowers like blue phlox, mayapple, cut-leaf toothwort, dwarf larkspur and trout lily are present. There is a plant checklist available at the visitor's center.

WESTERN

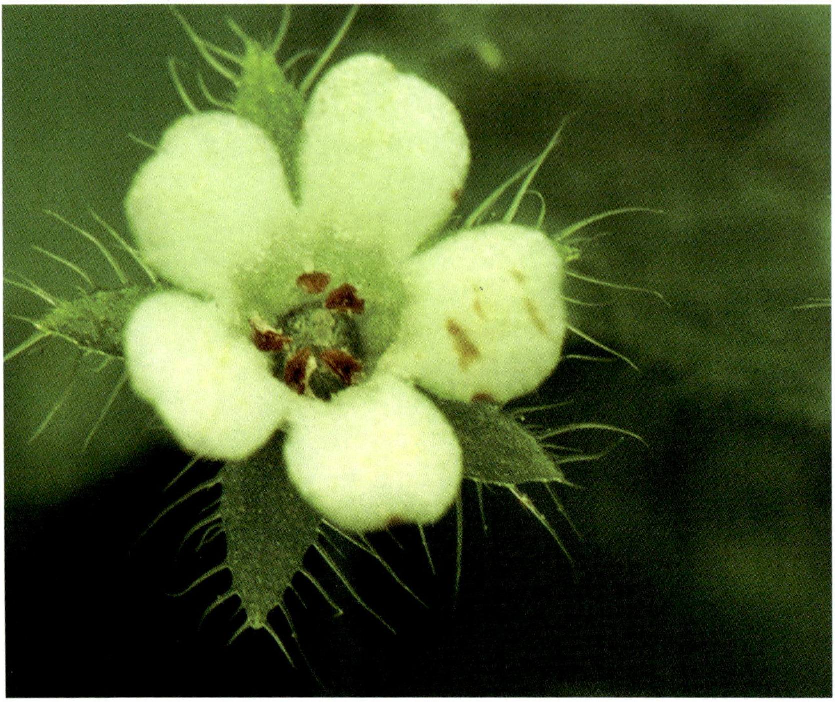

This is the best place in the state to see this rare plant, sweet baby blue eyes, as it can cover the ground in some locations along the trails.

To Get There

From I-64 travel south through Evansville, Indiana across the Ohio River on U.S. 41 to Henderson, Kentucky. Immediately after the bridge you will see the sign on your left for John James Audubon State Park. From the south continue north on U.S. 41 and the park entrance is on the right 1.7 miles from the intersection of U.S. 60. Lodging and meals are available in Henderson, Kentucky or Evansville, Indiana and there are five cottages available within the park for lodging.

Access Ratings

Hiking Trails	**EASY to MODERATE**

Yellowbank Wildlife Management Area

The trail at Yellowbank Wildlife Management Area is an old logging road that begins behind an iron gate near a pond on the south side of Kentucky 259 just after entering the management area. The first thing you will notice at the pond is the blue-eyed Mary in several nice patches that in a good year can be quite large. Walk around the pond, and turn right on the old road, and you will notice blue-eyed Mary right in the middle of the road. Continue up the first rise, and you will notice on your right some mesic woodland on fairly steep slopes. If you hug the road, you can find blue phlox, recurved and sessile trillium, Dutchman's breeches, squirrel corn, smooth yellow violets, yellow trout lilies and other typical spring flowers like wild ginger. The best flowers occur on the slopes, and you can find large patches of blue-eyed Mary in a good year and many patches of wood poppies. Because this is not a formal trail, you can wander around in these woods in search of bloodroot, spring beauties, stonecrop on the rocks and boulders, cut-leaf toothwort and a handful of other species. This is pretty productive for a short walk, and if you want to find the rare French's shooting star you must walk the trail from the information center on Highway 259, up over the ridge, and then down into the hollow where you will find many of these plants hugging the sandstone cliffline. The flowers in the rich woods can also be productive, and several of the boulders have lots of stonecrop on them with foamflower, hepatica, star chickweed, recurved trillium, rue anemone, and a handful of other species. This is a very scenic location and there are several wet-weather waterfalls coming over the cliffs and a nice stream in the bottom of the hollow as well. If you want to take a short diversion, take a run over to Otter Creek Park in late September and early October to photograph the Allegheny stonecrop. Go to the overlook (which is quite scenic), and as you walk along the edge on the trail, look over the side of the cliff and you can find a half dozen patches of this rare species. Because of their location you will need a long lens (300- to 500-mm) to get any decent images.

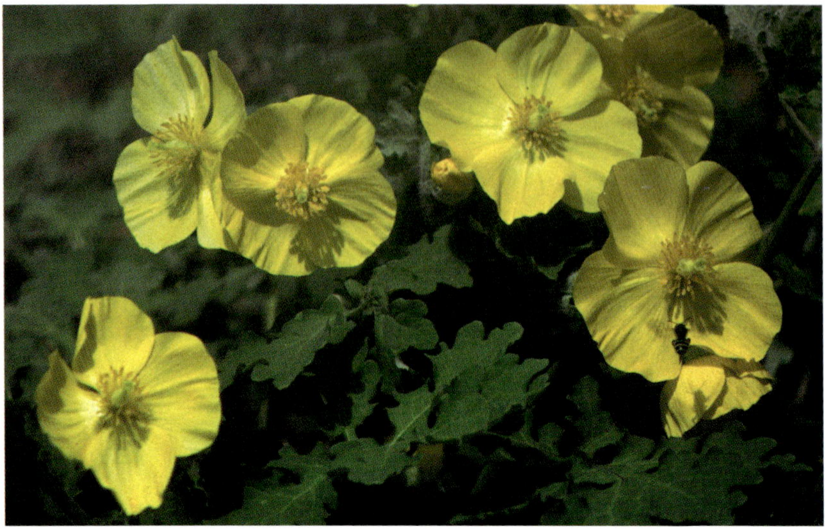

Wood poppies abound at this site, often in exceptionally large clusters in and around boulders.

WESTERN

To Get There

From I-64 in Indiana, take exit 105, and head south on Indiana 135. You will cross the Ohio River and enter Kentucky on Kentucky 79. Turn right on Kentucky 144 for 5.5 miles and turn left onto Kentucky 376 for 5.6 miles. Then turn back onto Kentucky 144 for another five miles and then turn right onto Kentucky 259 for four miles. It is best to get a map of the area prior to arriving because the pond is just off Kentucky 259 on the south side of the road, and it is an area that is open to horses. There are multiple lodging and meal choices about 20 miles north in Indiana or a few choices in Brandenburg, Kentucky.

Access Ratings

Hiking Trails	**EASY**

Ben Hawes State Park *(Owensboro)*

Ben Hawes State Park is best known for its golf course, but you can find more than four miles of hiking and mountain biking trails in this 297-acre park located about four miles west of Owensboro. The park is one of those places that do not support a great diversity of spring flowers, but it does have one outstanding feature; enough celandine or wood poppies that in a good year literally carpet the ground. The only trail worth walking from a photography standpoint is the Shipp Trail at the far end of the park. As you descend onto the trail from the road/cemetery, look for some nice patches of Dutchman's breeches and the only patch of false rue anemone I found in the park. When you get to the intersection of this trail with the Miss Sara Gray Trail, take a left and follow a small stream, and then ascend onto the top of the ridge. Once into the midsection, you will notice many "side" trails that are interconnecting without signage (signage is typically poor in the entire trail system at this park) which are there to accommodate mountain bikes. The best flower photography will occur on any of these unofficial trails. Look for yellow trout lilies, carpets of Dutchman's breeches and squirrel corn and some large patches of dwarf larkspur. Other typical spring flowers like rue anemone and blue woodland phlox can also be found here.

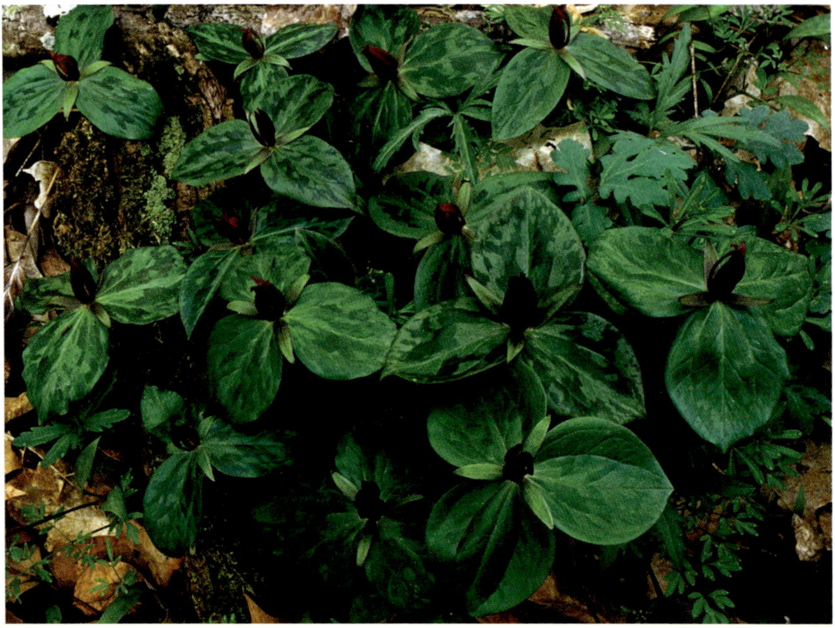

There are large populations of sessile trillium at this park.

WESTERN

To Get There

Travel west on U.S. 60 from the bypass for six miles (the park entrance is four miles west but you want to go the next right hand turn (Overstreet Road) and go approximately one mile north to the gate and park here.

Access Ratings

Hiking Trails	**EASY**

Yellow Creek County Park *(Owensboro)*

On the east side of town lies a true small gem of a place for wildflower photography. Yellow Creek Park is a typical county park filled with ball fields, picnic shelters, and a small natural area located in the rear of the park behind the Frisbee golf course. Most of the park's 152 acres are devoted to typical park recreation but the 51-acre natural area boasts more than 20 spring wildflowers found on "wildflower hill" in the early spring. There is even a miniature "cascades" or waterfall in the natural area. When you pull into the parking lot, you will see a bridge that takes you over the creek. From here take an immediate right across the covered bridge, and you will see wildflower hill right in front of you. It will be hard to miss because there are large numbers of wood poppies covering the hill. The most remarkable feature of this park is the huge populations of recurved trilliums, probably the largest populations of this species I have seen in the state. There is also a substantial number of dwarf larkspur in this park, and it is almost all the white form. I found several nice patches of the native chickweed as well on wildflower hill and some Virginia bluebells. Other species in the park include sessile trillium, Dutchman's breeches and squirrel corn, yellow trout lilies, yellow and blue violets, and a handful of other species. As you meander along the paths, you will ultimately come to another covered bridge and a swinging bridge, which makes this little 0.75-mile loop hike a nice diversion from photographing the flowers.

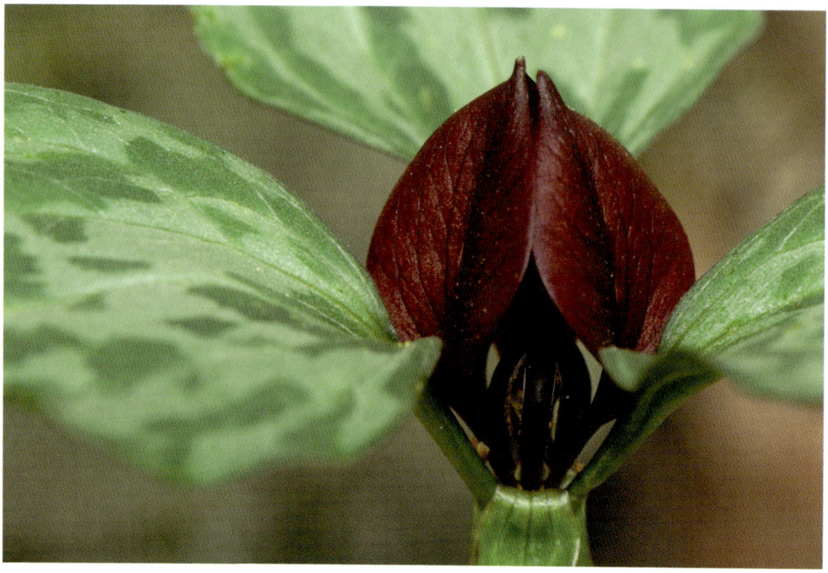

There is a large population of recurved trillium that is easily accessible at Yellow Creek County Park.

WESTERN

To Get There

Take U.S. 60 east of Owensboro and turn right onto Kentucky 144. The park will be on your right. Lodging is available in Owensboro and check out the world famous barbeque either at Moonlite or Old Hickory restaurants.

Access Ratings

Hiking Trails **EASY**

Land Between the Lakes

LBL, as it is affectionately known, is a 170,000-acre peninsula that ranges 40 miles long and eight to 12 miles wide. It is located between Kentucky Lake and Lake Barkley. The land was originally part of the TVA system but it is now managed by the U.S. Forest Service. For those interested in finding specific plants, I would recommend you purchase Ed Chester's excellent field guide, *Wildflowers of the Land Between the Lakes Region, Kentucky and Tennessee*, published by Austin Peay University. It has some wonderful information about the most common wildflowers you will encounter at LBL. The two sites I mention below are, in my opinion, the very best wildflower locations in LBL, but Ed's book has specific details on finding specific plants. For example, if you are looking for fire pink, Ed recommends you look along roadsides and wooded bluffs in Demumbers Creek off Brandon Chapel Road.

In addition to the areas I list below, here is some information for several showy and somewhat uncommon plants to photograph. If you travel west along U.S. 68 from Cadiz and cross Lake Barkley, just before you go over the bridge crossing over Kentucky Lake, pull off the road to the south and you will find a boat dock and recreational area (Fenton). Park along the road, and walk toward the face of the dam, pass by a few trees and look for a nice population of American snowbell, and the state listed Trepocarpus, and a few American wisteria vines.

Land Between the Lakes

The Trace

The summer wildflowers along the Trace, which is the major north-south road that bisects LBL, begin to be prolific in the Kentucky section between the intersection with U.S. 68 on the south and the north turnoff to the Nature Station (about 12 miles). You will have your best luck finding prairie or meadow flowers along this road between June 15 and the end of the growing season. The Trace is like a parkway, and there is minimal walking involved, with ample places to pull your vehicle completely off the road and park. In the spring, there are some very noteworthy wildflowers along this road, and in late April to early May look for the cream indigo. There are about two dozen plants scattered in this section. In addition, keep your eyes peeled for some dramatic patches of bird's foot violet. You will find all the color forms in some patches including the bicolor, deep purple, light lavender, and white forms of this showy violet. In the summer, if you enter the Trace at U.S. 68 look for Golden Pond (visitor's center on right) less than one-half mile from the intersection. At the edge of the pond, look for the diminutive spreading or prostrate eryngo in late July and August. Earlier in the season, mostly June and July look for the abundant scaly, spiked, and rough blazing stars, black-eyed Susans, and butterfly milkweed (at mile point 2.4 there is a large patch on the east side of the road) with their profusion of butterflies using these flowers. About the same time as the butterfly milkweed is in bloom, look for a proliferation of wild quinine, rosinweed, and whorled leaf coreopsis. Later in the season, from July through frost, if you travel north from the U.S. 68 entrance, look on the right-hand side for several very nice patches of southern blazing star with one of the best at mile 0.7 as you head north from the junction of U.S. 68/Kentucky 80. Mixed in with this flower, you are likely to encounter spreading aster and smooth aster and the very tiny flowered false pennyroyal in areas with no vegetation and rocks. Earlier in the flowering season, immediately across on the west side, is a large patch of wild bergamot. At mile 5.4 on the east side of the road (right side if traveling north), begins an extremely large patch of rattlesnake master, probably the biggest patch I have observed in the entire state. Finally, at the north road to the Nature Station, look on the right hand side by a group of autumn olive bushes for a good patch of slender blazing star. These are just a few of the species you are likely to encounter. Ohers I have seen include common milkweed, several different sunflowers, purple gerardia, gray goldenrod, several different sneezeweeds, and the native field thistle.

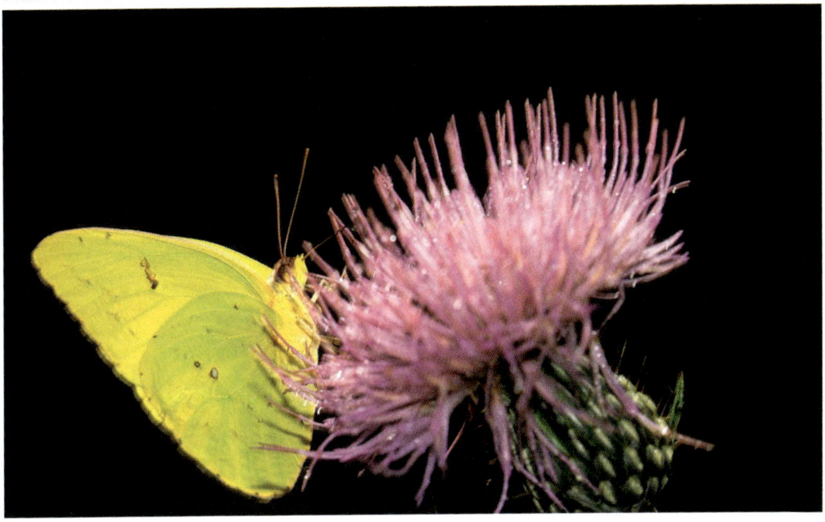

Cloudless sulfur butterflies are abundant during the late summer when the native field thistle and southern blazing star are in flower along the Trace.

WESTERN

To Get There

From I-24 on the north take exit 31 (Highway 453) to Grand Rivers. Proceed through Grand Rivers, and enter LBL on this highway in about four or five miles. The southern entrance into the Kentucky section is off U.S. 68/80, and the Trace is located about four miles after you cross either the Kentucky Lake or Barkley Lake Bridge.

Access Ratings

Driving Trails	**EASY**

Land Between the Lakes

Hematite Lake Trail

Spring is not the most spectacular season to hike the trail around Hematite Lake, but there are a few noteworthy flowers that occur primarily on the south side of the trail and near the back in the wetland area. As you approach the very back of the trail beginning on the north side, right before the boardwalk takes you out into the wetter areas, look on your right for the state-listed eastern blue star. As you walk around the boardwalk, you will notice large populations of spring cress and about midway along the boardwalk, look on the right-hand side for a very nice patch of recurved trillium. After you get off the boardwalk, the flowers get better, and you can find some nice patches of Jacob's ladder, blue phlox, dwarf larkspur, trout lilies, and spring beauties. As you get up on higher and drier ground and approach the dam, look for violet wood sorrel and several patches of dwarf crested iris. The best time to walk this trail is in July and August when the purple fringeless orchids are flowering in the back wetland area near the boardwalk. This is also the time of the year when the American lotus is in flower. Also look for lizard's tail, spider lily, Virginia dayflower and St. Andrew's cross, in both the upland and bottomland areas of the trail. The final flower to find is the state-listed grass-leaf mud plantain. This yellow-flowered wetland plant occurs in between the concrete stepping-stones as you cross over the dam spillway. If you have an inclination to carry a long lens, there is ample opportunity to photograph wildlife, particularly water birds like Canada geese and wood ducks along this trail.

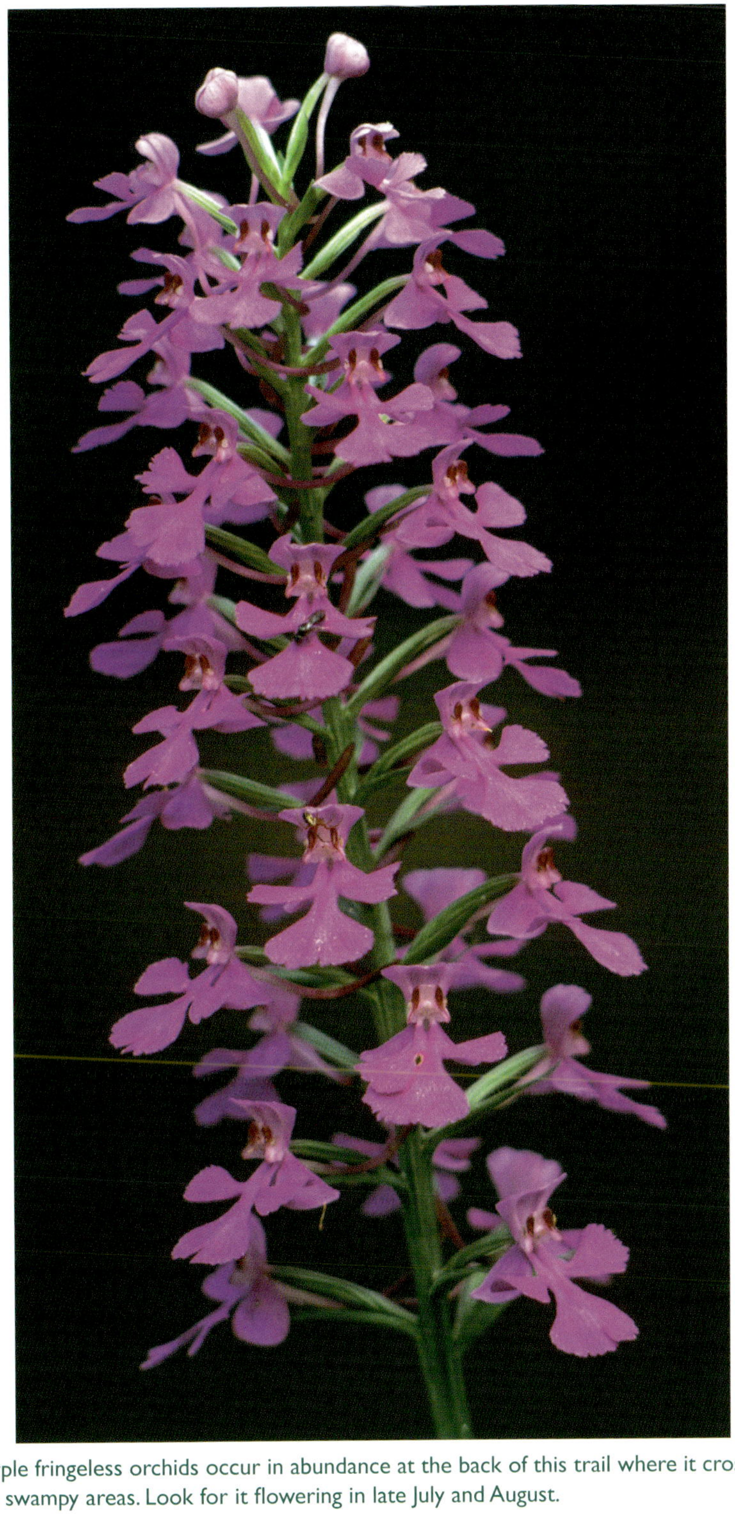

Purple fringeless orchids occur in abundance at the back of this trail where it crosses the swampy areas. Look for it flowering in late July and August.

WESTERN

To Get There

From I-24 on the north take exit 31 (Highway 453) to Grand Rivers. Proceed through Grand Rivers, and enter LBL on this highway in about four or five miles. The southern entrance into the Kentucky section is off U.S. 68/80, and the Trace is located about four miles after you cross either the Kentucky Lake or Barkley Lake Bridge. There are multiple state parks that have lodging available and I recommend Lake Barkley although Kentucky Dam Village and Kenlake also have rooms. There are many other lodging opportunities available at a multitude of exits on I-24. While in the area eating at Patti's 1880s Settlement is a treat and either come early or make sure you have reservations as they fill up fast. They are known for their huge pork chop dinner. Another good local joint is Leigh's barbeque on U.S. 641 just north of Grand Rivers.

Access Ratings

Hiking Trails	**EASY to MODERATE**

Ballard Wildlife Management Area and Swan Lake Bottoms

Summer is the best time to visit this area of far western Kentucky and both Ballard and the Swan Lake Bottoms are cypress swamp and wetland-dominated habitats. As you enter at the main entrance road, there is an exceptional stand of American lotus on the north side of the road. As you drive around the refugee and at Swan Lake Bottoms, look for large patches of both species of native rose or swamp mallows at the edge of the cypress swamps and in shallow water areas. In the spring as you enter the property on the south-side main entrance road there is a large population of the state-listed eastern blue star in the north ditch before you enter the refugee. There is also a small number of this species along the loop road. The next thing to look for is the feather foil in the second pond on the north side of the road. In late spring, drive the roads and you will find several nice patches of southern blue flag iris and at the Ohio River overlook (by the large pumping station) look for cut-leaf evening primrose. In late summer as you drive the roads through the refuge look for the occasional large white flowers of the spider lily in the woods. Other late-summer flowers to look for include cardinal flower, monkey flower, American frog bit (in the water at Swan Lake Bottoms Cypress Swamps), arrowhead, bur reed, tickseed sunflowers, button weed, common dodder, wild buckwheat vine, and passionflower.

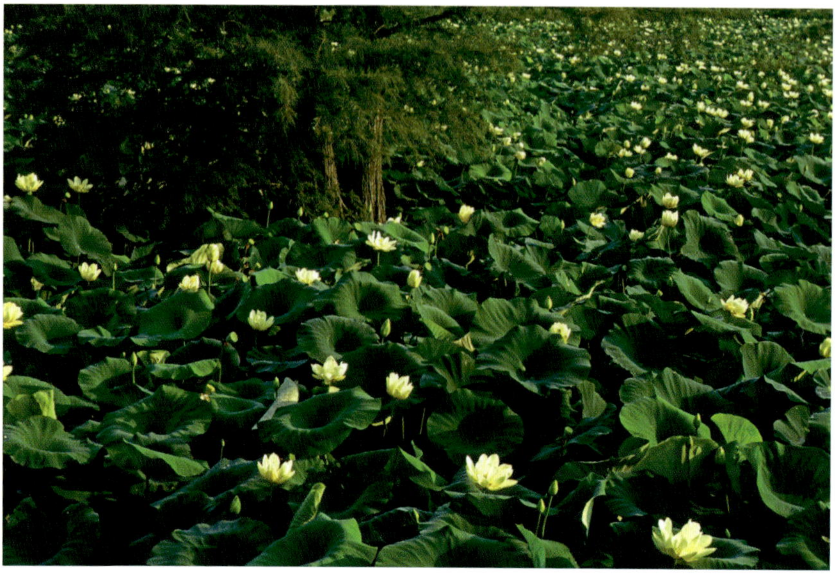

As you enter the Ballard WMA look for a pond on the north side of the road that is covered in American lotus.

WESTERN

To Get There

From the east on U.S. 60 from Paducah, travel 16 miles west and turn north on Kentucky 310 at LaCenter until you reach Kentucky 1105. This is the community of Oscar. Turn right until you reach Kentucky 473 (refuge road). Turn left and follow the road into the refuge. To get to Swan Lake Bottoms take U.S. 60 to Wickliffe and go through town following U.S. 60 until you see signs (small and brown) on the right. You will be on top of the levee. At the first or second brown sign turn right and drive down the gravel roads into the Wildlife Management Area. The wetlands are interspersed with large agricultural fields but keep going until the roads dead end. Meals and lodging are available in Wickliffe or LaCenter.

Access Ratings

Driving Trails **EASY**

Baker Natural Area *(Russellville)*

The Baker Natural Area is one of the better locations in the state for accessing prairie or grassland flowers. As you enter the property from the parking lot, the first significant plants to look for in the spring by a tree on the right about 50 yards from the parking lot is the state-listed Carolina larkspur. It flowers in early to mid-May. In early to mid-June, walk the trail back through the woods into a four or five acre opening that is literally covered with pale purple coneflower. The best time to visit this property from a photographic standpoint is June, July and August when the prairie flowers are in full bloom. As you walk along the trail and approach the weather station on the left, look for spiked blazing stars on the right and downy sunflowers on the left. Continue walking farther, and as you walk down the slope, look over to your right, and you will see several small "open" areas where it appears that no vegetation is growing. In these rocky open glades you should look for heliotrope and nodding wild onion in addition to some interesting mosses and lichens. Look farther west along the road and you will find the state-listed cut-leaf prairie dock. Other species to look for on this property include scaly blazing star, black-eyed Susan, rosinweed, and many other prairie or meadow species.

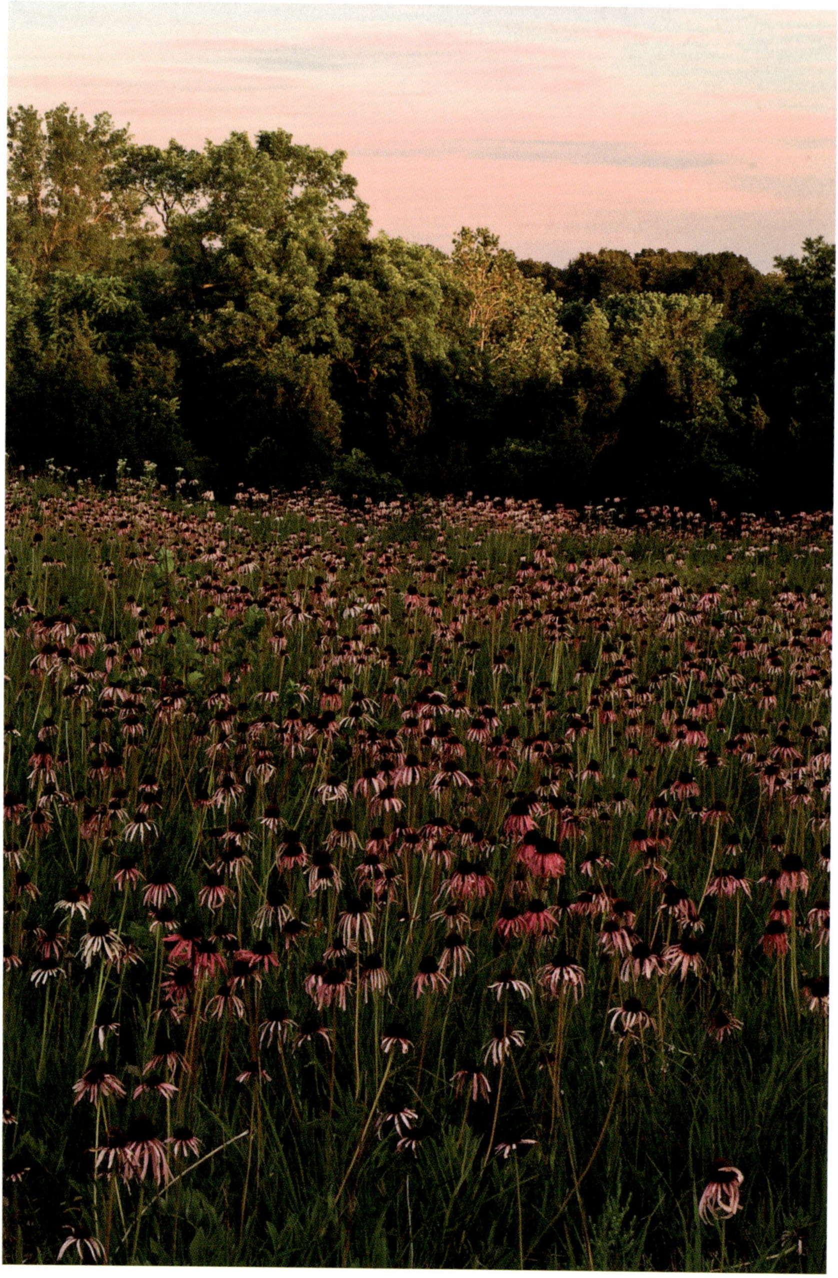

The pale purple coneflowers at the Baker Natural Area are in peak flower in mid-June.

WESTERN

To Get There

Baker Natural Area is easily accessible by getting on the Russellville northern bypass. From the east, go four or five miles to Sportsman Club Road and turn to the left. The parking lot is immediately on your left.

Access Ratings

Hiking Trails	**EASY**

Logan County Glade *(Russellville)*

This is an unlikely place to find spring or summer wildflowers; however, in the spring, the grassy openings and rock outcroppings provide quite a show with rocks covered in shooting star, bird's foot violet and hoary puccoon. As you begin the trail at the edge of the woods, you will notice the opening not more than a 100 yards in front of you. When you get to the edge of the opening, turn to the left, and proceed up the trail. On the left and right, you will find hundreds of shooting stars. Look carefully because you should be able to locate some pink-flowered specimens scattered very infrequently among the white-flowered plants. Continue around the loop trail, and you will notice bird's foot violet almost everywhere and you should be able to find all the color forms on the preserve, lavender, bicolor, deep purple, and white. Look for the bright yellow hoary puccoon mixed in with the violets. Other species that can be found on the glade include Carolina larkspur and Eggleston violet.

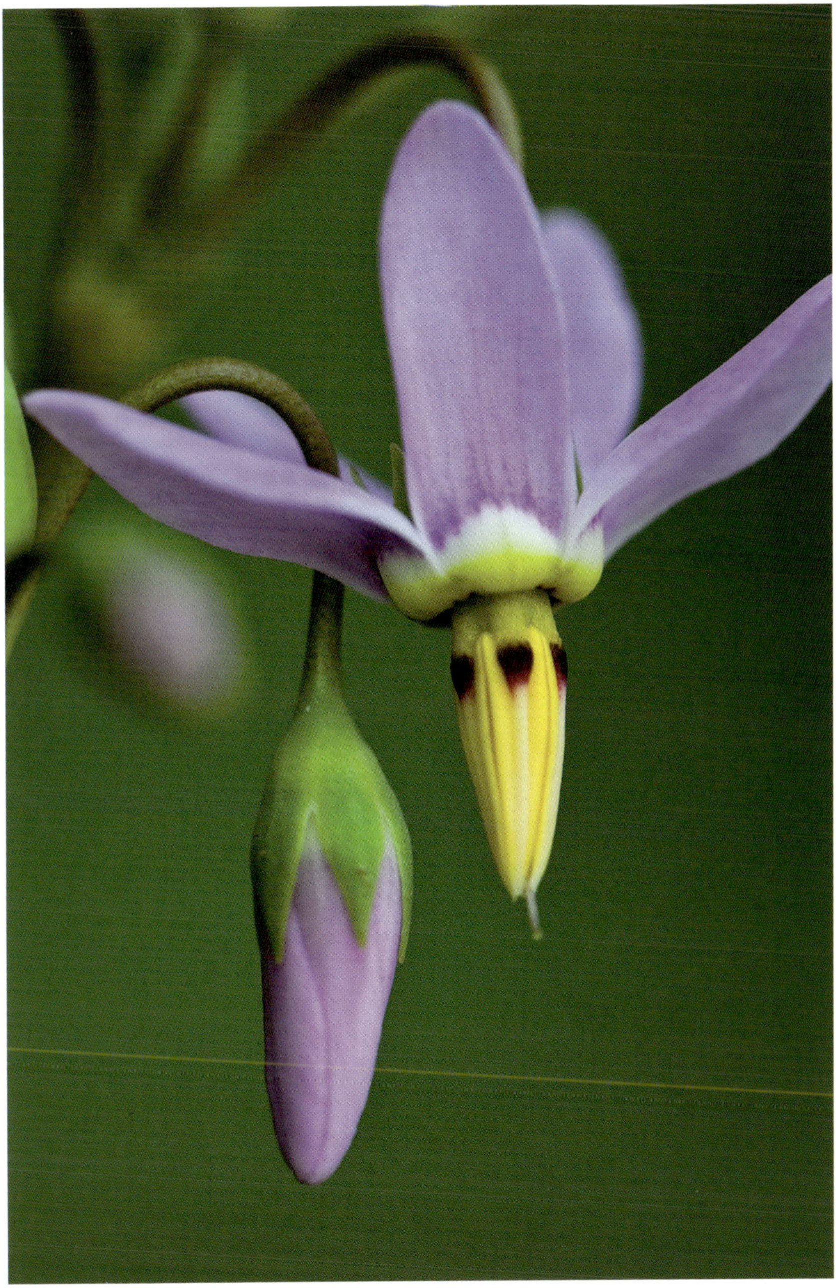

This is one of the few locations in Kentucky where I have found the purple version of the native shooting star, which normally has white flowers.

To Get There

Logan County Glade is accessible by coming into Russellville on U.S. 68/80 business highway from the east. Turn right into the parking lot between the health department and the old hospital. Lodging is available at the Comfort Inn or Best Western in Russellville and while in town eat at Roy's Pit Barbeque on the west bypass.

Access Ratings

Hiking Trails	**EASY**

Your Own Backyard

The final place to photograph wildflowers can be in your own yard. When I lived on Albemarle Road in Lexington, I grew more than 200 species of native wildflowers, many of them rare in their natural environments. Some of the images in this book were taken of the flowers that were in my backyard. One of the great attributes of growing wildflowers in the backyard is that you know when they are at their peak, and in perfect condition. You also know and are intimately aware of the lighting conditions in your yard. Thus you can predict when the best time photographic opportunities occur from a light perspective.

The best advice for designing a native wildflower garden is to use nature as your guide. Growing native wildflowers is no more difficult than growing horticultural flowers. You need to know sun, water and soil characteristics. For instance, you can grow a woodland garden on top of clay soils by placing four inches of pure compost on top of the clay and planting directly into the compost (that is what they do in nature, grow in composted leaves). Make sure you have dappled shade from a tree, not hard shade that you find on the north side of the home or building.

You can also grow many native water plants in a water garden and rain gardens are all the rage right now. These are perfect places to grow native plants like cardinal flower, great blue lobelia (in fact you can have a patriotic garden with red cardinal flower and the white and blue forms of great blue lobelia growing side by side). There are many excellent references to growing native plants and developing a native plant garden.

There are many great native plant nurseries that sell good quality plants. Do not, under any circumstances, except for salvage, remove plants from the wild to grow in your backyard. This is harmful for three reasons: you impoverish the local plant communities, you risk the possibility of introducing exotic plants or even worse pathogens or diseases, and there is no guarantee the plants will live or thrive. Most native plants, even some of our rare ones, are available from native plant nurseries and it just makes good sense to use those plants. From a photographic standpoint you can even photograph horticultural flowers using the same techniques I described below for photographing wildflowers.

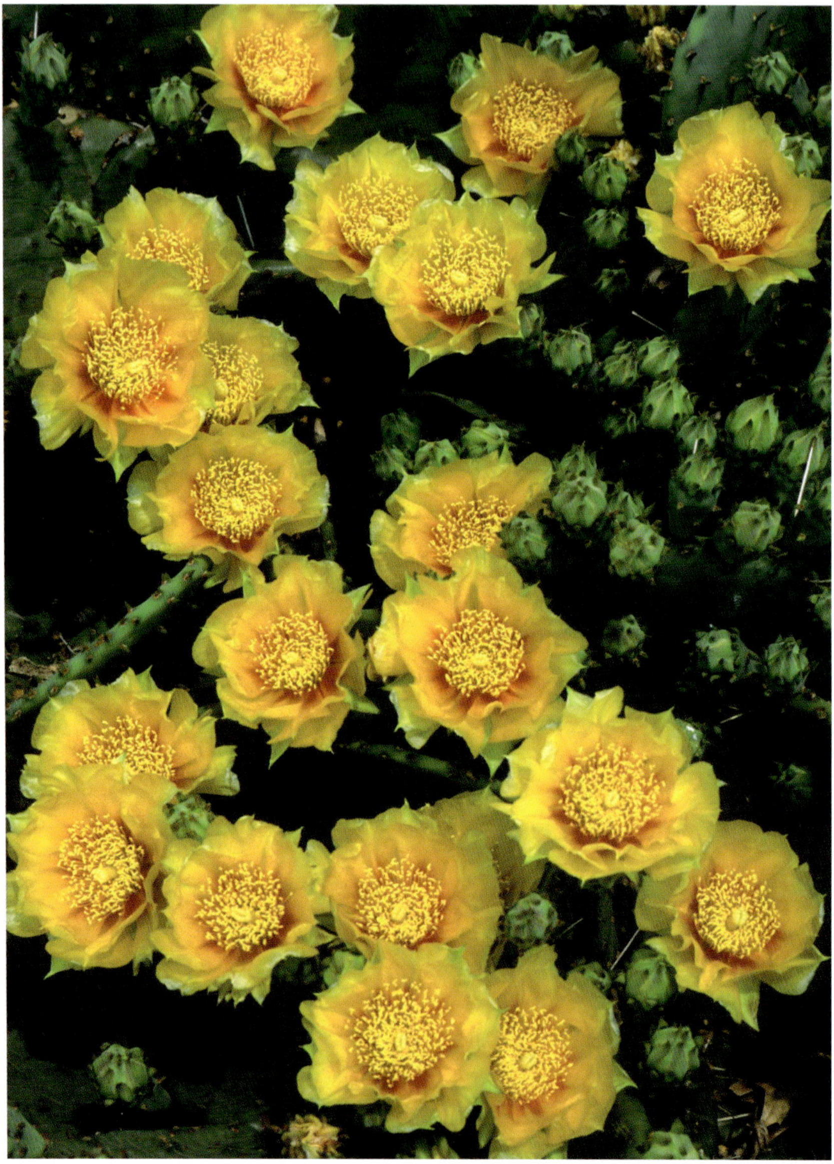

My neighbors loved walking by my patch of native prickly pear cactus when it was in flower. Having a nice patch in my yard allowed me the opportunity to reduce travel costs to photograph this species in the wild, plus since the flowers only remain open a single day, it allowed me to photograph when the most flowers were in bloom for the brightest and most colorful show of flowers.

Epilogue

As I write these concluding remarks, it is astonishing how technology moves ahead so quickly. New cameras, new software, new ways of looking at an old subject. Where technology will lead us is anyone's guess, but in concluding I would like to remind you of a couple of "old wisdoms" that I presented earlier in the book. I will take "technique over technology" anytime, anyplace. "Garbage in, garbage out." Equipment is just a tool. By the time you read this, much of the technology may have changed and gotten substantially better. Remember, it is your creative mind and the appropriate use of the technology that ultimately determines the final output from the equipment.

This final output is why I spent so much time emphasizing the "artistic" side of wildflower photography. Anyone can point and shoot and document what is in nature, but not everyone can "interpret" in a creative, expressive way what nature is saying to us. The great writer and diarist Anaïs Nin summarizes it well: "It is the function of art to renew our perception. What we are familiar with, we cease to see. The writer shakes up the familiar scene, and, as if by magic, we see a new meaning in it." The media guru Phil Cooke (www.philcooke.com) writes: "Don't give your audience what you think they want. Give them what they never dreamed possible." Finally Ansel Adams succinctly wrote: "You don't take a photograph, you make it."

Writing this has been a great journey spanning my 30-plus years travelling and photographing flowers and nature. I have learned much along the way from humble beginnings with a Pentax Spotmatic to new Nikon digital equipment. I have enjoyed every single flower I have ever seen and photographed. I have enjoyed every single minute I have spent outdoors photographing or even just watching the natural world. We definitely need the tonic of wild places, and I wish you the best in your efforts to share your vision of the natural world with humanity. In the end, remember what the great novelist and environmentalist Edward Abbey wrote: "Do not burn yourselves out. Be as I am – a reluctant enthusiast...a part time crusader, a half-hearted fanatic. Save the other half of yourselves and your lives for pleasure and adventure. It is not enough to fight for the land; it is even more important to enjoy it. While you can. While it is still there."

About the Author

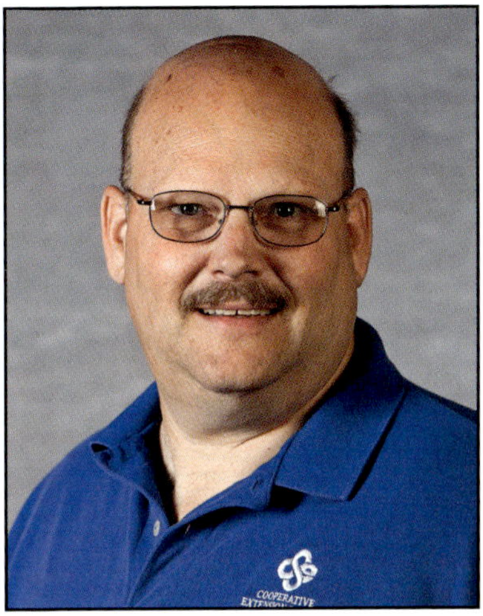

Thomas G. Barnes is a Professor in the Department of Forestry, University of Kentucky. Tom is the Kentucky Extension Wildlife specialist and the author of four regional natural history books about Kentucky. He has published more than 40 research papers and is an internationally published photographer with clients that have included The National Wildlife Federation, Time-Life, McGraw-Hill Publishers, Prentice-Hall, Brooklyn Botanical Garden, Chicago Botanical Garden, more than 40 federal, state, and city government agencies. His web site is www.tombarnes.org.

Glossary

Aperture

A circular opening in the lens that allows light to enter and reach the sensor as the image is being taken. The diameter of the opening is called an f stop and the larger the f stop the less amount of light enters and reaches the sensor. For example, f/2.8 lets in more light than f/16.

Aperture Priority (AE)

A camera mode where you set the aperture opening and the camera automatically sets the shutter speed.

Aspherical Lens

An aspherical lense has flattened edges so it is not a perfect sphere which produces higher quality images.

Bit

Short for binary digit and it is the basic information unit used in computing and telecommunications and has a value of 0 or 1. Monochrome images are 1 bit images where 0 = black and 1 = white. An 8 bit image, or 2 to the eighth power, has 256 tones.

Bit Depth or color depth

Bit depth refers to the color (or gray scale) of each individual pixel. For instance, a pixel with 8 bits per color of red, green, and blue gives a 24 bit image. 24 bit resolution is 16.7 million colors.

Bitmap

A method of storing information by mapping an image pixel bit x bit and includes the following formats: .BMP, .PCX, .PICT, .TIF, .TIFF, .GIF.

Buffer

Temporary memory storage in a digital camera that stores images prior to saving them to the memory card.

Center-Weighted Meter

An automatic exposure system that uses just the center portion of the image for determining overall exposure value of the image.

Charged Coupled Device (CCD)

One of two primary light sensitive chips used for image gathering.

Chromatic Aberration

Also called purple fringing, chromatic aberration can be common when using long telephoto lenses. You typically observed it when there is a dark area surrounded by a highlight and in between you see a band of purple pixels. It can be removed in post-processing software.

CMYK

Short for cyan, magenta, yellow and black, CMYK are the four colors used by photo quality printers. Cameras typically shoot in red, green, blue and the files are converted to CMYK for printing.

Compact Flash

A type of memory storage card for recording digital images.

Complementary Metal-Oxide Semiconductor (CMOS)

One of the two primary light sensitive chips used for image gathering.

Contrast

The difference between the lightest and darkest areas in an image and the greater the distance, the higher the contrast.

Depth of Field

How much of the photograph is in focus when the camera is fixed on the main subject. It is controlled by the aperture and focal length of the lens. Shallow depth of field refers to using a large aperture opening like f/2.8 where only the subject is in focus whereas deep depth of field refers to most of the entire image in focus.

Digital Zoom

A simulated zoom where the center 50 % of the image is magnified and the lens does not physically change length. Image quality is degraded and there is increased noise. Compare to optical zoom.

DPI

Short for dots per inch, DPI is a measure of the resolution of a digital device and in general the more DPI the higher the resolution. Most photographic prints are printed at 300 or greater DPI which is about the resolution the human eye can observe.

DSLR

Short for digital single lens reflex camera, DSLR has a viewfinder that sees through the lens (TTL) by way of a 45°-angled mirror that flips up when the shutter fires and allows the light to strike the image sensor. This semi-automatic moving mirror system allows the photographer to see the actual image through the lens and typically allows for the use of interchangeable lenses.

Dynamic Range

Similar to contrast in that it is the range of tones in a digital image and higher dynamic range gives more detail in both the highlights and shadows. Generally DSLR have greater dynamic range than compact point and shoot type digital cameras.

EXIF

Short for exchangeable image file format, EXIF is data such as time and date, shutter speed, aperture, etc. that can be read by web browsers and graphics programs.

Exposure

The amount of light that hits the sensor controlled by shutter speed, aperture, or ISO setting.

Exposure Value (EV)

A mechanism that allows the photographer to over-ride the auto-exposure system in the camera to either under or over-expose an image. Typically used with fill flash.

F stop

A number indicating the size of the aperture opening.

Fill Flash

A flash that is triggered, even in bright light conditions, to brighten deep shadows.

Histogram

A graphic representation of tones ranging from pure black (0) to pure white (255) and is used to determine exposure, contrast, and dynamic range.

Image Stabilization

A system built into a lens for reducing camera movement and is typically found in longer length lenses.

ISO

ISO refers to the sensitivity of sensor to light and is delineated by a number that typically ranges from 100 to more than 12,000. The higher the number, the more sensitive the sensor is to light and the higher the amount of noise.

JPEG

Short for the Joint Photographic Experts Group which designed this compression method that is used within the EXIF-JPEG file format and makes large files smaller. It is a lossy compression method meaning that some quality is lost during the compression. However, little loss in quality is noted by the human eye if a high quality, low compression JPEG setting is used.

LCD

Short for liquid crystal display, LCD is a low power monitor like a TV located on the rear of a digital camera that allows the user to view the image and other information about the photograph.

Megapixel

One million pixels.

Matrix Metering

An automatic exposure meter system that uses 256 areas across the image to determine overall exposure.

Noise

Randomly spaced or misinterpreted pixels that can appear when images are shot with a high ISO or a long exposure. It gives the appearance of speckles in the image.

Optical Zoom

A true zoom where the focal length of the lens extends or retracts so the image itself is magnified. These produce superior results when compared to digital zoom lenses.

Pixel

A single point in a digital image that is made of three dots, red, green, and blue which should converge at the same point and are arranged in a two dimensional grid. It is short for picture element which is the smallest unit of a picture that can be controlled.

Point and Shoot

These are compact cameras with a minimum of user controls that are simple to use and the photographer literally simply points the camera and trips the shutter.

RAW

The image that comes directly off the sensor at 12 bits per channel with no in camera processing. It is a lossless type of compression with no loss of quality during storage. It takes special software to view or print these files and allows the photographer to manipulate white balance, exposure, color balance, sharpness, contrast, and other data prior to saving as a TIFF or JPEG file.

RGB

Short for red, green and blue, RGB are the three primary colors that the human eye and digital cameras are sensitive to and from which all other colors are derived. See CMYK.

Resolution

The number of pixels per unit of length of an image.

Saturation

The vividness or richness of a color or how much it is undiluted by white light (more white light, less saturated).

SD Card (Secure Digital Card)

A type of flash memory card used for digital cameras and other devices. SDHC cards can store up to 32 GB of information and SDXC have a maximum capacity of 2 TB. See Compact Flash Card.

Shutter

A physical device that opens and closes a series of blades in front of the sensor that allows light to hit the sensor.

Shutter Priority

A camera mode where you set the shutter speed and the camera automatically sets the aperture opening.

Shutter Speed

A measurement of how long the shutter stays open as the photograph is taken. The faster the shutter speed the shorter the exposure time.

Spot Meter

An automatic exposure system that uses just the center one to two percent of the image for determining exposure value of the image.

TIFF

Short for tagged image file format, TIFF is uncompressed and is considered lossless meaning no information is lost and it contains no artifacts. See JPEG.

White Balance

A function in the camera that makes an adjustment to the red, green, and blue components of the image so that the brightest part of a scene appears white.

Index